CROSSCURRENTS IN THE GULF:
Arab, Regional and Global Interests

CROSSCURRENTS IN THE GULF

Arab, Regional and Global Interests

Edited by

H. RICHARD SINDELAR III and J.E. PETERSON

for

The Middle East Institute, Washington

ROUTLEDGE
London and New York

First published in 1988 by
Routledge
a division of Routledge, Chapman and Hall
11 New Fetter Lane, London EC4P 4EE

Published in the USA by
Routledge
a division of Routledge, Chapman and Hall, Inc.
29 West 35th Street, New York NY 10001

© 1988 Middle East Institute

Printed and bound in Great Britain by
Biddles Ltd, Guildford and King's Lynn

British Library Cataloguing in Publication Data

Crosscurrents in the Gulf : Arab, regional
    and global interests.
    1. Persian Gulf. International security
    aspects
    I. Sindelar, H. Richard III. Peterson, J.E.
    (John E.) II. Middle East Institute
    (*Washington, D.C.*)
    327.1'16

    ISBN 0-415-00032-7

Library of Congress Cataloging-in-Publication Data
Crosscurrents in the Gulf.

    Bibliography: p.
    Includes index.
    Contents: Foreign policy perspectives of the Arab
    Gulf States / Hermann F. Eilts — The Gulf Cooperation
    Council / John Duke Anthony — Soviet
    designs and dilemmas in the Gulf region / Roger F.
    Pajak — [etc.]
    1. Persian Gulf Region — Politics and government.
    2. Persian Gulf States — Politics and government.
    I. Sindelar, H. Richard. II. Peterson, John, 1947–
    III. Middle East Institute (Washington, D.C.)
    DS326.C76   1988   953   88-11408
    ISBN 0-415-00032-7

Contents

Part I: The Gulf in International Affairs

Part II: Significant Issues

Part III: Gulf States in Transition

Tables and Figures

Contributors

Dr. John Duke Anthony is President of the National Council on US-Arab Relations, headquartered in Washington, D.C., and has served as a consultant to various corporations and the US Departments of Defense, State, and Treasury. He has written extensively on the Gulf Cooperation Council and has been the only American invited to attend, as an observer, each of the GCC's annual heads of state summits since the organization was founded. He received his Ph.D. in international relations and Middle East studies from the School of Advanced International Studies (SAIS) of Johns Hopkins University, and is the author, *inter alia*, of *Arab States of the Lower Gulf: People, Politics, Petroleum* (Washington: Middle East Institute, 1975).

Dr. Zbigniew Brzezinski is currently Herbert Lehman Professor of Government at Columbia University, and a Senior Advisor and Counselor at the Center for Strategic and International Studies. As National Security Advisor to President Carter from 1977 to 1981, he was the architect of the 1980 Carter Doctrine, which enunciated US policy for the Gulf region. During his distinguished career, he has been an instructor in government at Harvard University (1953-1960), Professor and Director of Columbia University's Research Institute for International Change (1960-1977), a Guggenheim Fellow (1960), and a Ford Fellow (1970). He has served in many capacities, some of which include Director of the Trilateral Commission (1973-1976), member of the State Department's Policy Planning Staff (1966-1968), and member of the Board of Directors of the Council on Foreign Relations. Among many awards, he was the recipient of the Presidential Medal of Freedom in 1981. He received his B.A. (1948) and M.A. (1950) from McGill University, and his Ph.D. (1953) from Harvard University.

Professor Dale F. Eickelman is Professor of Anthropology at New York University. He has conducted extensive field research in Morocco and the Sultanate of Oman, as well as elsewhere in the Middle East. His publications include *Moroccan Islam* (Austin: University of Texas Press, 1976; Arabic translation, 1988); *The Middle East: An Anthropological Approach* (Englewood Cliffs, NJ: Prentice-Hall, 1981; 2nd ed., 1988; Japanese translation, 1988) and

Knowledge and Power in Morocco: The Education of a Twentieth-Century Notable (Princeton, NJ: Princeton University Press, 1985). He currently holds a fellowship from the MacArthur Foundation to write an anthropological study of political intelligence in the Arab Gulf.

The Honorable Hermann F. Eilts is currently Director of Boston University's Center for International Relations. He also serves on the Middle East Institute's Advisory Committee for the Research Center. He had a long and distinguished career in the United States Foreign Service, capping his career with stints as Ambassador to Saudi Arabia (1965-1970), and Egypt (1973-1979) during the years of Secretary of State Henry Kissinger's shuttle diplomacy. He holds a B.A. from Ursinus College and an M.A. in international relations from the School of Advanced International Studies (SAIS) of Johns Hopkins University.

Dr. David E. Long is currently Research Professor of International Affairs at Georgetown University, on detail from the Department of State. He was previously Associate Director of the office of the Ambassador at Large for Counter-terrorism. Prior to that, he was a member of the Secretary of State's Policy Planning Staff and Chief of the Near East Division in the Bureau of Intelligence of Research. He has a doctorate in international relations from George Washington University, is a widely recognized expert on Saudi Arabia and is the author of a number of books and articles on Saudi Arabia and the Gulf, the latest of which is *The United States and Saudi Arabia: Ambivalent Allies* (Boulder, CO: Westview Press, 1985).

Dr. Roger F. Pajak is National Security Adviser for Soviet and Middle East Affairs in the Office of the Secretary of the Treasury. He was formerly Senior Foreign Affairs Adviser with the US Arms Control and Disarmament Agency (1971-1980), and Associate Research Fellow at the National Defense University, and has lectured widely. Among his publications are *Soviet Arms Aid in the Middle East* (Washington: Georgetown University Press), and *Nuclear Proliferation in the Middle East: Implications for the Superpowers* (Washington: National Defense University Press, 1982).

Dr. J.E. Peterson is an author and consultant on Middle Eastern affairs in Washington, D.C., and Adjunct Fellow in Middle Eastern Studies at the Center for Strategic and International Studies (CSIS).

He received his Ph.D. from the School of Advanced International Studies (SAIS) of the Johns Hopkins University, and has taught at Bowdoin, William & Mary, Penn, and Portland State. His books include *Oman in the Twentieth Century* (New York: Barnes & Noble, 1978), *Yemen: The Search for a Modern State* (Baltimore: Johns Hopkins University Press, 1982), *The Politics of Middle Eastern Oil* (editor; Washington: Middle East Institute, 1983), and *Defending Arabia* (New York: St. Martin's Press, 1986). His latest publication is *The Arab Gulf States: Steps Toward Political Participation* (New York: Praeger, 1988, for the Center for Strategic and International Studies; Washington Papers, No. 131).

Professor Rouhollah K. Ramazani has taught at the University of Virginia since 1954, where he is the Harry F. Byrd Professor of Government and Foreign Affairs. He has also been a Visiting Professor at Cambridge University, Agha Khan Professor of Islamic Studies at the American University of Beirut, and a Visiting Professor at the Johns Hopkins School of Advanced International Studies (SAIS). He has authored ten books and numerous articles on Middle Eastern affairs. His two latest books are *Revolutionary Iran: Challenge and Response in the Middle East* (Baltimore: Johns Hopkins University Press, 1986), and *The Gulf Cooperation Council: Record and Analysis* (Charlottesville: University Press of Virginia, 1988). Professor Ramazani serves on the Middle East Institute's Board of Governors, and on the Board of Advisory Editors of the *Middle East Journal*.

H. Richard Sindelar III, as a Pearson Program Fellow, served as the first Director of the newly-created Middle East Institute Research Center during 1985-1986. Among other projects at the Institute, he inaugurated the Center's annual series of lectures. His posts as a Foreign Service Officer have included Tel Aviv (1974), Jerusalem (1974-1976), and the Sinai Field Mission (1978-1979). During 1976-1978, he was a political analyst for Lebanon and Palestinian affairs in the State Department. A lawyer, he currently serves as a Division Chief in the Legal Affairs Branch of the Visa Office in the Bureau of Consular Affairs.

Joseph C. Story is President of Gulf Consulting Services, which provides political and economic analyses on the states of the Gulf Cooperation Council. He was formerly a Senior Economist with Wharton Econometric Forecasting Associates, and has also worked for ARAMCO, the Federal Energy Administration, and the Agency for International Development. He holds a B.S. degree from Indiana University and an M.A. in international economics from the University of Illinois.

Wayne E. White is currently the senior analyst in the Arab-Israeli affairs division of the Department of State's Bureau of Intelligence and Research. He previously served as the analyst with primary responsibility for advising State Department principals on the course of the Iran-Iraq war. He holds an M.A. degree in Middle East history from Pennsylvania State University and served as a Foreign Service Officer from 1973 to 1981.

Preface

The Arabian Gulf ?
The Persian Gulf ?
Or, more simply, just "the Gulf" ?
The name given this crucial body of water depends on which side of the Gulf one is. The bitter dispute over terminology mirrors one of the enduring schisms which have helped to keep this distant part of the world on the periphery of global awareness.[1] Most Americans seem to view the Gulf region as a somnolent, distant place of peaceful dhows, endless sand, and flowing oil, punctuated by recurring crises. The unprovoked Iraqi assault on the *USS Stark* on May 17, 1987, resulting in the loss of 37 American lives, was one of these crises.

Once again, policymakers and the media around the world were compelled to focus their attention on a growing number of intractable and inter-related concerns which have characterized this region in recent years:

—the prolonged and largely stalemated conflict between Iran and Iraq, now in its eighth year;
—the increasingly dangerous impact of the Iran-Iraq war on the other states of the region, demonstrated most recently by the July 1987 riots in Mecca, in which several hundred pilgrims died, and
—the Iranian Silkworm missile attacks on Kuwait in September and October 1987;
—the vital importance of the Gulf as a primary source of oil supplies (some 60% of the world's total proven oil reserves are located in the Gulf);
—the inescapable reality that most of this oil must be exported in tankers passing through the vulnerable Strait of Hormuz;
—the issue of freedom of the seas and the concomitant decision of the United States government to provide US naval escorts for Kuwaiti oil tankers re-registered under the US flag;
—the build-up of US military forces in the Gulf in mid-1987, to more than 40 ships and 20,000 personnel, and the deterioration of the situation into violent clashes with Iran;
—the continuing US-Soviet strategic rivalry for the upper hand in this economically and politically crucial region; and
—the corollary concern that regional conflict can suddenly spin

out of control and escalate beyond the crisis-management abilities of world leaders, as happened in the Balkans earlier in this century and provoked World War I.

Such attention has not routinely been the case. Even observers of the Middle East are much more likely to have followed the events, politics, debates, and conflagrations surrounding the Arab-Israeli dispute, or the sorrowful history of Lebanon and its violent disintegration. Those who truly know the region are few in number. It is the rare diplomat who specializes in the area. A few businessmen, particularly from the oil and construction industries, are conversant about Gulf history, economics, and affairs generally, out of commercial necessity and occasionally later personal interest. The occasional scholar follows the region in some depth, but the primary interests of even scholars often lie elsewhere.

If global interest should wane again, it is possible that the emergence of future crises in this region may well affect the world in fundamental ways we cannot readily comprehend at this time. That the Gulf is crucial and vital to the well-being of the Western world is axiomatic. We must thus remain aware of history's repeated lessons that such regions on the periphery of civilizations and empires have often spawned cataclysms that have not only severely affected those civilizations, but also fundamentally altered the world's course.[2] To the list of minor but historically relevant place-names associated with these historic sea-changes could well be added at some future time such names recently in the news as Basra, Shatt al-'Arab, Majnun, Ahvaz, al-Faw, Kharg, Farsi, and Hormuz.

Even though the Gulf may be on the periphery of our awareness, it possesses many of the characteristics of those marginal regions which, in history, have spawned influential developments and evolutions far beyond the perceived intrinsic importance of the region. It is, at one and the same time, on the geographic periphery and at a geostrategic center of the globe. If conventional analysis is to be believed, the epicenters of Western interests lie in North America, the Soviet Union, China and Japan, and in Europe. The Gulf is situated much away from these centers. The barriers of time and distance thus make conducting affairs with these countries in any continuous, significant way a difficult exercise. The advent of aviation and telecommunications has shrunk these distances to some extent, but transportation of people and goods still is a time-consuming process relative to dealing with other less peripheral areas.

Yet throughout history the Gulf has been and continues to be a vital land bridge between two of these epicenters — the West and the East. Like the Balkans in times past, it is strategically located on or near trade routes and sea lanes. Like the American colonies, it possesses important natural resources for the economies of the epicenter powers. Like the Mediterranean, it is the means by which continents are connected and the route through which invaders must pass.

If, in the perception of most Westerners, the Gulf is on the periphery in most things, it certainly is not on the economic periphery. The Gulf's oil resources are crucial to the industries and economies of much of the Free World. The waters of the Gulf and its approaches constitute a major sea lane, principally for the transport of this oil but also for the large volume of imports into the Gulf's littoral states. The investments of many Gulf states have helped bolster the economies of many Western and Third World countries, just as Western countries and firms have staked their prosperity on the economic development of the Gulf states.

Traditionally, the Gulf has also been on the political periphery — except for brief interludes, such as playing out of European rivalries at the turn of the century, the use of the Gulf and Iran as a corridor for aid to the Soviet Union during World War II, the Arab oil embargo of 1973-1974, the Iranian revolution in 1979, the outbreak of the Iran-Iraq war in 1980, and the crisis in 1987. World leaders pay scant attention until an event threatening strategic security unfolds. With the passing of the immediate threat, attention soon wanes again.

Such has been the case, for instance, with the Iran-Iraq war. The Western world's early concern faded once it became apparent that neither side would carry the day and thus there was no need to make hard political, military, and strategic choices. The same brief burst of attention occurred at the start of the "tanker war" in 1984, but then concern slackened as the oil continued to be exported. Upheavals and conflicts in the Gulf have often been thought of as minor annoyances by those in Western capitals seized with global issues deemed much more significant. Witness the Dhufar rebellion in Oman in the 1970s, which received scant attention and then only because of the perceived strategic threat of Communist influence. The *USS Stark* incident has once again placed the Gulf at center stage in the West's eyes, but the lifespan of this attention is likely to be ephemeral — to the chagrin of the states of the Arab littoral.

A principal intention of this volume, and the lecture series on which it is based, is to sound again the warning that we must pay more attention to the Gulf region, to try in some small way to generate greater — and especially more profound and enduring — interest in the region, and to contribute to better understanding of the forces, both internal and external, which shape events there. Our interest must not be transitory; rather, we must devote sustained diplomatic, economic, and cultural resources to improving our ties to this region and raising, permanently, American awareness of its vital centricity.

This volume has sought to gather the analytical expertise and interpretations of some of the best scholars, writers, analysts, and diplomats familiar with this sensitive and simmering region. The authors represented herein, some of the best and the brightest in Gulf affairs, have contributed their time and views in an effort to paint a better picture of the Gulf region and its importance.

The genesis of this volume lies in a project begun in 1982 to renovate the Middle East Institute's George Camp Keiser Library. The renovations, completed in 1985, returned the building, an old carriage house, to its original Victorian splendor. Incorporated within the building was a modern facility for research and study. But the many who contributed to the renovation wanted to leave more than an amalgam of brick and mortar, and hence the idea was born of creating an active and continuing research arm of the Institute. With the generous support of several private Omani citizens, the Sultan Qaboos Research Center, located on the second floor of the library's newly renovated quarters, was created in 1985.

Among the center's programs inaugurated at the outset was a lecture series on issues and problems of the Gulf region. An Advisory Committee for the Research Center was instrumental in helping to guide and nurture this early program. Special thanks for their part in this inaugural effort, and their expertise and guidance, must go to committee members James H. Critchfield, Dr. Dale F. Eickelman, Dr. Omar Zawawi, and Dr. Robert McC. Adams.

In addition, the generous contributions of time and scholarly effort by our lecturers were crucial to launching both this volume and the Research Center as a whole. The Institute is deeply indebted to these distinguished scholars, diplomats, and writers for their willingness to help an embryonic enterprise get off the ground with quality and class. We want especially to single out for appreciation the friendship and critical guidance offered throughout the project by two key contributors, Dale Eickelman and Wayne White. Each helped this effort along in ways too numerous to catalogue.

Just as crucial was the volunteer assistance by a number of helpers. Nancy Wood became over time our indispensable resource for the project, contributing many, many hours on tasks great and small. She, and MEI interns Barbara Johnson, Bruno Schneider, and Doug Maguire, were invaluable in editing the papers, checking facts, doing lengthy word-processing and script preparation, and more. Without them, and the early advice of MEI publisher Kay Manalo, this volume would not have been possible. A special note of thanks also goes to Alexia Suma, whose assistance in helping update some of the materials as events unfolded was, above all, a professional effort. We are indebted to Daniel L. Kiser and Christina N. Morrow for the preparation of the maps.

This volume is divided into three integrated sections. Part One provides an overview of the international and foreign-policy environment of the Gulf, including external interests and regional responses. Part Two offers detailed examinations of three of the most significant issues that presently affect the region, and thereby the decision-making process of both the Gulf's leaders and key outside governments, including the United States. Part Three consists of illustrative looks at three key countries of the Gulf littoral. These states are undergoing dramatic internal changes at the same time as they are playing central roles in the present and future development of the region.

Inevitably, when this volume appears in print, the narratives of the following chapters will have been overtaken by the rapidly unfolding events in the Gulf at the time of writing. Nevertheless, we fully expect that the underlying analyses, ideas, and interpretations will continue to serve as useful guides and references with which analysts, scholars, and policy-makers may examine regional events, trends, and foreign-policy formulations, and ascertain, with as much certitude as possible in this volatile region, what directions forces and events will take in the future.

We begin with an introduction outlining one of the fundamental cornerstones of recent United States foreign policy — the Carter Doctrine and its antecedents — written by one "present at the creation," Dr. Zbigniew Brzezinski. The Carter Doctrine, really no more than a few phrases in a broader State of the Union message by President Carter, has become, like the Monroe Doctrine before it for Latin America, the centerpiece of United States policy for the

Gulf. It is a balance of needed toughness, with a willingness to help the region achieve calm without the necessity of resorting solely to military might. It has stood the test of time and a myriad of challenges, including Soviet activities in the region, the outbreak of the Iran-Iraq war, the emergence of the tanker war, recent concern over the possible closing of the Strait of Hormuz by Iran's use of Silkworm missiles, and developments arising out of the reflagging of Kuwaiti tankers. Whatever the outcome of this and future debates on specific challenges and confrontations, the doctrine itself is likely to be the strategic foundation on which tactical decisions of the moment are based.

NOTES

1. In an attempt to remain terminologically neutral, the generic term, "the Gulf," is employed in this volume.

2. See, for example, Carroll Quigley, *The Evolution of Civilizations* (New York: Macmillan, 1961), pp. 39–93. Quigley's theory extends much beyond the mere notion that an isolated event or series of happenings can severely influence a central empire's course. His analysis includes empirical evidence that whole new civilizations often evolve over time on the periphery of older, decaying ones. These newer states are nurtured by some of the ideas of the old, amalgamate them with their own social, cultural, religious, economic, political, military, and philosophical ideas, and combine this mixture with influences from elsewhere. The birth of Rome on the periphery of the decaying Greek empire, the rise of Islam between the declining Roman and Persian empires, the growth of the Ottoman empire at the boundaries of Byzantium, and the impact on Western thought of Islam's furthest expansion into the fringes of Europe, are all examples of this phenomenon.

Abbreviations

ADDF	Abu Dhabi Defense Force (UAE)
ARAMCO	Arabian-American Oil Company (Saudi Arabia)
ASRY	Arab Shipbuilding and Repair Yard (Bahrain)
AWACS	Airborne Warning and Control System
BAPCO	Bahrain Petroleum Company
bd	barrels per day
BENELUX	Belgium, Netherlands, Luxembourg
CENTCOM	Central Command (US)
CENTO	Central Treaty Organization
COMIDEASTFORCE	Commander, Middle East Force (US)
DDF	Dubai Defense Force
EEC	European Economic Community
EGPC	Emirates General Petroleum Company (UAE)
EIU	Economist Intelligence Unit
FBIS	Foreign Broadcast Information Service (US)
FNC	Federal National Council (UAE)
GARMCO	Gulf Aluminum Rolling Mill Company (Bahrain)
GCC	Gulf Cooperation Council
GDP	gross domestic product
GIC	Gulf Investment Corporation
GIF	Gulf Investment Fund
GOIC	Gulf Organization for Industrial Consulting
IMF	International Monetary Fund
NATO	North Atlantic Treaty Organization
OIC	Organization of the Islamic Conference
mbd	million barrels per day
MEED	*Middle East Economic Digest*
OAPEC	Organization of Arab Petroleum Exporting Countries
OAS	Organization of American States
OECD	Organization for Economic Cooperation and Development

OPEC	Organization of Petroleum Exporting Countries
PDRY	Peoples' Democratic Republic of Yemen (South Yemen)
PFLO	Peoples' Front for the Liberation of Oman
SAF	Sultan's Armed Forces (Oman)
SAIRI	Supreme Assembly of the Islamic Revolution in Iraq
SAM	surface-to-air missile
SCC	State Consultative Council (Oman)
tbd	thousand barrels per day
TOS	Trucial Oman Scouts (UAE)
UAE	United Arab Emirates
UDF	Union Defense Force (UAE)
UEA	Unified Economic Agreement (GCC)
UK	United Kingdom
UN	United Nations
US	United States
USAF	United States Air Force
USGPO	US Government Printing Office
USSR	Union of Soviet Socialist Republics

Map 1: Middle East

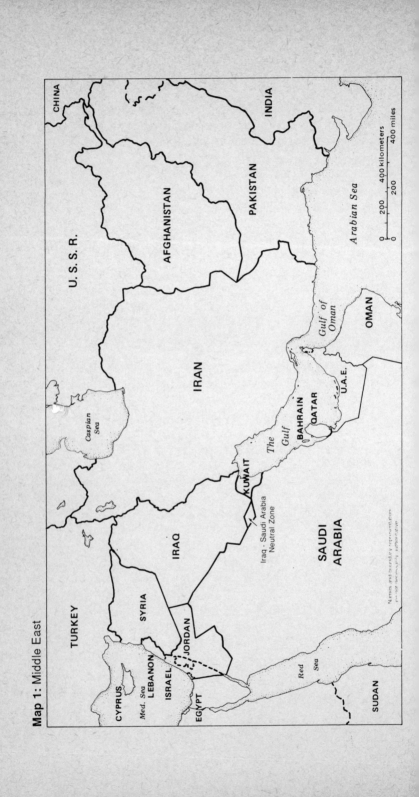

Map 2: The Gulf Region

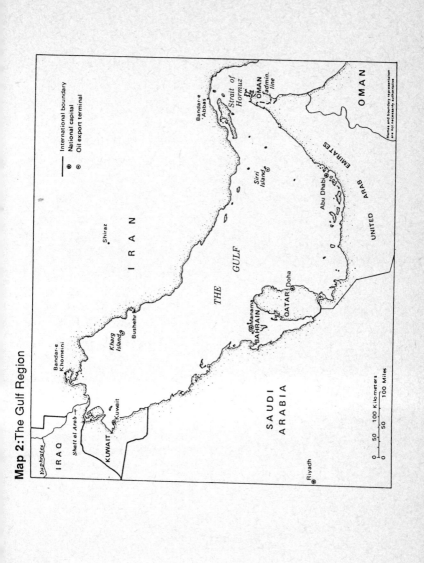

1

After the Carter Doctrine: Geostrategic Stakes and Turbulent Crosscurrents in the Gulf

Zbigniew Brzezinski

The Gulf has been a geostrategic focal point of global significance for nearly a century. The United States has been aware of its importance ever since American merchantmen first made port calls in Oman at the end of the eighteenth century. But US concern with developments in the Gulf has intensified with the events of the last two decades. Similarly, the Soviet Union has been aware of the importance of the Gulf since the days of Great Russia and the Tsars. Once the scene of Dutch, French, British and German rivalries, the Gulf now is marked by American-Soviet superpower competition.

To appreciate fully the extent of the global context in which events in the Gulf region are played out, one must approach the issue with a geostrategic perspective in mind. The longstanding US-Soviet rivalry is one that we can anticipate will endure for many decades and perhaps generations to come. There have been three key strategic fronts in the forty-year contest between the superpowers: Europe, the Far East, and the Gulf. Europe has been marked by a stand-off since the conclusion of the Second World War, with massive conventional forces, backed by both intermediate and strategic nuclear forces, facing each other along a long line from northern Germany to the Balkans. In the Far East, we confront Moscow's surrogates in Vietnam and neighboring countries, face a longstanding stalemate in Korea, and can see the beginnings of Soviet naval and commercial expansion into the Pacific basin.

In recent years, however, the most alarming confrontation has been in the third of these geostrategic centers: the Gulf. It is here that the US has suffered two major strategic reversals in the last decade alone: the loss of position and influence in Iran, and the Soviet invasion of Afghanistan. There are three major stakes in the region of primary concern to the United States. First and foremost is oil, with all its political, economic and military ramifications. The second stake is the Soviet Union's age-old search for access to a warm-water port, which has been combined in recent years with a growing naval and political presence in the Indian Ocean. The third consideration involves the moderate states in the region, which could be toppled by local upheavals that would diminish US influence and leverage, as happened with Khomeini's ascendancy in Iran, and also provide fertile ground for Soviet adventurism at American expense.

The Gulf countries contain nearly two-thirds of the free world's proven reserves of crude oil and export one-quarter of all oil traded in the world today. In 1986, Western Europe received some 30 percent of its oil imports from the Gulf, while Japan received 60 percent and the United States five percent. The great bulk of these oil exports must pass through the narrow and exceedingly vulnerable chokepoint at the Strait of Hormuz, and it is vital to Western interests that this shipping lane be kept open. In the event of a large-scale conventional confrontation in Europe or elsewhere, the region's oil supplies would quickly become a determining factor in whether Western military forces prevailed or ground to a halt as a result of the military planners' classic nightmare: a lack of fuel to keep the machines of war running.

This dependence will only grow in the future. It is estimated that in 1995 the free world will receive between 30 and 45 percent of its oil from the Gulf states. Were the Soviet Union ever to achieve predominance over southwest Asia and the Gulf itself, Moscow would be in a position to exert tremendous leverage over our allies in Western Europe and Japan. Analysts have only to look at the tremendous impact of the Arab oil boycott of the 1970s on the economies of both West and East to appreciate the true chokehold any hostile foreign power could have over our wellbeing merely by controlling this crucial resource area.

The second major concern for the US in the Gulf is the reasonable assumption that Moscow still covets an all-season warm-water port. The value of access to the Indian Ocean has long been evident. Eighteenth-century American traders, whose need for free shipping lanes and commercial entry to the world's ports served as an important factor in the young nation's foreign policy, were quick to recognize the advantages and importance of the Indian Ocean and its position between the markets of the West and the goods and resources of the East. One of our longest continuing diplomatic relationships, established over 150 years ago, has been with Oman, once a maritime power throughout the eastern Indian Ocean and East African waters. In the nineteenth century, the importance of Indian Ocean access via the Gulf was discernible in "the Great Game" played out between the British and the Russians in Persia, Afghanistan, and the Northwest Frontier of India.

The Soviet Union's search for access is no less crucial to Soviet strategic planners now than it was in the time of Peter the Great. An outlet on the Indian Ocean littoral would permit Soviet naval units to bypass the often frozen waters and inhospitable climes of Murmansk, and to escape the geographical strangleholds encircling Soviet naval bases at Vladivostok and in the Black Sea. It must be remembered, even in an era of modern strategic forces, that Soviet military planners still have as a part of their intellectual software an almost encyclopedic remembrance of the old and trusted axioms. There is no doubt that an Indian Ocean outlet today would give the Soviets a new, shorter route for much of their commerce and trade, and a vital naval position near the heart of some of the free world's most heavily travelled shipping lanes in one of the globe's most crucial oceans.

Perhaps the most elusive, and yet potentially the most dangerous, policy consideration confronting the US is dealing with internal and regional disruptions, whether they be from the left or from Islamic fundamentalism. No greater lesson of how these forces can dramatically shift the balance of power exists than that of Iran, where a longtime and progressive friend of the United States was transformed into an unpredictable fundamentalist regime whose leaders disavow the old rules of the diplomatic game and display considerable skill in attacking the United States and the West in unorthodox ways. As the Iranian revolution graphically demonstrated, it is very difficult for Western policy-makers to develop an effective response once new and powerful social, religious, and political attitudes gain widespread acceptance, the hold of a leader or government begins to slip, and a crisis erupts.

The immediate aftermath of such an upheaval is often a great reduction in the power, leverage, and influence of Western nations. Diplomatic, commercial and military ties may be tossed aside along with the fallen regime. More profound and threatening, however, is the fact that these upheavals provide the sort of political climate in which Soviet intrigues can blossom and Soviet influence expand. In the confusion following the eventual death of Ayatollah Khomeini, for example, any number of opportunities might appear for the Soviets to gain additional leverage and influence, if not for

3

elements sympathetic to Soviet ideology to gain control of this strategically important country. Sudden leadership changes, no matter their causes, in other states of the region, might also afford similar opportunities.

At least three scenarios come to mind in which the United States' position in the Gulf could slip precipitously as a result of largely internal political dynamics — and thereby endanger our global position. First, moderate Arab regimes could be destabilized by fundamentalist and Iranian-backed social and political upheavals. Second, Iran might decisively defeat smaller Iraq and assume the threatening position of unchallenged regional military power. Third, the Soviet Union might evolve into a principal regional arbiter, particularly if alarmed Arab regimes were to perceive that a timid US could not, or would not, afford them protection and consequently turned to Moscow for such succor.

It was with this superpower context in mind that, in late 1979 and early 1980, the Carter administration began the complex process of putting together a long-term United States foreign policy for the Gulf and Indian Ocean region. The end result was.President Carter's enunciation, in his 1980 State of the Union message, of what came to be known as the Carter Doctrine.

The fall of the Shah had ended the United States' efforts to promote Iran as the dominant regional power and the focal point of our security belt across the south of the USSR. Iran's collapse, in turn, undoubtedly smoothed the way for the Soviet invasion of Afghanistan. For the first time since the advent of the direct Soviet-US rivalry in the aftermath of World War II, the insertion of Soviet forces into Afghanistan had breached the accepted lines between the superpowers. A deep Soviet wedge had been driven into the defensive arc nurtured by the West to span the southern front between the other two crucial centers of confrontation: Europe and the Far East. I was convinced at that time, and remain so now, that this event was at least in part brought about by an increasing confidence in the Soviet Union that the US, in the wake of the Vietnam experience, was becoming more acquiescent.

A number of elements needed to be included in an American response to these negative developments, in particular the watershed of the Soviet invasion of Afghanistan. First, whatever else was decided, our response had to display a requisite firmness, sense of strength, and commitment to the region. Second, the United States needed to seek some sort of regional security framework through which and with which to prepare for, analyze and respond to crisis in the region, whether Soviet-inspired or generated from within. Third, this toughness needed in turn to be backed up by concerted efforts to enhance our military capabilities and lessen our military reaction time to any regional crisis. Fourth, in the broader global arena, this needed to be supported by an overall strategic renewal, both in terms of strategic thinking and in terms of the nuts-and-bolts rebuilding of United States global forces.

After much planning, and political and bureaucratic maneuvering, our efforts bore fruit when President Carter, on January 23, 1980, made the following statement at a crucial portion of his State of the Union address:

Let our position be absolutely clear: An attempt by any outside force to gain control of the Persian Gulf region will be regarded as an assault on the vital interests of the United States of America, and such an assault will be repelled by any means necessary, including military force.

The speech also spoke in this context of a need to create collective efforts to meet the new Soviet threat to the Gulf-Indian Ocean region. President Carter concluded a litany of projected US responses to potential Soviet aggression by declaring:

Finally, we are prepared to work with other countries in the region to share a cooperative security framework that respects differing values and political beliefs, yet which enhances the independence, security and prosperity of all.

With these pronouncements, President Carter established the essential elements of US policy. The first pronouncement, picked up as a central theme by the press, quickly was dubbed the Carter Doctrine. It was directly descended from both the nineteenth-century Monroe Doctrine, cordoning the Americas off from European machinations, and the post-World-War-II Truman Doctrine, which responded similarly to a Soviet threat against Greece and Turkey.

The doctrine possessed, first of all, the necessary resolve. A clear line across which the Soviet Union or others were not to tread had been drawn, and it was backed by a direct statement that our interests would be defended by military force if need be. It was purposefully vague as to how, where, and when such a military response might be made. This was my concept of designing options which might involve both vertical and horizontal escalation, in which the United States would be free to choose either the terrain or the tactic or the level of our response. In this way, our military planners could keep the Soviets and others guessing about how we might retaliate against any adventurism in the region. In turn, this uncertainty, we believed, would heighten Soviet military leaders' wariness about confronting us in a region we had formally declared vital to our interests.

Backing the Carter Doctrine's toughness was the second facet of the three-cornered US response: the idea of a regional security framework, by which the United States could lend additional credibility to the policy as a whole. The idea was not a formal alliance, but a less defined but nevertheless crucial amalgam of security cooperation arrangements with various regional nations. In this way, tangible steps would be taken to reinforce the US commitment to the area, without bullishly charging ahead, oblivious to the political sensitivities of already small and vulnerable states.

At least in the early going, then, this regional security effort would best be nurtured by moving forward with the third key element in the US response: enhancing our military capabilities specifically as they related to the Gulf region. It was during this time that military cooperation, on a variety of matters and in a multitude of ways, was expanded appreciably with regional states. In 1980, we agreed on heightened military cooperation with several states, including joint military exercises and access to support facilities at Ras Banas (Egypt), Berbera (Somalia), Mombasa (Kenya) and al-Masira Island (Oman). Early-warning capabilities were enhanced through joint AWACS programs with the Saudis, and other avenues of military cooperation, including military sales, were discussed at length with then-Crown-Prince Fahd and other Saudi leaders. Access to forward bases in Oman was negotiated.

Prepositioning of military stockpiles against the eventuality of a conventional confrontation, joint military exercises with regional states such as Oman and Egypt, increased US naval and air deployments to this southwestern front, and efforts to build the Rapid Deployment Force were all decisions designed, at least in part, to emphasize that the words of the Carter Doctrine could and would be backed up with military clout if push came to shove. We would not for a long time, if ever, be able to match the Soviet Union battalion for battalion or tank for tank on the southwest front. The Soviets' job is made easier by dint of proximity of supply lines from their home bases or Afghanistan. US military leaders would be faced with great distances to cover, strung-out supply lines and other logistical difficulties. Despite all this, the deterrent effect of the Carter Doctrine's words themselves, coupled with the sundry efforts to expand our regional capabilities and cooperation, have made clear that any Soviet adventurism in the Gulf or Indian Ocean would come at a high cost to Moscow.

The vastly enlarged US naval forces rushed into operation in the Gulf and northern Indian Ocean in summer 1987 was the price we all had to pay for the lack of international credibility in American resolve. If American power were truly feared, not a single American warship would have been necessary. In other words, the Gulf naval armada bespoke a significant erosion in the US capacity for deterrence.

Rather than an aggressive, assertive policy and actions, the US posture was reactive. Large numbers of US naval vessels were assembled for escort duty. To the Iranians and to others closely watching around the globe, both the numbers and the type of duty signalled a defensive, reactive, Maginot-line type of military philosophy.

We were not, at the same time, positioning ourselves to strike swiftly, hard, frequently, and with decisiveness in an offensive fashion should the Iranians seek to test our resolve. A defensive mode signals concern and fear. An offensive posture, poised to strike at the heart of an opponent, signals resolve and strength. In other words, we were prepared to provide defensive firepower against a given attacker, in a situation where the latter would choose the time and place of his action. We should have been less interested, in a tactical sense, with the fate of one or two ships carrying the US flag; let them sail on alone. But, if any one of them were attacked, our armadas should have been in position to retaliate on our terms, in our way, at our chosen time, and against our chosen targets.

An appropriate US response should have concentrated adequate military power to inflict serious damage on the potential opponent and quietly conveyed to that opponent its intentions. In this particular case, Washington should have informed Tehran, perhaps through a responsible third party, that: (1) US-flagged ships will continue to use the Gulf; (2) the United States will respond with military means against Iranian assets if any US-flagged ship is harmed; (3) the US will react similarly if any US facilities are subject to Iranian-sponsored terrorist action; and (4) the United States has the capacity to destroy not only important Iranian military assets but also vital economic facilities, and to impose a total naval blockade of all Iranian maritime trade. Following such a message, the United States pointedly could have sent in an unescorted freighter or tanker, even informing Tehran of its schedule.

We need to revitalize the world's belief and confidence in the viability and credibility of United States' deterrence. Deterrence is the threat of counterviolence designed to negate the capacity of our opponent to compel us to fulfill his will, where war is violence intended to compel an opponent to submit to our will. In both Europe and the Far East, our positions are stronger, the game more static, the rules of political engagement discreet and understood, and the changes likely to be incremental and small. The Middle East, on the other hand, is in a state of rapid and uncertain flux, thus posing a much greater array of opportunities and dangers.

Much was done toward the end of the Carter Administration to revise American strategic thinking away from the notion of preparing almost exclusively for a brief Armageddon-like nuclear conflagration. Instead, we substituted a more flexible use of our strategic and conventional forces, the development of a rapid deployment force to respond to crises, and modifications in the command, control, communications, and intelligence (C^3I) functions central to a successful military response on all levels of conflict.

More needs to be done, however. First and foremost, our conventional military thinking needs to evolve away from its fixation on Europe. The economies of our NATO allies are able to assume a greater portion of these nations' own defense burden. We should move to restructure and reallocate some of our conventional force assets away from the static defense of Europe and more toward enhancing our abilities to inject our forces quickly into areas where we cannot, or do not wish to, station permanent forces. As an integral part of this rethinking, the Pentagon should push forward with enhancing our sea and airlift capabilities, and expanding light, quick-response units such as the US Central Command.

In the policy arena, it is therefore also best for US foreign-policy formulators to focus their efforts in the broader southwest Asia region, seeking both ways to control any further erosion in the American position and to exploit advantages as they surface. The Gulf, Iran and the Afghanistan-Pakistan axis are the keystones of this region, and the potential steppingstones to things greater or lesser.

With this in mind, I have previously outlined a five-point effort to build on the Carter Doctrine in response to the challenges of this region.[1] I think it appropriate to conclude by reiterating these five points. The United States needs:

(1) to reinforce the anti-Soviet resilience of the region's key countries, notably Pakistan and Iran, and to cooperate with China to improve Pakistan's security;

(2) to increase the US capacity to mount a prompt military response should the Soviets attack;

(3) to keep the Afghanistan issue alive by sustaining the resistance, while simultaneously probing for Soviet willingness to restore genuine neutrality and internal self-determination to Afghanistan;

(4) to engage India in at least diplomatic efforts for the resolution of the Afghanistan problem and to promote a less tense Pakistan-Indian relationship; and

(5) to help stimulate a more distinctive political consciousness among the Soviet Muslims as a deterrent to the further Soviet absorption of Islamic peoples.

These components of a long-term geostrategy will require collectively a major political, military and economic undertaking. Such an effort is justified by the huge stakes and is facilitated to some extent by the relatively favorable trends on the other two central strategic fronts. Accordingly, for the United States to concentrate its initiative and resources on this region is both justified and feasible.

NOTE

1. *Game Plan* (Boston: Atlantic Monthly Press, 1986), p. 222.

Part I:
The Gulf in International Affairs

Introduction

Much as an artist sketches his work in preliminary "studies," this opening portion seeks to outline the broad global and regional concerns, and ways in which the Gulf is viewed by the Arab Gulf states. The following sections add depth, flavor, and color to these sketches. The treatments here of the sweeping perspectives set certain central issues and themes which recur periodically through the volume, such as the Iran-Iraq war, and the ambitious experiment of the Gulf Cooperation Council (GCC). By first taking a broad look at the Gulf of yesterday and today, we hope to provide a framework for gauging the impact on the Gulf of tomorrow of the specific significant issues examined in the following sections.

Hermann Eilts examines how the Gulf countries view the world, "looking out" from their corner of the globe. Each Gulf country has a unique perspective, drawn from its national interests, its history, and its relations with both its neighbors and countries outside the region. Yet many of their concerns are shared as well. Ambassador Eilts also pays particular attention to the outlook of the Sultanate of Oman, which was chosen for a variety of reasons.

Oman is one of the Gulf's most strategically important states. It has a long and proud history as both a regional power and a great seafaring nation. Its economic, political, and military circumstances reflect in many ways the Gulf as a whole; it is neither the largest nor the smallest in terms of these aspects, but representatively in the middle. Oman has had friendly relations with the United States for more than 150 years, and, in recent years, it has been the Gulf country on which US leaders could count the most for security assistance and cooperation. As a consequence, as a friend, Oman's views ought to carry an extra bit of weight and should be of particular interest to US policy-makers.

At the same time, Ambassador Eilts uses Oman as a filter to examine those forces which most influence the foreign-policy decisions debated in the councils of Gulf governments. How do they see their positions within the Gulf? Beyond the Gulf? Which players, through their views and lobbying, carry the most weight in these councils? How do Gulf leaders view the superpowers — and their own national security concerns? As the world becomes more reliant on the Gulf's resources, what leverage do these countries believe they can muster to seek acceptance of their views and deference to their concerns? How will these decision-making processes evolve in the years ahead?

Next, John Duke Anthony discusses and analyzes a major Gulf experiment: the cooperative effort within the framework of the GCC to pool resources, ideas and people to better achieve common regional goals. While unity is an omnipresent theme in Arab politics, the only working experiment in this regard, on either a regional or subregional level, is that of these six Gulf states.

Will the GCC evolve into an integrated, perhaps supranational, authority? Or will it go the way of so many other cooperation or unity schemes? Or, perhaps, will it evolve over time as the European Community has — a step at a time, each painfully taken, but each a step forward toward more unified policies and a step away from the historical reluctance to link in any way the destinies of independent, sovereign nations?

How will the broad economic issues of the region influence the GCC's course? Will local economic provincialisms prevail — such as duplicative industrial concerns and transportation facilities in many countries? Will tribal centrifugal forces, endemic for centuries, push the organization back toward more fragmentation of its constituent parts? The success or failure of the GCC is likely to have a substantial bearing on the degree and direction of the political and economic power that the Gulf will project in the years ahead. How will formidable issues such as the Iran-Iraq war affect the organization's unity, when each country has its own political, military, and religious perspectives and concerns? Does a regional group such as the GCC complement or conflict with larger organizations, such as the Arab League and OPEC?

Part One ends with Roger F. Pajak's examination of another key foreign-policy problem: the Soviet Union's role, influence, and aspirations in the Gulf. If the Carter Doctrine, described in Dr. Brzezinski's introductory chapter, enunciates the principles upon which the United States bases its actions in the region, what is the parallel for Moscow? How much concern should there be over Soviet inroads? Can a socialist system coexist in constructive ways — for the Soviets — with more traditional, Islamic, and tribal societies?

To what extent will Gulf countries, either individually or in concert, seek to play the superpowers off against one another, and to what extent can Gulf countries be relied upon by the United States to decide that their interests more closely align with those of the Western and Pacific nations? Does Moscow have the skills to exploit opportunities in the Gulf, or will an inexpert hamhanded approach, as demonstrated in Egypt, eventually dissuade Gulf leaders from significant cooperation with Moscow? Given the bloody fighting of January 1986 in the Peoples' Democratic Republic of Yemen (South Yemen), might many observers be overestimating the Soviet potential for mischief in the region?

Even if Moscow can be smooth and polished in its handling of its relations with the Gulf, will Moscow's decision-makers, in their list of priorities, see fit to devote the considerable effort, resources, and political capital necessary to take full advantage of opportunities? To what extent, if any, would it be wise to seek more, not less, Soviet involvement and cooperation in the region, as an effort to coopt Moscow into playing a positive role?

2

Foreign Policy Perspectives of the Gulf States

Hermann Frederick Eilts

The foreign policy concerns of the Arab states of the Gulf — Iraq, Kuwait, Saudi Arabia, Bahrain, Qatar, the United Arab Emirates (UAE), and Oman — are of three kinds:

(1) Those that are immediate, urgent and compelling;

(2) Those still unresolved Gulf-area disputes that already existed prior to the Iran-Iraq war and affected relationships of various Gulf states with one another; and

(3) Those emotionally charged disputes plaguing the Arab world as a whole, the Gulf states and peoples included, and either significantly or marginally affecting Gulf states' security.

Oman, as an Arab state, and a founding member of the Gulf Co-operation Council (GCC) since 1981 shares to some extent virtually all of the foreign-policy concerns of its Gulf neighbors. Yet, circumstances of Omani geography and recent political history perforce nuance the Omani perspective on most of these common foreign-policy problems. Thus, Oman, located as it is in the southeastern part of the Arabian Peninsula, senses less imperatively certain foreign-policy issues, especially those flowing from the Iran-Iraq war, than do, for example, its Kuwaiti and Saudi Arabian GCC partners.

The Omani political and geographic coign of vantage is inevitably somewhat different from those of its GCC partners, although Oman is in principle supportive of its Arab neighbors in the Gulf and doubtless is in earnest in avowing this. In order to contrast the Omani perspective with that of other Arab states of the Gulf, it is necessary first to sketch the foreign policy concerns of the latter group of polities, and subsequently to assess the Omani view of these issues, as well as those foreign policy problems peculiar to Oman itself.

PRIMARY CURRENT CONCERNS OF ARAB GULF STATES

At present the overriding and immediate foreign policy concern of the Arab states of the Gulf can be only one thing: the ongoing Iran-Iraq war. To Iraq, which is not a member of the GCC, and its Ba'thist leadership, sheer survival is at stake. Iraq has repeatedly in the last few years unsuccessfully proffered peace to Iran. While Iraq's defense capability remains high, a protracted war of attrition would be difficult to withstand. Hence, persistent Iranian rejection of any honorable peace breeds an Iraqi determination to force a cessation of hostilities by intensifying air attacks on Iranian strategic targets.[1]

To the remaining Arab states of the Gulf — Kuwait, Saudi Arabia, Qatar, Bahrain, the UAE and Oman — the heightening of Iran-Iraq hostilities during 1985 and the subsequent al-Faw offensive in early 1986 and in the Fish Lake area early in 1987 raise the possibility of flailing Iranian military retaliation against one or more of them and, concurrently, the need to continue substantial financial support for Iraq at a time when their own oil revenues are sharply reduced and their domestic development programs perforce much curtailed. Kuwait and Saudi Arabia are especially vulnerable on both scores. Should Iran seem to be establishing its hegemony in Iraq as a whole or even only in southern Iraq, Kuwait's very existence as an independent entity could be jeopardized.

Were this to happen, Saudi Arabia, in particular, would be faced with the unenviable alternatives of joining in the war against Iran or having on its northeastern doorstep a hostile Shi'a neighbor, flushed with military success, and whose current leader proclaims the invalidity of "kingship" in Islam. An Iranian military success would put fundamentalist Shi'a in even closer proximity to the kingdom's already restive Shi'a minority. Since Saudi Arabia's military assets are few, and those of Kuwait even fewer, they would need outside help to defend themselves.

In theory, four possible sources of aid exist: (1) the GCC military collectivity, (2) one or more friendly Arab states inside or outside the Arab League context, (3) the US, or (4) a combination of all three or parts thereof, plus perhaps French and/or British naval forces in the area.

17

Taking each of these in turn, the GCC is scarcely likely to be able to mount effective military action against a victorious Iran, all the more so since some of its member states, like the UAE, have already been hedging their bets by maintaining quiet dialogue with Tehran and assuring the latter of friendship. For all practical purposes, the Arab League is badly fractured. Its derivative Arab Collective Security Pact has been moribund for years, while military planning in the Arab League Military Committee, such as it is today, has focused almost exclusively on an Israeli threat. To be sure, individual Arab states outside of the Gulf area, especially Egypt, might be willing to assist. Both the late President Sadat and President Mubarak have on occasion indicated a willingness to deploy Egyptian troops for the defense of threatened Gulf states, although any Egyptian military formations sent abroad are likely to be limited in number. They are more likely to be trainers and advisers than Egyptian combat units.

The US, whose presidents from Truman to Reagan have issued *ad seriatim* official statements of support for Saudi Arabian political independence and territorial integrity, has deep economic and political interests in that country. The US has also resumed diplomatic relations with Iraq,[2] although the quality of the bilateral tie with that country has diminished since Iranscam and the inadvertent Iraqi attack on the *USS Stark*. Past covert American arms shipments to Iran notwithstanding, one assumes that the US would see its Gulf interests seriously threatened by a likely Iranian victory. American concerns are shared, indeed to some extent promoted, by Saudi Arabia. Kuwait, with whom the US has no security commitment, and which has often opposed overall US Middle East policy, has since the reflagging of Kuwaiti tankers in the spring of 1987 been upgraded in preferential status. At least the seaward part of a US security umbrella has been extended to it. However, since neither Saudi Arabia nor Kuwait is yet prepared to allow the establishment of a long-sought forward command post for the US Central Command (CENTCOM), such a tactical operational headquarters has had to be put aboard a US naval vessel positioned in the Gulf of Oman.

Past Saudi political sensitivities on according indigenous military facilities to the US, especially since the closure of an airbase at Dhahran in 1962, might reasonably be expected to be subsumed temporarily in the need for rapid tangible US (and perhaps Egyptian) support and the US requirement for in-kingdom facilities if it is to function effectively in a defense support role. US "over the horizon" defense assistance to Saudi Arabia, while symbolically useful in the absence of hostilities, is hardly practical in an actual conflict situation. The US probably would also urge Egyptian and/or GCC military participation. For Saudi Arabia, Egyptian participation would be easier to take if the US were a co-partner in any such defense effort. Precisely how such a scenario would play out would depend upon the circumstances of an Iranian breakthrough in Iraq and whether or not such an Iranian success would be followed by an early move against Kuwait. Granted, the foregoing is a worst-case scenario, but fatalistically minded leaders and peoples of the Arab states of the Gulf must and do speak about such a contingency, while at the same time fervently hoping it will not take place.

A more realistic and immediate worry, especially in view of the apparent Iraqi intention to stop the export of Iranian oil by destroying or crippling the Kharg Island loading facilities, is the possibility of Iranian retaliation against one or more Arab states of the Gulf. The Iranian president and the speaker of the *Majlis*, among others, repeatedly have warned that, if Iran's oil exports are seriously impeded, all Gulf oil exporters will be made to suffer. Despite its limited capability to project force beyond its borders, Iran has already in the past few years conducted several "token" bombings of Kuwaiti facilities. These were clearly intended to be minatory.

More recently, Iran stopped vessels bound for Kuwait and Saudi Arabia, allegedly in order to search for contraband cargoes. Such cargoes, when found — and the judgment of what was contraband was made solely by Iranian boarding parties — have been confiscated. Moreover, an Iranian head of the War Information Department, Kamal Kharrazi, in the autumn of 1985 ominously warned that Kuwaiti actions in assisting Iraq were tantamount to a state of war existing between Iran and Kuwait.

Iran also began attacking Kuwaiti tankers carrying oil out of the Gulf in 1987. This prompted a Kuwaiti appeal to both the US and the Soviet Union for assistance, contending that the international community has an obligation to keep the sea lanes open. Both superpowers responded, the Soviets by chartering three tankers to Kuwait and the US by permitting 11 Kuwaiti tankers to fly the American flag. The latter arrangement enabled an augmented US naval force in the Gulf to convoy such reflagged Kuwaiti tankers between Kuwait and Khawr Fakkan in the Gulf of Oman. Iran responded to American convoy operations by sowing mines in the western Gulf sea lanes and off the port of al-Fujayra on the Gulf of Oman. Unpublicized Saudi and Kuwaiti assistance was provided to the US in mine-clearance operations. Tensions rose in the entire Gulf area as Iran publicly denounced Kuwait and Saudi Arabia as US lackeys and threatened unspecified punitive actions against those states and American interests in the region.

Are these harbingers of contemplated direct Iranian military or subversive actions against Kuwait? And, should such Iranian actions transpire, what do the GCC states, including Oman, do to implement their mutual security planning in support of one of their member states threatened by or subjected to outside assault? Exposed as Kuwait is, and without any outside security umbrella, an understandably alarmed Kuwaiti leadership has heightened the alert status of its air defense forces. These include its American-supplied I-HAWK missile batteries and newly acquired Soviet-supplied Strella-2s, SAM-7s and SAM-8s. The latter, which have been urgently commissioned, were purchased by Kuwait from the USSR because of American refusal to sell more sophisticated ground-to-air missiles. An Iranian air attack is thus likely to draw Kuwaiti counter-fire, which could lead to further escalation.

Notwithstanding occasional joint military exercises among groups of GCC states, one detects little real enthusiasm on the part of most of them to shift from joint maneuvers, conducted in a non-hostile environment, to an actual combat operation, be it defensive or offensive, with Iran as the enemy. All of the unresolved, or at best partially resolved, GCC problems of command and control, joint planning, logistic support, lack of equipment standardization, priority of defense of national territory over that of the commonwealth, would sharply emerge. One cannot escape the conclusion that the GCC military dimension, such as it is — and without denigrating its potential significance — is for the time being more suited for *ad hoc* limited military interventions related to possible internal insurgencies in a member state than it is for major conflict against an aggressive outside non-Arab (or Arab) state. This may change in the future, but such is patently the present situation.

Next to Kuwait, Saudi Arabia is viewed by Iran as unfriendly to its interests. Saudi Arabia provides the largest financial support for Iraq. Its ports, too, have been used to off-load material destined for Iraq. Although Foreign Minister Sa'ud al-Faisal's mission to Iran in May 1985 suggested some easing of Saudi-Iranian strains, the two countries are essentially deeply distrustful of each other and are likely to remain so. The Saudi success in 1984 in shooting down an

Iranian aircraft, which intruded into the Saudi side of the Gulf, seems to have had a deterrent effect upon Iran — at least up to now. No Iranian aircraft incursions into Saudi waters have since been reported, though such have taken place in the nearby waters off Qatar.

The Saudi success in warding off Iranian air threats must be viewed as a positive development in an otherwise negative litany of conflict escalation in the Gulf. It was made possible through effective US-Saudi defense collaboration, manifested through round-the-clock USAF-crewed AWACS operations in the Gulf area off Saudi Arabia, through American-provided weapons systems, and through the skill of Saudi Air Force pilots in using those systems. Saudi Arabia seemed almost apologetic about the incident when it happened, and it certainly did not seek that aerial confrontation. There was also considerable worry at the time, including in the US, about resultant possible widening of the conflict. This did not happen. In fact, the effects of the downing of the Iranian aircraft have been generally salutary.

Despite indications of a quiet improvement in Saudi-Iranian relations as a result of King Fahd's acquiescence in Iranian-proposed OPEC oil-production quotas, the underlying tension between the two states persists. It manifested itself in violent form on August 2, 1987, when Iranian pilgrims attending the annual *hajj* (pilgrimage) staged a demonstration attacking the United States, Israel and the Soviet Union. Although the demonstration had been permitted by the Saudi authorities, it erupted into a melee and was forcibly broken up by Saudi Arabian security forces. In the ensuing scuffle and panic, some 200 lives were lost and many others were hurt. Most of the casualties were Iranian, although numbers of Saudi police were apparently stabbed by Iranian pilgrims. In the wake of that incident, Iran renewed its virulent attacks against Saudi Arabia and questioned the legitimacy of the house of Sa'ud. By late August 1987, the Saudi authorities showed signs of responding in kind and spoke of eliminating the Iranian "monster." Relations between the two states became seriously roiled.

Bahrain is concerned that Iran still retains a claim to it and is alive to Iran's potential political capability to incite the Shi'a majority of Bahrain to revolt. These are currently less imminent dangers, considering the plethora of hostilities elsewhere in the Gulf, but their re-emergence in more acute form also depends upon whether or not Iran succeeds in the war. With the completion of the causeway between Saudi Arabia and Bahrain, Saudi military support for any government of Bahrain threatened by Iranian-inspired indigenous Shi'a dissidence will be facilitated. The small US naval force based on Bahrain is hardly in a position to play much of a role in generally escalating Gulf hostilities or in Bahrain itself. Nevertheless, at a minimum, the US Command Middle East Force (COMIDEASTFORCE), like the several US military missions in Saudi Arabia, symbolizes US concern for the independence of Gulf states, especially Saudi Arabia and Bahrain.

The UAE has its own preferences on dealing with Iran. It maintains dialogue with Iran, ships goods to Iran, and in general quietly propitiates the Iranian behemoth, somewhat to the annoyance of its fellow GCC partners. The UAE leadership finds it politically prudent to do so, and in present circumstances it may not be entirely wrong. Dubai, although officially a member of the UAE, acts largely on its own and maintains regular trade and other contacts with Iran.

THE STRAIT OF HORMUZ

Iran has sometimes specifically threatened to close the Strait of Hormuz as a means of making other oil producers in the Gulf suffer, should its own oil exports be seriously restricted. Any such action would affect all Arab states of the Gulf, except Oman. Even for Oman, however, whose disconnected sovereign territory in the Musandam Peninsula places part of the Hormuz chokepoint in its territorial waters, any such prospect is worrisome. It is doubtful that Iran has the military capability to block effectively the Strait of Hormuz, but this does not mean that Iran might not at some point — especially in a state of desperation — attempt to do so.

President Reagan has indicated that the US will use military means, if necessary, in order to keep the strait open, and one must assume that he means it. Should the US renege or equivocate on that commitment, its image in the Gulf region — and elsewhere — will be sorely damaged. While permanent closure of the Strait of Hormuz is highly unlikely, military action on one or the other side of the "Quoins" rock outcroppings, which divide the strait, could disrupt for a time the flow of oil out of the Gulf. This marginally would hurt Arab oil-exporting states of the Gulf, especially at a time of already reduced oil incomes. Apart from Japan, however, it would not seriously hurt European states or the US, whose oil imports from the Middle East already have been sharply reduced. Thus far, to be sure, despite repeated Iraqi air attacks on the Kharg Island oil facilities, Iranian oil exports have remained high, which probably reduces the danger of an attempt to close the strait. But this could change if Iraq, on its part, becomes increasingly desperate to prevent a war of attrition and inflicts more destruction on Kharg or on other Iranian petroleum production or export facilities.

The dangers were illustrated by escalations in the war in the Gulf during 1986 and 1987. Following the Iranian seizure of the Fish Lake area in southern Iraq in February 1987, an increasingly alarmed Iraq concluded that Iran would have to be forced to negotiate peace through economic strangulation. Iraqi air attacks on Kharg Island, the Iranian oil-reloading facilities at Sirri and Larak islands, and petroleum installations in Iran accelerated. Iran responded by attacking Kuwaiti tankers on the grounds that Kuwait provided financial support to Iraq and allowed its ports to be used to offload military supplies consigned to Iraq. An Iranian *pasdaran* (Revolutionary Guards) speedboat base was constructed on Farsi Island from which rocket and machine gun attacks on Kuwaiti vessels in the northern Gulf were made. Two Saudi-owned vessels and a number of foreign ships bound for Kuwait were also attacked.

By late spring of 1987, hostilities at sea had extended to the southern portions of the Gulf and to the Gulf of Oman. Iranian-acquired Chinese Silkworm missiles were positioned on Qishm Island and on the nearby Iranian coast and threatened closure of the Strait of Hormuz. Resultant tensions caused the deployment of sizeable American naval forces to the Gulf and the Gulf of Oman, as well as Soviet, British and French naval flotillas. Although a UN Security Council resolution was passed unanimously, calling for a ceasefire between Iraq and Iran, which Iraq accepted, the Iranian Islamic government failed to give a positive response. Following a six-week lull in Iraqi and Iranian air attacks after the passage of the UN resolution, Iraq, in late August, resumed air attacks on Iranian oil facilities and tankers, charging it could not wait indefinitely for an Iranian response. In turn, Iran attacked an unescorted Kuwaiti vessel in the Gulf. More attacks by both sides against each other's interests and states friendly to Iraq seemed likely.

SECONDARY FOREIGN POLICY CONCERNS OF THE ARAB GULF STATES

Although eyes of Gulf leaders are currently glued on the evolving, and seemingly escalating, Iran-Iraq war, Arab leaders of the Gulf

23

states have not forgotten past issues that involved their security, even if these have in the last five years lost some of their immediate saliency. Contrary to the Reagan Administration's belief, and despite events in Afghanistan, a Soviet incursion into the Gulf is not considered a real problem by Gulf leaders. On the contrary, Iraq still receives needed military equipment and spare parts from the USSR, while Kuwait has had a Soviet Embassy for nearly a quarter-century and regularly urges GCC partners to recognize or to establish diplomatic relations with the Soviets as a counter to what is portrayed as an uncritically pro-Israeli US. Rightly or wrongly, both Iraq and Kuwait take considerable pride in what they perceive to be their ability to manage a relationship with the Soviets without harm to their independence. Oman and the UAE, too, have acted to establish diplomatic relations with the USSR.

Those problems that have been temporarily subordinated, but have in no way disappeared, have to do mainly with conflicting territorial claims of one Arab Gulf state against another. Thus, the Iraqi claim to *all* of Kuwait, based upon past Ottoman sovereignty over Kuwait, even when the latter was a British protected state, has not been definitively disavowed. When the Iran-Iraq war began in 1980, and it looked for a time as if the Soviet-equipped Iraqi army would soon defeat Iran, there was deep concern among official and private Kuwaitis that an Iraqi victory would soon be followed by a move against Kuwait. That danger was forestalled by the Iranian success in throwing back the initial Iraqi surge and the ensuing protracted conflict still underway.

Nevertheless, the Iraqi claim continues to cast its shadow. Should Iraq win, or should the war end with the Iraqi military machine still reasonably intact, Kuwaitis fear that they might again be pressured by their stronger neighbor for total subservience or territorial concessions. At a minimum, the protracted negotiations prior to the Iran-Iraq war over Iraq's demand for the Kuwaiti islands of Warba and Bubiyan would doubtless have to be resolved quickly in Iraq's favor. Kuwait obviously hopes that by providing financial and other support for Iraq, it is buying the latter's goodwill. But goodwill is an effervescent commodity in Gulf politics, as it is in international politics anywhere and as the Kuwaitis well know.

Although the Kuwaitis have not publicly voiced this, one continues to hear of their continuing displeasure that the British, when signing the treaty of 'Uqayr with Ibn Sa'ud in 1922, gave part of their southern areas to Saudi Arabia. Kuwaiti-Saudi relations, despite common 'Anayza origins, have seldom been very close.

Among other things, Saudis allege Kuwaiti smuggling, including of pilgrims seeking to avoid *hajj* tariffs, into Saudi Arabia. The Saudi leadership has been worried also over the precedential effect of the elected Kuwaiti National Assembly on their own public's growing demand for a greater participatory role in politics,[3] and is uneasy about Kuwaiti flirtations with the Soviets.

Further to the south, Saudi Arabia still has border claims against Qatar, Abu Dhabi and Oman. These have been quiescent of late and the GCC provides a forum to keep them from spilling over and again badly straining relations among member states. But most have not been definitively resolved and, in the absence of the erstwhile British protector, the lingering concern persists that sooner or later the Saudi colossus will insist on such claims being settled in accordance with Saudi wishes. Also, various UAE component states have sought to give oil concessions in territory which Oman claims, and Omani military forces have in the past been deployed to assert the Omani claim to such disputed territory. GCC mediation helped to quiet the dispute between Bahrain and Qatar over the Fasht al-Dibal islet in the summer of 1986.

To these boundary questions must be added unresolved median line issues of the Gulf. Of fifteen such lines needed in the Gulf area, only seven are agreed upon; eight must still be negotiated. Among those agreed upon is the Oman-Iran line; among those still in dispute is the line between Oman and the UAE. There is no immediate necessity to arrive at further median line agreements, given the current oil glut, but at some point in the future the issue of these unresolved lines will again have to be faced.

On a more abstract level, the Arab states of the Gulf are also affected by the unresolved Arab-Israeli issue. Some, like Kuwait, feel deeply about the Palestinian cause, partly because of the large number of émigré Palestinians living in their country. So does Saudi Arabia, even though its Palestinian expatriates are smaller in number. Paradoxically perhaps, but hardly surprisingly, while Palestinians in many countries of the Gulf tend to be segregated — and to some extent distrusted by local officials and the public — considerable official and private sympathy exists for their cause. They are fellow Arabs who, in the eyes of Gulf peoples, have been unjustly treated. There is also concern on the part of Gulf states that, unless a Palestinian state comes into being, the Palestinians will always be a potential threat to Gulf Arabs' job opportunities and, on another plane, to their internal security.

It is utter nonsense to suggest, as some do, that the Gulf Arab states and peoples are indifferent to the Arab-Israeli problem. Granted, it is lower on their priority list of concerns than are more immediate Gulf problems and some would like to be rid of it, but it is omnipresent in one form or another. Even in Oman, where Palestinians have been kept out, public sympathy is for Palestinians and their cause. This is no new development; it has been the case for forty years or longer. Even during World War II, the few Americans serving at the RAF base at Salala, Dhufar, heard local criticisms of Jewish actions against Arabs in Palestine. Isolated though Oman has been for a large part of this period, the transistor radio long ago made its way into Oman and enabled Omanis to keep abreast of Arab political concerns in the Middle East area.

For Saudi Arabia, in its self-appointed role as guardian of the holy places of Islam, the issue of Israeli occupation of Jerusalem is a major foreign policy concern. Saudi Arabia may be expected to try to rally its GCC partners to supporting it on this issue should occasion arise. No Arab state of the Gulf, Oman included, would fail to support Saudi Arabia on this Islamic canonical issue.

OMAN'S PERSPECTIVES

In a sense, Oman's position in relation to its Gulf partners is peculiar. It is *of the Gulf*, mainly because of its Arab character, its geographic location, and because it shares sovereignty over the Strait of Hormuz with Iran, but it is not, strictly speaking *in the Gulf*. Apart from its strategically important Musandam Peninsula, separated from the rest of Oman by the UAE, Oman fronts entirely on the Gulf of Oman and the Arabian Sea. Its land borders are with the UAE, Saudi Arabia and the Peoples' Democratic Republic of Yemen (PDRY). Its territorial disputes such as they have been, have been mainly onshore rather than offshore. Its non-Arab neighbor across the Strait of Hormuz is Iran, larger in size and strength, an exporter of Islamic revolution, at war with Iraq, and hostile to several of Oman's GCC partners.

In Oman, as elsewhere in the Middle East, the burden of history lies heavy. Educated Omanis recall that Persia occupied coastal Oman in the past. Might an aggressive Iranian Islamic Republic, if given a chance, they ask, not seek to re-establish in some form erstwhile Persian suzerainty or domination over all or parts of Oman? Given past Iranian interest in making the Gulf an Iranian-controlled body of water — as evidenced by the Iranian seizure of the Tunbs and Abu Musa islands in 1971, by the late Shah's unacceptable "closed sea" concept, and by the "Islamic Gulf" idea more recently adduced by some Iranian clergy — Omanis have cause to be concerned. An Iranian military victory against Iraq would in all likelihood before long prompt Iranian pressure on Oman to conform to Tehran's foreign policy wishes, if Oman wished to maintain some semblance of national identity. Meanwhile, however, the war in the northern Gulf is for Omanis somewhat remote.

Nevertheless, controlling as it does maritime traffic through the Strait of Hormuz, and having to do so under Iranian eyes, Oman must maintain a low profile and take a passive, unassertive, even equivocal role in the Iran-Iraq conflict, lest any rash act be perceived by Iran as hostile and cause a spillover of Iranian retaliation against Oman. Several Iranian naval craft operate in the Iranian sector of the Strait of Hormuz, and at least one has without seeking permission transited the Omani zone of separation into the Gulf of Oman.

Iranian naval craft have intercepted foreign flag vessels in the approaches to the Gulf in search of contraband destined for Iraq. Such Iranian actions have taken place in what are nominally high seas. Oman might make a weak and mainly postural diplomatic demarche to Iran for violation of its territorial waters without seeking prior permission, but prudence dictates that this be the extent of its response, its GCC partners notwithstanding.

Actions caused by Iran on the high seas, Oman points out, cannot be its concern and, if deemed sufficiently disturbing by the West, Oman assumes they will be countered *on the high seas* by US and other Western naval forces patrolling the area without involving the sultanate. To be sure, US naval P-3 surveillance aircraft, "transiting" at Masira Island and, on occasion, al-Sib, maintain surveillance over the Gulf of Oman area, including over Iranian naval vessels, and this regularly results in Iranian protests to Oman. Such Iranian protests are a source of embarrassment to Oman, but in present circumstances can be fended off.

The extension of the Iran-Iraq conflict to the southern portions of the Gulf and the Gulf of Oman, and the resultant presence of large foreign naval flotillas in the area, has accentuated Omani concerns. Whatever their GCC sympathies may be, they have sought to avoid provoking their Iranian neighbor and have attempted to maintain a posture of neutrality in the management of maritime traffic through the Strait of Hormuz. As American naval convoys escorting reflagged Kuwaiti tankers have passed through the Omani zone of separation in the strait, Omani naval forces have insisted upon strict compliance with prescribed procedures. Oman is clearly worried about the presence of Iranian Silkworm missiles and Iranian naval vessels in the strait area, and the possibility that an armed clash could occur between Iran and US naval forces there. It can but hope that this will not happen.

Aware of its physical vulnerability to Iran, Oman for a long period urged its GCC partners to adopt a more realistic security posture, one which acknowledged more openly a need for integrated defense forces and a putative need to depend upon outside, specifically US and Western, military support. It has been unsuccessful in this regard, but — despite earlier strong Kuwaiti and less severe Saudi opposition — it has sought to enhance its own margin of security by signing agreements with the US. In 1980, it accorded the latter contingent rights at Omani military facilities at Masira Island, and more limited usage privileges at al-Sib, Thamarit and Khasab airfields, the last in the Musandam Peninsula.

Such rights of access however, are not automatic and require Omani approval. Separate and parallel agreements were signed with the US for American economic and military assistance, the unofficial *quid pro quo* for such privileges. The Omani military facilities at the above locations have in fact been improved and extended with Congressionally appropriated US funding.

Some controversy persists, nevertheless, as senior British military advisers to the sultan of Oman have sometimes sought to limit American use of such US-financed Omani military facilities. Nevertheless, Oman has permitted its military facilities to be used for emergency purposes by disabled US naval aircraft unable to return to their carrier platforms in the Gulf of Oman, thus saving them from having to ditch at sea. This Omani courtesy is reminiscent of similar courtesies extended by the sultan's great grandfather, Sayyid Sa'id bin Sultan, to American commercial vessels visiting his ports a century and a half ago.[4] Apart from American lives saved, recovery of crippled aircraft has saved the US Government millions of dollars indeed, as much or more as is involved in American economic and military aid to Oman.

For Oman, as for Saudi Arabia and Bahrain, some American military presence in the country represents a "plate glass" window, in lieu of a formal US military guarantee, which Oman hopes will prove to be an indirect deterrent against Iran or any other putative aggressor. By the same token, the presence of US military forces on

Omani territory, however limited in number, creates not only criticism from some Arab states and Iran, but also some domestic criticism. American military bases on Arab soil, Oman included, have become politically controversial in the Arab world and lend themselves to the charge of clientage to the US. For the moment, this risk is manageable, but should the Iranian threat at any time recede, the acceptability of a US military presence in Oman will become more domestically charged. In contrast, US naval units in the Indian Ocean are a politically more acceptable "over the horizon" protection for Oman, not being on sultanate territory, but by the same token are operationally less effective in case of need. Critical response time from such US naval assets would be slower.

Should Omani military facilities be used at any time for US military actions against Iran, Oman's political vulnerability is likely to increase. Put another way, so long as no Iranian attempt is made to close the Strait of Hormuz, such Omani-Iranian tensions as exist because of the limited US military presence in Oman are acceptable risks. Should Iran at any time attempt to close the Strait of Hormuz, and thereby evoke a US military response to reopen them in whole or in part, utilizing for this purpose Omani military facilities (as opposed to US naval assets in the area), Iranian hostility to Oman, as host to US military forces, will unquestionably intensify.

Although Iran may not be able to do much to chastise Oman in the immediate wake of such an action in the Strait of Hormuz, the Americans will not always be there and the Omanis know that the possibilities for Iranian retribution are likely to endure for some time. They can only hope, therefore, that whatever escalation of hostilities takes place in the northern Gulf, the situation at the Strait of Hormuz will remain relatively quiet. Sadly, they can do little on their own to achieve such an outcome. Meanwhile, despite war tensions relatively near at hand, Oman continues to manage inbound and outbound maritime traffic through its zone of separation in the strait with commendable competence, and its small naval force in the area effectively assists in this endeavor.

Apart from the Iranian shadow, Oman's longer-term foreign-policy concerns are a function of its historical legacy. It will be recalled that Oman, whatever its early nineteenth-century role may have been in the Arabian Sea and in the greater Indian Ocean area, had opted under Sa'id bin Taymur (1932-1970) for a position of relative isolation in the world at large. It steadfastly had refused to engage in Arab issues — indeed, the Arab League had in the 1950s sought to censure Oman for refusing independence to the so-called

Inner Oman — Palestinians had been barred almost entirely from Oman, and expatriates had been limited to Baluch, Pakistanis, Indians and Britons. The country in effect had remained a political recluse.

Although Oman was independent, a British security umbrella had offered protection of sorts for many years. The five-year period of civil war from 1954 to 1959, precipitated by an Imam of (Inner) Oman asserting rights of independence, was crushed, but only with British support. That rebellion, Omanis remember, was supported by Saudi Arabia and other Arab states. The subsequent long Dhufar rebellion, from about 1962 to 1975, eventually was brought to an end through a combination of indigenous Omani forces, British officers seconded or on contract to Oman, an Iranian expeditionary force, some Jordanian assistance, and astute civic action leading to defection of Dhufari tribal leaders and tribesmen from insurgent ranks.

The Dhufar insurgency, Omanis also remember, was initially supported by Iraq and, after 1967, by the newly formed PDRY. The first sent weapons to the insurgents; the second provided strategic depth, and logistic support and training bases. Although Iraqi aid to Dhufari insurgents stopped in 1973, and PDRY support and sanctuary to such insurgents ended as the revolt eventually dissolved of its own weight, Omanis cannot forget the hostile role these states played in inciting and perpetrating it. Might one or the other or both seek at some point to re-encourage Dhufari insurgency? Whatever protestations of current friendship emanate from either Iraq or the PDRY, Oman looks at these states — one remote, the other its next door neighbor — with wariness rooted in past experience.

Since the advent of Sultan Qaboos in July 1970, Oman has in large measure, though not entirely, opened itself and become a member of the international community of the Middle East and of its Gulf political sub-system. Its oil production, begun in 1967, has been modest, but has produced reasonable revenues. The sultan has utilized these to develop the country to a point where domestic political pressures for change are fully containable. The miserly mentality of his father, which had evoked widespread domestic discontent, is a thing of the past. As with every other monarchical ruler of the Gulf area, however, Ayatollah Khomeini's charges that "kingship" is illegal in Islam must be of concern to the sultan, all the more so since there were similar Ibadi charges during the civil war with the so-called "Imamate" of Inner Oman in the 1950s. For now, however, Oman is not the principal target of such Iranian vituperation.

Oman, at the direction of Sultan Qaboos and thanks to the efforts of Sultan Qaboos's uncle, the late Sayyid Tariq, became a member of the Arab League in 1971, although it plays no more than a nominal role in that largely atrophied organization. It has not, for example, subscribed to the virtually dormant Arab League Collective Security Pact. It also became a member of the United Nations that same year.

Whatever his own and his peoples' sympathies may be, the sultan has carefully steered clear of active involvement in the Arab-Israeli problem, has continued his father's policy of excluding Palestinians from the country, and has supported — admittedly mutedly — the American-brokered Camp David agreement of 1978 and the subsequent Egyptian-Israeli peace treaty of 1979. These actions have earned him the occasional displeasure of some other Arab states, including nearby Saudi Arabia and Kuwait, but he has remained quietly steadfast in support of those instruments. Occasional Egyptian offers of military assistance, in case of need, have quietly been parried — in part because Oman does not want to become more actively involved in intra-Arab politics; in part because some doubt exists as to exactly what kind of military aid Egypt might provide in an emergency; and in part because, since the end of the Dhufar insurgency, there has been no need to call for outside military assistance.

Oman has been a member of the GCC since the inception of that organization in 1981. It has participated in the meetings of the GCC, where it generally has favored a more comprehensive security structure — including seeking assistance from non-Arab sources — than most other GCC members, especially Kuwait, are at this time prepared to countenance. Oman's limited military relationship with the US is the primary case in point.

Following the final dissolution of the Dhufar insurgency in 1975, and doubtless also due to fortuitous changes later in leadership in the PDRY, Oman's relationship with its southwestern neighbor has thawed. Thanks to Kuwaiti mediation, talks began in 1983 between Oman and the PDRY on defining their border. These negotiations have proceeded desultorily, but they do suggest the possibility of arriving at some *modus vivendi* between Oman and the PDRY — if the latter can be trusted. Oman, in any case, seems prepared cautiously to probe for some settlement of its outstanding problems with the PDRY, and non-resident ambassadors have been exchanged.

Although Oman established diplomatic relations with Saudi Arabia in 1971, they have improved greatly since the death of King Faisal in 1975. Faisal could never forget Saudi Arabia's humiliation at Buraimi in 1955, nor historical Saudi hegemony over parts of Oman during the last century. Sa'id bin Taymur was seen as a British puppet and was anathema to him. Since his accession to power in Saudi Arabia, King Fahd has shown a greater willingness to deal with Oman and its ruler as equals. To be sure, territorial issues remain regarding the common frontier of the two states, and these have of late created some new frictions in Saudi-Omani relations. Oman considers Saudi Arabia excessively rigid in its claim to disputed territory and unwilling to compromise.

Oman also has territorial disputes with some of the UAE component states, but most of these are currently in limbo. On its part, Oman would like a land-corridor connection between it and the Musandam Peninsula through al-Fujayra and Sharjah. Since al-Fujayra is already tiny, and such a land corridor would mean giving up its economically important Gulf of Oman frontage or, alternatively, dividing the tiny principality in two, al-Fujayra — supported by its UAE fellow states — has refused. The issue is not urgent, however, and Oman's access to Musandam is assured, either through land transit through al-Fujayra and Sharjah or by sea. For al-Fujayra and the smaller UAE principalities, Oman is a relative colossus in much the same manner that Saudi Arabia is to its neighbors, but without the latter's taint of trying to export rigid Islamic social doctrines.

Such territorial disputes will at some point have to be resolved, and the GCC seems a good forum in which to move in that direction. For the moment, at least, the existence of the GCC has taken some of the "sting" out of those issues, and reduced the urgency of achieving final settlement of boundary controversies.

Oman does receive some criticism from its fellow GCC states for its continued heavy dependence on the British. The sultan is surrounded by British advisers who, presumably with his concurrence, control all access to him, especially during the six months that he spends in Salala. To be sure, they are there entirely at the sultan's pleasure, yet their influence, real or imagined, projects an image of British dependency.

The British, it must be admitted, have done much for the sultan, although not *all* of the advice given by British advisers in various fields has been the best. Large sums of money have been squandered through infelicitous advice from some such British advisers, at least so a former official in Oman charges.[5]

Undeniably, however, the British Government has provided Oman with security help of a direct and immediate kind, especially in times of internal insurgency, such as the US never would. The US might help in case of external aggression against Oman, but its likely role in the case of internal rebellion is more problematical. For the US, the thicket of British advisers around the sultan sometimes has been felt to make ready access to him difficult.

The British, although they have reluctantly come to accept an American military presence in Oman, never have been especially enthusiastic about such a presence. To them, it represents US competition in a state in which their influence long had been predominant. Now that the British have left the Gulf, Oman remains for them the major British position of influence in the Arabian Peninsula. British and American firms are strong commercial competitors in the Omani economy. It is an awkward situation, to say the least, for Omanis, British and Americans alike.

Like other Third World states, Oman is sensitive — perhaps hypersensitive — on issues involving national sovereignty. This is natural and should be expected. Two recent developments have again demonstrated that the Omani leadership is not prepared to be taken for granted by anyone and that, despite its military ties with the United States, it objects to being projected as an American puppet. Both have to do with Oman's relationship with the superpowers.

First, early in 1985, negotiations took place between Oman and the United States over renewal of the five-year access agreement to Omani military facilities. The negotiations were more difficult than many American officials had anticipated. As so often happens in such cases, Department of Defense lawyers sought stronger "status-of-forces" provisions and endeavored to include provisions that would have made these Omani facilities virtually American bases. Not only did the Omanis reject this, but on their part, they sought to limit more closely US use of Omani military facilities. They were concerned for several reasons. One was that the US Air Force, in their view, increasingly seemed to assume that it had a legal right to the routine use of Omani military facilities without advance Omani political-level approval. Likely Iranian reaction to routinized USAF usage of these facilities doubtless was a related factor. So was shortsighted American publicity on the Omani role in

33

US security planning for the Indian Ocean and Gulf, and on the involvement in the country of ex-CIA officials, the net effect of which was to embarrass the Omani leadership before its own public, its Arab neighbors and Iran, and which Omanis deeply resented.[6] Although joint Omani-US military exercises had taken place in 1983 and 1984, there was Omani concern about the Pentagon's proclivity to want to give these wide publicity.

Washington, with its penchant for public relations, can sometimes be its own worst enemy in dealing with Oman and likeminded Arab states, who for reasons of their own do not want their cooperation with the US blazoned all over the media.

There was also Omani annoyance that the US, at least in their view, had not given the sultanate in the previous five years the kind of treatment that the "special relationship" which presumably exists between the two states deserved. In an effort to allay this, Vice President George Bush visited Oman in May 1984 and April 1986. He was the first and only senior US official who had done so for many years. The Omanis, like other friends in the Gulf, need regular diplomatic hand-holding, given the risks that they perceive they take in providing military assets to the US. They feel that they are too often ignored by American officialdom. They believe that their "special relationship" with the US, despite its relative newness, warrants a closer, higher-level bilateral dialogue than currently exists. Perceived US failure to recognize this is another factor in current strains between the two countries.

To be sure, arrangements were worked out eventually which left the essence of the earlier access agreement intact, although US personnel perquisites at Omani military sites were somewhat curtailed and advance Omani approval for American usage privileges tightened. The negotiations left a slightly sour taste in some Omani and American (Pentagon) mouths, and residual strains persist in the relationship between the two countries. In some American quarters, too, the belief exists that the British advisers in Oman may have encouraged the tough Omani negotiating stance. Since Omani facilities are still needed, in whatever form, the US has had to make the best of the situation. While both countries want to retain their mutual relationship, one wonders what Oman's negotiating posture will be when the access agreement again requires renewal. Much will depend upon the area situation at that time and on US sensitivity these next few years to Omani concerns when exercising usage privileges at Omani military facilities. One may hope that both sides will use good judgment in working out access modalities.

Also distressing to the US has been Oman's interest in a rapprochement with the Soviet Union, evidenced by the establishment of diplomatic relations in September 1985. It was announced by the Omani Foreign Ministry in August 1985 that the Omani minister of state for foreign affairs would meet with his Soviet counterpart in New York during the forthcoming UN General Assembly session, in order to discuss establishing diplomatic relations between the two states. The statement was made without any consultation with or notice to the US and an American government spokesman subsequently commented that the US had been taken by surprise by the announcement. Oman, as a sovereign state, is of course at liberty to contract diplomatic relations with any other state that it wishes, but the Omani action in substance and procedure was especially embarrassing to an administration that sees the Soviets as irrevocably evil, that is determined to keep them out of the Gulf area, and that sometimes myopically expects all friendly governments to see the Soviets in the same light that it does: as solely responsible for every political problem that exists in the Middle East area.

Adding to the Omani desire to balance somewhat its relationships with the US and the USSR is the fact that Omanis, like other Arabs, are not entirely sure of US reliability. Distant though it was, the US misassessment and consequent failure in Lebanon was not lost on them.

Coming on the heels of the difficult access-renewal negotiations, US annoyance, while perhaps slightly naive, is comprehensible. There is little evidence, however, that Omani displeasure over what were perceived to be excessive US demands is mainly responsible for Oman's action. The latter is in fact consistent with Sultan Qaboos' established policy of "opening" Oman to relationships with all states. Oman considers itself non-aligned, despite the agreements with the US, and a number of Arab and Gulf factors doubtless account for Oman's decision to establish relations with the USSR. Omani-Soviet relations are not likely to alter Oman's basic reliance on the British and Americans for outside security support.

The close personal dialogue between Sultan Qaboos and King Hussein of Jordan, who has found occasional flirtations with the Soviets to be an effective countervailing mechanism after Congressional rebuffs on American arms sales, also may have had some influence in encouraging the Omani ruler to establish a formal relationship with the USSR. An equally plausible reason is an Omani desire to show Saudi Arabia, which, as indicated above, has been difficult of late on border issues, that Oman is prepared to go its own way. Saudi Arabia, despite occasional statements of its leaders about resuming diplomatic relations with the USSR, usually has opposed in GCC forums Kuwaiti urgings that this be done. Oman also may hope that diplomatic relations with the USSR may facilitate successful border negotiations with the PDRY, generally believed to be a Soviet client state.

If the Soviets follow the pattern of conduct that has characterized their presence in Kuwait, i.e., carefully avoiding any encroachment on indigenous sovereignty, they will be accepted in Oman. If they are perceived as openly or covertly seeking to interfere in Oman, they will have difficulties. In any case, Oman clearly believes that it can manage a Soviet diplomatic presence in its capital without detriment to its security. It remains to be seen how any incipient Omani-Soviet relationship will affect the Omani-US link in longer-range terms. At the very least, it is an Omani signal to the US that the sultanate intends to pursue its own foreign policy, based upon its calculation of its national interests, and that it will not docilely follow American leads on international issues, however much it needs US military and economic help.

The US-Omani association, which began as a commercial interest, goes back to 1790 when the first American vessel touched at Muscat. Generally, relations between the two states have been correct, but not extensive in scope. In the past few years, what was heretofore largely a commercial and humanitarian relationship has been broadened to include a strategic dimension. But Oman insists it must determine how its national interests are best pursued and resents any suggestion that any such sovereign prerogative has been curtailed as a result of its recent closer security links with the United States. It wants to be treated as a sovereign equal, not as a surrogate of either superpower or of any of its Arab neighbors. For its GCC partners, for the US and for others, Oman is indeed the "sentinel of the Gulf."[7] To date, it has played that important geopolitical role with considerable skill.

NOTES

1. For a detailed analysis of the war, see the chapter by Wayne White elsewhere in this book.

2. Diplomatic relations between Iraq and the United States, which had been broken as a result of the June 1967 Arab-Israeli war, were re-established in November 1984.

3. The National Assembly was suspended indefinitely in July 1986.

4. In a letter to President Jackson written in 1833, following the signing of a treaty of amity and commerce with the US, Sayyid Sa'id bin Sultan stated that the president might "depend that all American vessels resorting to the ports within my dominions shall know no difference in point of good treatment between my country and that of his own most happy and fortunate country, where felicity ever dwells." See Rudolph Said-Ruete, *Said bin Sultan* (London: Alexander-Ouseley, 1929), p. 128.

5. John Townsend, *Oman: The Making of the Modern State* (London: Croom Helm, 1977), pp. 82–83.

6. See, for example, *New York Times*, March 25 and 26, 1985.

7. This description was first used in Liesl Graz, *The Omanis: Sentinels of the Gulf* (London: Longman, 1982).

3

The Gulf Cooperation Council: A New Framework for Policy Coordination

John Duke Anthony

More than six years after its establishment in May 1981, the Gulf Cooperation Council (GCC) — an organization that groups together Saudi Arabia, Kuwait, Bahrain, Qatar, the United Arab Emirates (UAE), and Oman — continues to develop and pursue its goal of creating an integrated, common market. It is widely acknowledged that in terms of measurable cooperation on region-wide issues of interest and concern to its members, the GCC has already achieved more than the European Economic Community (EEC) did in its first decade.

Beyond its political and economic ramifications, the GCC stands as proof that regional accord among Arab countries on a host of developmental, strategic and security issues is possible. Moreover, the experiment thus far demonstrates determination among six Arab governments to assume a steadily increasing measure of responsibility for dealing with a broad range of regional challenges, with the concomitant diminution of the need or pretext for intervention by outside powers.

Fundamental to the success of the GCC to date has been the capacity of its leaders to benefit from all the failed past attempts at Arab integration, such as the United Arab Republic, which joined Egypt and Syria (1958-1961), the South Arabian Federation (1959-1967), the Maghreb Permanent Consultative Committee (1964-1971), and the Confederation of Arab Republics (1972-1975). These and other unsuccessful attempts to establish durable instrumentalities in the name of pan-Arabism provided the GCC's founders, to paraphrase Rudyard Kipling, with "no end of a lesson," and one which, collectively, has done them "no end of good." These lessons imply that incremental increases in Gulf integration can be achieved only through a slow, steady, and frequently painstaking process of forging consensus on a series of issue-specific agendas.

BASIS FOR CONSENSUS

As a first step, the collective need for sensitivity to the particular dynamics, sovereignty, and separate national interests of the individual states was agreed to by the members as the *sine qua non* for any successful *modus operandi*. Accordingly, at no point has there been any effort to merge massively or quickly as in Arab integrationist schemes attempted elsewhere. The approach of the GCC's architects, acknowledging the extent of intra-GCC diversity in terms of differing local traditions, resources, and circumstances, essentially has been one of seeking to coordinate the members' policies and positions on issues of importance to the GCC as a whole. Without such flexibility at the outset, it is doubtful whether the GCC would ever have come into being.

Various disparities between and among the members not only exist but, in several cases regarding economic differences and commercial competition, they are especially pronounced. Some of these disparities, such as forms of economic dependence or complementarity, undoubtedly have facilitated the integrative process. Others, rooted in different historical traditions or contemporary circumstances, have slowed the momentum. In this light, it is not surprising to note periodic divergences of viewpoint among the members as, for example, over pricing arrangements for oil and a variety of other export products, including petrochemicals, liquefied gas, fertilizers and aluminum products. Finally, different population bases, education levels, and other factors related to development potential have naturally resulted in different domestic concerns and national priorities.

The competing, and at times divergent, interests, however, at no point have been so great as to reverse the forward momentum of intra-GCC cohesion. A common language, religion, and culture and many attributes of a shared history have been subtle but strongly influential factors in undergirding a sense of togetherness necessary for a common approach to a range of contemporary challenges and future uncertainties.

The compact land mass which defines the GCC — an expanse considerably larger than all of Western Europe — provides for a sense of common identity, much as the similarity of much of the members' history offers a common perspective on the outside world. Indeed, consensus as reflected in the existence of broadly similar viewpoints among the members on the benefits to be gained from addressing a range of common external threats and domestic concerns have served as much as anything else to propel the cooperative process forward.

This commonality of shared interests was recognized by GCC leaders many years ago. Efforts to coordinate positions and pursue mutually beneficial policies in specific trade and security matters pre-date the formation of the GCC. For example, in 1953, eight years before it attained full independence, Kuwait pioneered regional resource-sharing activities by creating the General Board of the South and Arab Gulf to provide cultural, scientific and health services to the nine lower Gulf amirates which, like Kuwait, were then part of the British protected-state system in the Gulf.

More recent examples date from the mid-1970s. For example, in 1976, the United Arab Emirates (UAE), Bahrain, Saudi Arabia, Iraq, Qatar and Kuwait established the United Arab Shipping Company to stabilize intra-regional shipping operations. In the same year, the UAE, Saudi Arabia, Qatar, Kuwait, Oman and Iraq formed the Gulf Ports Authority. In 1979, Bahrain, Kuwait and Saudi Arabia incorporated the Gulf Petrochemical Industries Company in order to establish a petroleum by-products industry, and in 1980, the UAE, Bahrain, Saudi Arabia, Qatar, Kuwait and Iraq agreed to establish an Arabian Gulf University in Bahrain, where students throughout the Arab Gulf states could acquire a broadly similar training in different scientific and professional fields.[1]

Other important joint projects launched prior to the GCC's establishment include the Arab Shipbuilding and Repair Yard (ASRY), Gulf Air, the Gulf News Agency, the Gulf Organization for Industrial Consulting (GOIC), the Gulf Joint Production Institute, the Gulf States Information Documentation Center, the Gulf Radio and Television Training Center, the Gulf Television Corporation, the Regional Project for the Survey and Development of Fisheries Wealth, the Joint Gulf Organization for Marine Meteorology, and the Gulf Postal Union. Although the slow but steady accumulation of these achievements escaped the notice of many Western, especially American, observers at the time, it is clear that these institutional and infrastructural units provided a solid base on which the GCC itself could build.

ENVIRONMENTAL FACTORS

Numerous external factors affected the six countries simultaneously and sufficiently to compel the formal establishment of the GCC.

One was the perceived threat of either Soviet or US military intervention. The 1973 Arab-Israeli war, the following oil embargo and higher petroleum prices, the 1979 revolution in Iran, and then the Soviet invasion and occupation of nearby Afghanistan all intensified superpower rivalry in the region.

In January 1980, President Carter, reacting primarily to the Soviet invasion of Afghanistan a month earlier, announced that the US would apply force, if necessary, in response to any attempt by a foreign power to control the Gulf region. The Soviet Union replied to the new Carter Doctrine with what became known as the Brezhnev Doctrine. The latter called for international respect for the region's sovereignty, as well as independent local control over its natural resources. In addition, it stated that no foreign military bases should be established in the area.

The Gulf leaders, under no illusion as to their capacities for self-defense in the event of a superpower conflict in their midst, were apprehensive about the prospect of Western powers and the Soviet Union trying to further their national interests in the region at the expense of the local states. Many of them voiced their concerns with an African proverb which states, "when two elephants fight, it is rare that one is able to defeat the other. But one thing is certain: the grass underfoot always gets trampled." These concerns crystalized in what would become known as the GCC Doctrine which, in essence, holds that responsibility for stability and security in the region belongs to the states themselves and no one else.[2]

Another factor was Tehran's declared intention to export the Iranian revolution. Soon after Ayatollah Khomeini assumed power, it became clear that his country's militants, far from being content with having overthrown the secular establishment in Iran, were covetously casting their eyes across the Gulf. The militants not only challenged Saudi Arabia's authority as leader of the Islamic world, but proclaimed the governments of virtually every Arab Gulf country to be "corrupt" and "illegitimate." Confronting all of the GCC states in the face of such provocations was a haunting demographic reality. The ubiquitous shortages of labor made them dependent on alien, immigrant workers, including tens of thousands of Iranians — with the concomitant risk of externally-inspired subversion.

A third factor was the absence of another organization comparable to the GCC. Such an organization might have provided a credible alternative, were it to have shown any likelihood of being able or willing to address the concerns of the Gulf States with any degree of effectiveness. However, political divisiveness in the Arab and Islamic worlds at the time was especially pronounced and showed no signs of early abatement. Moreover, the challenges facing the Gulf countries and the Arab world as a whole, ranging from an expansionist Israel and Iranian radicalism to the prospects for superpower intervention, appeared to be on the rise.

In addition to responding to a commonly perceived region-wide threat, the GCC's founders were also inspired by the knowledge that each of the members would be able to enhance various aspects of its national interests through participation in the council. In this regard, the GCC's continuing ability to protect and promote the individual interests of its member states has played an integral role in the success of the organization.

Indeed, the greatly diminished revenue from petroleum beginning in 1983 and thus not present when the GCC began was a subsequent, unanticipated factor in this regard. Beyond reducing the spending power of each state, this factor required a far more careful and creative approach to economic development — and even to savings and investment — than had previously been acknowledged as necessary. On grounds of lessened duplication and increased cost effectiveness alone, it became quickly and abundantly clear that each GCC state stood to benefit greatly, at least potentially, if all agreed to cooperate in their developmental efforts.

ORGANIZATION AND FUNCTIONS

The organizational structure to serve such an ambitious design is rooted in indigenous political values, the Islamic faith, and traditional local skills and approaches. GCC activities emphasize consultation and consensus-building, gradual change, and respect for individual sovereignty and concerns within a context of support for the region's political *status quo*. The GCC is composed of a bureaucratic structure with well-articulated responsibilities and functions. Its charter details the goals and laws of the council and its division into three main bodies: the Supreme Council, the Ministerial Council and the Secretariat-General.[3]

The Supreme Council, the GCC's highest authority, is composed of the heads of the member states. The council's presidency is rotated yearly and each member has one vote. The function of the council is to set the domestic and foreign policies for the GCC and, if necessary, to amend the GCC's charter and internal rules.

At the time of the GCC's founding in Abu Dhabi, a separate Commission for the Settlement of Disputes, attached to the Supreme Council, was envisioned. The commission's functions would have been to seek to settle any disagreement among the member states that could not be resolved within the Ministerial or Supreme Councils. In the course of implementing the charter, however, it was agreed among the heads of state that creation of a separate commission, beyond resulting in costly bureaucratic proliferation, was actually unnecessary inasmuch as the Supreme Council itself, with a broadened mandate, would be able to perform the requisite functions.[4]

Since establishment of the GCC, the heads of state have met for working sessions lasting two or more days at the annual GCC heads of state summits, as well as at the pan-Arab summit conferences at Fez in 1981 and 1982, at the annual summit meetings of the Organization of the Islamic Conference and the bi-annual sessions of the Non-Aligned Movement. No comparable number of other Arab heads of state met to discuss inter-Arab affairs on any other issues with anything near this degree of frequency during the same period.[5]

The GCC's Ministerial Council is composed of the foreign ministers of each member state; its presidency is rotated annually along the same lines as the Supreme Council and the council is convened quarterly. Each country has one vote. Resolutions of substantive matters must be reached by unanimous vote, but procedural issues can be passed by a majority. Beyond implementing the policy decisions of the Supreme Council, the function of the Ministerial Council is to encourage and further member cooperation.

To this end, the members early on delegated Kuwait and the UAE, on behalf of all six countries, to seek an end to the prolonged enmity between member state Oman and neighboring South Yemen. The successful effort, manifested in an accord which the two governments signed in Kuwait in September 1982, was followed by other, less successful attempts to mediate between Iraq and Iran, at war with one another since September 1980. In 1986, another success was registered when Saudi Arabia and Oman helped to mediate between Bahrain and Qatar on a matter of disputed offshore territory.

A majority of the individuals in the Ministerial Council have been members since the GCC began. In late 1987, the council had met for regular, intensive working sessions on more than two dozen separate occasions, in addition to conferring with one another at the seven aforementioned meetings of the heads of state. Placing this observation in its historical context reveals an interesting insight into the internal dynamics of this newest of Arab regional organizations. With the much more highly publicized meetings and officials of the United Nations, the League of Arab States, the Organization of the Islamic Conference, the Non-aligned Movement, and even OPEC and OAPEC as points of reference, it is doubtful whether a group of any other Arab leaders in this century has set aside as extensive an amount of time to deliberate issues of common concern as have the GCC's foreign ministers during the past six years.

The six council members share a combined experience spanning several decades in practically all of the major developments of the period inside such organizations as the Arab League, OIC, OPEC, OAPEC, and the UN. Their competence includes extensive first-hand familiarity with such questions as regional and national strategies toward such issues as security, technology transfer, human and natural resource development, foreign investments, and relations with both superpowers, as well as Western Europe and literally dozens of other countries in Africa and Asia.[6]

The secretary-general and two assistant secretaries-general are appointed by the Supreme Council. The functions of the Secretariat-General itself include preparing studies related to cooperation and coordination and integrating plans and programs for member states' common action. The secretariat also oversees the administrative and financial regulations of the GCC as a whole.

The secretariat, which is based in Riyadh, is divided into a half-dozen operational units. The most influential include the office of the secretary-general and the offices for economic and political affairs. The organization's secretary-general, former Kuwaiti diplomat 'Abdullah Bishara, was the unanimous choice of the Supreme Council when the GCC was founded. Prior to assuming this position, Bishara served with distinction for ten years as Kuwait's Permanent Representative to the United Nations.

The Office of Economic Affairs deals with a range of activities pertaining to financial, investment and industrial planning in the GCC, including such questions as customs, transportation and communications, oil and other energy-related matters, agriculture and livestock management. The office's primary goal is the furtherance of integration through enhanced coordination among the individual development plans of the member states.

The day-to-day administration of GCC economic affairs during the 1981-1987 period was headed by Assistant Secretary-General Dr. 'Abdullah El-Kuwaiz, a former deputy minister in Saudi Arabia's Ministry of Finance and a frequent spokesman on issues of economic importance to the GCC at meetings of the International Monetary Fund, the World Bank, and other agencies.[7] In addition, a coordinator for GCC economic consultations with Western European countries and the United States was appointed in 1985. Ma'mun al-Kurdi, concurrently a career diplomat with ambassadorial rank and the title of deputy assistant secretary for economic affairs in the Saudi Arabian Ministry of Foreign Affairs, holds this position. Ambassador al-Kurdi has headed several high-level GCC delegations engaged in consultations with officials in European capitals and the United States in an effort to forge greater linkages between the GCC and its major economic partners.

Former Omani Ambassador to India Ibrahim Sobhi was the assistant secretary-general for political affairs during the GCC's first six years. In early 1987, he was succeeded by former Omani consul-general in Geneva, Sayf al-Maskari. The sector which he heads deals with political and strategic matters concerning the member states and is especially involved in efforts to enhance GCC security coordination. This sector is subdivided into individual departments dealing with Arab relations, international affairs, security issues and information. These departments, in concert with a separate military committee headed by Saudi Arabian General Yusuf Madani, study and make policy recommendations for such issues as mutual security and weapons purchases, the Iran-Iraq war, joint training maneuvers, and other international questions bearing on the collective and individual effectiveness of the GCC states in regional and world affairs.

ECONOMIC ISSUES: INTEGRATION, DEVELOPMENT AND TRADE

The GCC, despite its youth and geographic size, already stands as one of the world's most economically influential organizations. Its members possess nearly half the world"s proven oil reserves, lift the bulk of petroleum produced by OPEC, and are major actors in world trade and international finance. Together they function as a powerful bloc in the World Bank and the IMF, in OPEC and

OAPEC, and in such organizations as the Arab Monetary Fund and the Arab Fund for Social and Economic Development.

In the past two or three decades, the six GCC states have made phenomenal strides in developing their basic infrastructures and public services. With these accomplishments behind them and the GCC in place, there is now at hand an unprecedented vehicle for pursuing more complex future development. The GCC's economic mission is to coordinate and integrate the policies of the six member states toward a common market, with the prospect of an eventual merger into a single economic entity. Within this context, the major goals are to diversify the six economies away from dependence on crude oil exports for national income; to industrialize, both "downstream" in the petroleum sector and into non-oil sectors; and to increase exports and reduce the heavy reliance on imported goods.

The position and role of the GCC in the development planning of the member states is critical to these goals. Consolidation of the local markets is necessary to support import substitution industries, and all the industrial schemes will depend on economic cooperation to avoid wasteful duplication. Opening up foreign markets to GCC industrial exports — a far more difficult task — will necessitate the combined bargaining power of the entire group. GCC-orchestrated joint ventures will benefit from location in the state with the greatest economic rationale for the particular industry, a lack of local competitors, an enlarged local market protected from foreign competition, and assistance in reaching potential consumers overseas.

Blueprint for integration: the Unified Economic Agreement

The power of economic integration is outlined in the 1981 Unified Economic Agreement (UEA), which superseded all previous bilateral and multilateral agreements among the members on economic issues. The UEA calls for intra-GCC freedom of travel for the nationals of each state, freedom of commerce between member states, and the construction of a common economic infrastructure.

Additional provisions of the agreement include elimination of customs duties between GCC states, provided the goods satisfy a criterion of a minimum local value-added content; coordination of import and export policies and regulations; free movement of labor and capital; coordination of oil prices; coordination of industrial activities and standardization of industrial laws; coordination of policies for technology, training and labor affairs; a cooperative approach to land, sea and air transportation policies; and, finally, establishment of a unified investment strategy and the coordination of financial, monetary, and banking policies, including the possibility of introducing a common currency.

As a means of helping to implement the agreement, the GCC's Supreme Council, at the 1982 summit in Bahrain, agreed to establish a $2.1 billion Gulf Investment Fund (GIF) and a companion body to administer the fund, the Gulf Investment Corporation (GIC), based in Kuwait. The six states appropriated the money for economic development and industrialization, and to facilitate joint economic projects among GCC members in agriculture, commerce, mining and general investment.

The first stage of the agreement was implemented in early 1983 when customs duties were rescinded for agricultural produce, animals, industrial products and natural resources of national origin traded among the member states. Owing to Bahrain's much greater dependency on customs revenue than any of the other members and the need to protect several infant industries in Oman from unfair competition, certain exceptions were made. In addition, the transit of goods from one member state to another would be similarly exempted from duties and taxes. In another breakthrough, professionals in medicine, law, accounting, engineering and consulting registered in one GCC country were permitted to practice in the other member states as well.

Another early step to implement the 1981 accord was the tasking of Saudi Arabia's Weights and Measures Organization with responsibility for establishing a uniform system of industrial standards that would apply to the GCC member countries as a whole. In 1983, in a move that underscored the immediate and tangible benefits of cooperation, the GCC also saved its citizens millions of dollars by collectively making bulk purchases of rice at lower prices for the member states. In addition, electricity and telecommunications companies have all moved closer to harmonizing their previously widely disparate prices.

On the other hand, exporters of natural gas have proceeded at a slower and more uncertain pace of price standardization, owing to fluctuations in the international price for petroleum. And the once ambitious goal — one with immense symbolic as well as practical importance — of creating a unified currency throughout the GCC has continued to elude consensus.

47

When the UEA was announced, its implications instantly became the subject of widely different interpretations by nearly every economic interest group imaginable, both foreign and local. A flood of questions ensued from all corners as to the meaning of the agreement in terms of the cost of imported goods; the impact of development plans in one state on plans underway in another state; the kind of system that would be erected to enforce the agreement and when it would be in place; whether the timetable was realistic; and whether the GCC's more affluent members would be able to take advantage of the less affluent and vice versa.

It soon became evident, however, that the UEA was intended not for immediate implementation but, rather, to serve as the principal regional document for member states' planning from that point forward. The extensive economic turndown in the region occurring subsequent to the UEA, but in no way related to it, made it difficult to realize more of these cooperative objectives than otherwise might have been the case.

In 1983, in the midst of the economic recession, the GCC's industry ministers acknowledged publicly the difficulties they were encountering in implementing a unified industrial policy. In calling nonetheless for unified industrial legislation and an integrated approach to industrial development, they conceded that competing national self-interests were sufficiently real and extensive as to preclude a blanket policy at that stage. Instead, the ministers recommended a strategy that distinguished between medium and large projects. They foresaw no harm in small and medium-size industries of a similar nature operating in their respective states, but desired coordination on major industrial projects. The ministers thus sought to satisfy the economic needs of individual states while at the same time placing a limit on the degree to which any one of them would be permitted to pursue new industrial policies without regard to the impact of such policies on the others.

The GCC secretariat and more than a dozen ministerial-level committees in fact have made substantial progress in allocating specific new GCC-wide industries to member states according to agreed-upon priorities and "relative advantages." Saudi Arabia, for example, should continue to lead on matters pertaining to petrochemicals and wheat, egg, and livestock production, as well as the establishment of industrial standards, and the development of manufacturing strength in general. Qatar is the likely site for a major regional gas-gathering facility, while Kuwait seems certain to retain a pivotal influence in foreign investment and regional economic assistance.

Oman, for obvious reasons, figures heavily in any scheme to by-pass the Strait of Hormuz by an oil pipeline with a terminus on the Indian Ocean. Bahrain is mentioned frequently as a site for regional health services, for the treatment of certain diseases, and for various research facilities. The UAE, headquarters of the Arab Monetary Fund and the one GCC country with the greatest expertise in offshore petroleum operations and liquefied natural gas production for export to Europe and Japan, is interested in applied solar energy research and also figures in schemes for intra-GCC pipelines and ship repairing.

Trade policies

While the number of joint industrial projects undertaken thus far remains very limited, there has been progress in coordinating trade policies. A region-wide consensus has been reached that stipulates a tariff range applicable to imports from non-GCC countries. This policy alone has helped to facilitate the long term planning needs of the GCC's regional and global suppliers.

In addition to adopting a common external tariff, the 1981 UEA accelerated movement toward a more comprehensive duty-free trade agreement within the GCC. Following a consensus that basic items should be dealt with first, a new GCC-wide tax was imposed on several imported products, including iron, steel, cement, and food staples, in order to protect local production. Another boost to GCC producers has been a 1982 resolution requiring all government projects in the member states to utilize to the fullest possible extent products manufactured locally.

Another UEA trade feature called for the creation of a "collective negotiating force" to strengthen the GCC's position in dealing with foreign suppliers. Added in late 1985, it focused on institutionalizing negotiations with leading European exporters to the GCC and creating a mechanism for discussing similar economic issues with the United States. In addition to several sessions with leading European economic officials, three rounds of meetings between high-level GCC delegations and their American counterparts have been held: in December 1985 in Riyadh, in May 1986 in Washington, DC, and in February 1987 in Bahrain. Further meetings on a fairly regular basis are anticipated for the remainder of the 1980s.

The purpose of these exchanges and meetings of specialist working groups with the United States, Western Europe and Japan is to place the GCC's economic relationships with its major trading partners on a solid long term footing.

Petroleum: the engine of GCC development

The foregoing clearly indicates that the GCC, within seven years, has made impressive strides toward implementing the 1981 economic agenda. However, as individual members readily admit, far more remains to be accomplished. With most member states dependent on oil for over 90% of their export earnings and government revenues, diversification away from reliance on crude oil exports stands as the most daunting challenge.

Even continued dependence on exporting such a critical commodity as oil has been difficult for the GCC to manage. The success of industrialized countries in launching energy conservation programs and the degree to which some have been able to switch to non-oil alternatives has complicated matters. Some major consumers, particularly the US and Western Europe, have re-oriented the sources of a portion of their oil to suppliers outside the Gulf. Reduced international demand in the mid-1980s due to the recession and the introduction of competition from several new non-OPEC oil producers caused the price of Gulf oil to fall. From 1980 to 1983, GCC oil revenues declined by half: from $145 billion to $72 billion.

The altered economic situation has affected every GCC state. Saudi Arabia's oil exports have dropped by well over 50 percent since 1982. The kingdom's gross domestic product has contracted and government spending has been cut five years in succession. The UAE and Qatar have undergone similar experiences.

Kuwait, Bahrain and Oman, on the other hand, have fared differently. Kuwait has had a cushion in the form of continuing high yields on its extensive overseas investments; Bahrain continues to receive financial largesse from Saudi Arabia and Kuwait; and Oman, not an OPEC member, has been able to pump more oil to offset lower oil prices.

In light of the altered economic circumstances, GCC planners have focused on enhancing the prospects for expanding member states' activities in international oil operations. The breadth of the mandate to increase GCC involvement in the petroleum sector is evident in a resolution passed at the first GCC summit meeting in Abu Dhabi in May 1981. The resolution called for joint cooperation in order to establish an integrated oil industry, including exploration, refining, marketing, industrialization, pricing, transport, utilization of gas and development of energy sources.

Individual GCC states have made impressive gains toward these goals. The efforts of Kuwait, Saudi Arabia and the Amirate of Abu Dhabi to diversify sources of revenue through worldwide financial investments are well known. Kuwait has been especially successful in increasing its international holdings. It penetrated the European market in 1983 when it purchased the facilities of the Gulf Oil Corporation — comprising some 1,600 retail gas stations — in the Benelux countries and Scandinavia. Kuwait also purchased refineries in Rotterdam, Copenhagen, and Milan, two lube-oil plants and eight terminals in Denmark, a 50-percent interest in 30 terminals in Sweden, and 1,500 retail outlets in Italy. It also bought equity in the International Energy Development Corporation, a Geneva-based consortium of companies involved in overseas oil exploration, primarily in less developed countries.[8]

In the United States, Kuwait purchased the Santa Fe Company, an oil service firm with a large inventory of drilling rigs, extensive oil leases in the US, the Gulf of Mexico, and the South China Sea, and holdings in the North Sea. Kuwait also bought an oil and gas exploration firm in Oklahoma, Occidental Petroleum Corporation's geothermal electric plant in California, and two large construction firms. Future Kuwaiti acquisitions are expected to take place in Japan, Taiwan and South Korea.

Industrialization strategies for the future

An important long term step toward economic diversification has been to focus efforts beyond the sale of crude petroleum to the building and maintenance of industries such as petrochemicals, fertilizers, aluminum, iron, steel and cement. Joint economic investment and development plans in these areas, again, pre-date the formation of the GCC. In most instances, they were spearheaded by the Qatar-based Gulf Organization for Industrial Consulting, which acted as an information clearinghouse and undertook feasibility studies for proposed projects.

The move toward elimination of tariff barriers and the concomitant freer flow of products, labor and capital, plus provisions for the establishment of joint ventures, have all helped to accelerate industrialization. Although the GCC's industrial sector at present contributes less than ten percent of the states' total gross national product (GNP), there is widespread agreement that new region-wide industries will develop, to which increasing amounts of new and advanced technology will be transmitted.

Although many outside observers are pessimistic about the GCC's future prospects in this realm, it is significant that in the midst of the recession, the non-oil sector of the economy in some GCC states was the only sector to register economic growth. For example, in Saudi Arabia, growth in the petrochemical sector has exceeded 20 percent annually in recent years, and in Oman, the percentage of the non-oil industrial-related GNP has increased ten-fold from a small base.

The nucleus of the GCC's basic industries in the mid-1980s lies in chemical fertilizers, aluminum rolling, and iron castings. Under free-trade conditions, the GCC possesses all the necessary natural resources and capital to be very competitive in the international market. In chemical fertilizers, which require large amounts of natural gas and sulphur, the GCC holds about 10 percent of the world's known natural gas reserves and exports approximately 4 percent of total world output.

The GCC's holdings in sulphur are so abundant that it is able to export the bulk of its production to countries in Asia and Africa with enough left over to supply the sulphur needs of the entire Arab world. As a result of the petroleum-driven development schemes of the 1970s, every GCC state is involved to some degree in the production of chemical fertilizers. In such important derivative products as ammonia and urea, the GCC produces 35 percent and 51 percent respectively of the overall needs of the Arab region.

Aluminum rolling has also played an important role in the GCC's pursuit of industrial diversification and development. Bahrain pioneered in the production of aluminum in the Gulf. In 1981, in a cooperative move spearheaded by Saudi Arabia to avoid industrial duplication, Saudi Arabia, Bahrain, Kuwait, Iraq, Oman and Qatar established the Bahrain-based Gulf Aluminum Rolling Mill Company (GARMCO). The company is capable of producing 40,000 tons of aluminum sheets annually, an amount sufficient to cover much of the Gulf's domestic demand.

Iron and steel play a similar role in GCC development plans. For several years, the annual consumption of these two commodities by the GCC averaged about five million tons, of which approximately

11 percent is produced locally. Only in the past six years have the GCC states begun in earnest to construct iron and steel plants, although Qatar built a small factory in 1974. In 1983, Saudi Arabia undertook the most ambitious project by constructing a complex with an annual capacity of 800,000 tons of reinforced steel. The consumption of iron and steel is projected to increase to as much as 21 tons per year by the next decade. The GCC anticipates that 30 percent of the expected increase will be met by domestic production.[9]

Industrialization and trade

A major hurdle confronting the GCC's efforts to export its petrochemical products is a range of protectionist measures either already enacted or under active consideration by some Western governments.

The economic arguments behind such measures notwithstanding, there is no denying that such measures, coming at the moment the GCC has reached the "take-off" point in export capacity, have engendered the suspicion that Western countries have gone beyond looking out for their own industrial interests and are determined to keep the Arab world economically dependent on European or American goods, services, and technology. In the face of such impediments, the GCC has signalled its intent to challenge what it considers to be unfair trading policies. Such issues are among those included in the aforementioned Euro-Arab and GCC-US economic dialogues that have become commonplace in the mid-1980s.

The extent to which the GCC would be capable of responding to European or American tariff barriers is illustrated by the following. Trade figures show that GCC imports consist of 42 percent capital goods, 34 percent industrial products, and 12 percent foodstuffs. In the mid-1980s, Europe provided 37 percent of the GCC's commodity requirements, followed by Japan at 17 percent and the United States at 11 percent.[10] This diversity of suppliers permits a certain degree of maneuverability for the GCC member states in the international marketplace.

The diversity also implies the need for GCC suppliers to recognize that, with the Gulf having entered its second stage of development, expectations regarding the nature and overall orientation of the GCC's international trading relations are certain to change. As the GCC states move toward the 1990s, one country that may lose considerably, if it proves unable to adapt successfully to the altered environment in which GCC foreign-trade relations occur, is the United States. The US already has seen its once dominant market position in several fields seriously challenged by European and Japanese firms. The complaint expressed most often by GCC corporate representatives and chamber of commerce officials is that American businesses are not meeting the new economic challenges and the changed circumstances for commercial relations in the Gulf, a complaint not limited to the perennial one of American firms charging too high a price for their goods and services.

From the foregoing, it is clear that Western leaders would be exceptionally short-sighted to dismiss the GCC's economic goals as fantasy or impractical, or to reject without appropriate analysis the rationale behind the organization's industrial priorities and policies.

Despite the continued dominance of oil and oil by-products in the GCC's economy and trade, a fundamental consequence of the successful development schemes of the last decade is the GCC's emergence as a permanent competitor in the international marketplace. The GCC is determined to diversify its economy and, to this end, there is no way to avoid the fact that the expansion of the non-oil sector will hinge largely on exports.

THE SECURITY DIMENSION

Any economic plan necessitates a predictable and stable environment if it is to be a success. Accordingly, despite the original and continuing focus on economic issues, the GCC has had no choice but to turn its attention increasingly to security concerns. These have been exacerbated by the Iran-Iraq conflict, an instance of Iranian-supported subversion in Bahrain in 1981, several cases of Iranian-inspired terrorism in Kuwait since 1983, Iranian bombings of UAE offshore oil platforms in 1986, Iranian-provoked demonstrations and riots during the 1987 *hajj* in Saudi Arabia, and repeated, indiscriminate attacks by Iran on neutral and non-belligerent shipping in the Gulf since 1984 — including even attacks on tankers carrying Iranian oil.

In the face of these and related challenges to the region's governmental *status quo*, the GCC's leadership early on enunciated five principles that continue to guide the security policy of the member states. First, the GCC was established and exists not as a military bloc against any power, but rather as a regional organization seeking nothing more than the welfare, stability and security of its people. Second, collective security binds the GCC together: a hostile act against any single GCC country will be interpreted as an attack against every one of the six member states. Third and fourth, the GCC was established as a defensive measure against the possibility of externally inspired domestic subversion and against foreign, especially superpower, intervention. Fifth, GCC military policy is inseparable from that enshrined in the charter of the League of Arab States, an organization in which each of the GCC countries are also full-fledged members.

In keeping with these principles, joint defense policies are mapped out in meetings between defense ministers, armed forces chiefs of staff, and other senior military personnel. The defense ministers meet at least once yearly but their top aides and specialized technicians meet with considerably greater frequency to implement defense policies, coordinate strategies and prepare recommendations for the ministers.

Typical of the importance of such meetings was the meeting of the GCC chiefs of staff in Riyadh in June 1984. At previous meetings, there had been discussion of coordination among their armed forces and practical means of implementing the resolutions passed by the defense ministers. On this occasion the chiefs of staff evaluated the results of the previous fall's joint "Peninsula Shield" maneuvers in the UAE, discussed the idea of forming a unified military force, and studied ways to protect the GCC's oil exports. It was recognized that improvement of overall GCC security would necessitate progress on the establishment of a joint defense system, the development of a common military infrastructure, and joint policies on arms purchases and joint military maneuvers.[11]

Subsequently, the GCC has moved to implement each of these four prerequisites to collective security. GCC military units, collectively and bilaterally, have conducted a number of exercises in addition to the aforementioned maneuvers in the UAE in 1983. Other bilateral exercises have included Saudi-Kuwaiti air maneuvers in 1983 and 1984, and joint air and naval exercises between UAE and Omani forces in 1984 and 1985, and additional full scale exercises involving units from all six states in Saudi Arabia in September 1984 and in Oman in March 1987.

Separate bilateral maneuvers aimed at facilitating cooperation between and among the member states' respective naval forces took place in the summer of 1987. In addition, the ministers on numerous occasions have discussed the need to forge a more credible deterrent to the maritime escalation of the Iraq-Iran war, which has wreaked havoc on their oil-production and oil-export industries.

Although the establishment of a joint defense strategy has not been officially announced, common sense indicates that contingencies have been worked out to address various potential security threats that confront the GCC. Indeed, the fact that top military personnel meet regularly to discuss how best to implement their public goal of forming a unified — some GCC planners prefer the word "coordinated" — military force suggests that common defense policies have been concluded. The fact that the GCC holds regular joint military exercises and that a combined force with contingents from all six member states has been permanently stationed at Hafr al-Batin in northeastern Saudi Arabia since 1985, is its own evidence that mutual security policies indeed are being implemented.

As defense planners in the North Atlantic Treaty Organization (NATO) and other multinational organizations will immediately acknowledge, achievement of these last two prerequisites for establishing a credible collective security mechanism — a common military infrastructure and a common arms acquisition policy — has proven exceptionally difficult. The elusiveness of this goal to date can be explained by the fact that its attainment and the merging of each member state's security concerns with those of the GCC community as a whole would require each state to relinquish a substantial degree of its national sovereignty and independence. Whether the benchmarks are NATO, the Organization of American States (OAS) or the Association of South East Asian Nations (ASEAN), such actions do not come easily to contemporary nation-states.

Moreover, a common arms acquisition policy would require all six states to purchase their weapons and long-term, follow-on training and support systems from a single source. As a consequence, the GCC would become intimately and critically dependent on one supplier, something which very few, if any, countries outside the Soviet bloc, would be prepared to do. This, to be sure, is only part of the problem. An equally, if not more important, consideration is that such a relationship inevitably would be perceived as a *de facto* alliance and send important — and, undoubtedly, controversial — political messages throughout the Middle East and international community.

Like any other group of countries faced with a comparable security situation, the long-range foreign relations implications of a common arms acquisition policy and development of a common military infrastructure — as well as regionwide awareness of the possible serious consequences of a single mis-step in this most controversial and complicated of all GCC endeavors — have had their own effect on regional defense planning. On balance, such considerations have tended to accentuate differences of viewpoint within the GCC and have slowed the movement toward consensus on matters pertaining to defense and security.

Based on the discussions and deliberations that have taken place thus far, three competing trends toward GCC defense policies, as represented by different member states, can be discerned. More than any other GCC state, Kuwait has resisted attempts by suppliers to commit it to a common arms acquisition policy. In an effort to present an independent, non-aligned foreign policy, Kuwait maintains close diplomatic ties with the United States and the Soviet Union.[12]

Oman, on the other hand, has embraced joint military exercises with foreign forces, primarily the United States and Britain. Various Omani strategists have sought a GCC military policy closely aligned with the West in defense of the Strait of Hormuz. In contrast to the much longer-standing defense relationship between Oman and Great Britain, US-Omani military cooperation arose out of a 1980 agreement that provided the US with limited, conditional access to Omani military facilities in exchange for funds and related assistance to modernize the sultanate's military bases.

Since the agreement was signed, Washington has spent $256 million to lengthen runways at four of the sultanate's air bases, harden concrete aircraft hangars, and install storage tanks capable of holding over a million gallons of jet fuel. Pursuant to the agreement, American transport and tanker aircraft have been permitted routine use of Omani facilities to supply US naval task-force ships in the Indian Ocean, and American P-3 antisubmarine reconnaissance planes have been permitted to operate out of the Masira Island base.

Saudi Arabia seeks a third path somewhere between Kuwait and Oman. In a cautious but persistent approach, the kingdom has aimed at consensus for the view that the GCC should become increasingly self-reliant in as many areas pertaining to defense as possible, while remaining sensible enough to recognize that the record of successful contingency planning in this century, in general, has been rather abysmal. Accordingly, pragmatism alone suggests that various kinds of conflicts could erupt in the future which may require the assistance of outside forces, regardless of the wishes of GCC military planners.

Saudi Arabia's approach, which appears to have the support of Bahrain and Qatar — and Kuwait too, following its 1986 decision to seek US and Soviet naval protection for its oil tankers — may well be the course which GCC defense policy eventually will follow. If so, this would mean that the achievement of a unified arms acquisition policy and the formalities of a collective security pact will come later rather than sooner. It also implies that explicit basing rights for foreign forces or the permanent, large-scale presence of foreign troops in the GCC will continue to be forbidden.

CONCLUSION

It may be instructive to place the GCC's achievements to date in perspective by making some comparisons to the EEC, the principal prism through which most Westerners, often erroneously, have insisted on viewing the GCC. The comparison denotes that the GCC has had no choice but to proceed in a milieu that has been and continues to be vastly different from that of the EEC at the time of its establishment. At the end of World War II, the EEC countries faced economic devastation. The miracle allowing full recovery was the US-financed Marshall Plan. Such circumstances hardly could have been further removed from those confronting the GCC at the time of its inception.

Second, the GCC has moved forward as far as it has without the formal assurance of a great power protective security umbrella, such as that which the American-backed NATO provided for the EEC. Third, the process has occurred among countries which, certainly in the beginning, lacked a stimulus comparable to that present in the case of the European countries — broad economic-resource complementarity and a long-standing history of interstate trade relations in industrial fields, as manifested by the European Coal and Steel Community.

Fourth, the GCC has taken root and registered its achievements at a time and in a place where two far more populous neighbors, Iraq and Iran — each with nearly six times more men under arms than the GCC's combined defense forces — have been warring with one another throughout the GCC's entire existence. The Gulf is only 19 minutes away by plane at its widest point (between Iran and Saudi Arabia) and less than ten minutes at its narrowest point (between Iran and the UAE and Oman). Since 1984, tankers and freighters en route to or coming from GCC states have come under attack regularly.

Viewed in this light, the GCC stands out as the most prominent example of successful Arab regional collaboration in an era which has seen numerous other attempts at such an ideal fail. Its achievements are all the more remarkable when one considers that at the time the council was founded in 1981, many, if not most, observers predicted its speedy demise. Now in its second half-decade of cooperation and progress, it is evident that the GCC has not only contributed significantly to the stability of the region and to the welfare of its people but has been a force of reason and responsibility for the Arab world as a whole.

When Gulf events of recent years, problematic on many fronts, are considered in light of this reality, the result is a cautiously optimistic outlook for the organization and its member states. Such a guardedly upbeat prognosis applies not only to the GCC's hopes for further economic coordination, but also to the prospects for maintaining local security in the absence of a spillover from the Iran-Iraq war. It is certain that the will to do so exists on both fronts and that the impetus to follow the necessary course to achieve these goals is strong.

A wider international consideration of the GCC and appropriate support for it undoubtedly would enhance its chances of success. A successful GCC poses no credible threat to anyone and would do much to enhance the cause of both Gulf and global security. Regardless of its long-term efforts, the GCC in the mid-1980s already can be reckoned as the most unifying and cohesive multinational unit that the modern Arab world has ever attempted.

NOTES

1. As an Arab Gulf state, Iraq participated in many pan-Gulf cooperative activities. But, not being a member of the GCC, it has been excluded from many Gulf organizational developments since 1980.

2. Authors's interviews.

3. For more information on GCC organization, and the text of the charter, see John A. Sandwick, ed., *The Gulf Cooperation Council: Moderation and Stability in an Interdependent World* (Boulder, CO: Westview Press; Washington: American-Arab Affairs Council, 1987).

4. Author's interviews.

5. As of 1987, the members of the Supreme Council consisted of: King Fahd bin 'Abd Al-'Aziz Al Sa'ud of Saudi Arabia (since 1982); Shaykh Jabir al-Ahmad Al Sabah of Kuwait (since 1978); Shaykh 'Isa bin Salman Al Khalifa, Amir of Bahrain (since 1965); Shaykh Khalifa bin Hamad Al Thani, Amir of Qatar (since 1972); Shaykh Zayid bin Sultan Al Nahyan, Amir of Abu Dhabi and President of the United Arab Emirates (since 1966 and 1971 respectively); and Sultan Qaboos bin Sa'id Al Bu Sa'id of Oman (since 1970).

6. The members of the ministerial council are as follows: Shaykh Sabah al-Ahmad Al Sabah, since 1961 the foreign minister of Kuwait and, in that capacity, long the doyen of all the 21 Arab foreign ministers; Prince Sa'ud al-Faisal Al Sa'ud, Saudi Arabia's minister of foreign affairs since 1975; Shaykh Mubarak bin Muhammad Al Khalifa, minister of foreign affairs of Bahrain since 1971; Shaykh Hamad bin Khalifa Al Thani, minister of foreign affairs of Qatar since 1984; Shaykh Rashid bin 'Abdullah al-Nu'aymi, minister of state for foreign affairs in the United Arab Emirates since 1981; and Yusuf bin 'Abdullah al-'Alawi, minister of state for foreign affairs of Oman since 1982.

7. In mid-1987, Dr. El-Kuwaiz became president of the Arab Monetary Fund, at which time his GCC post fell vacant.

8. Author's interviews.

9. Author's interviews.

10. Author's interviews.

11. Author's interviews.

12. For more information on developments in this regard in mid-1987, see the chapter by Hermann F. Eilts elsewhere in this volume.

4

Soviet Designs and Dilemmas in the Gulf Region

Roger F. Pajak*

OVERVIEW

Since Moscow became embroiled in the Third World in the mid-1950s, the Gulf area has ranked high on the list of Soviet regional priorities. It is a region where demand for arms and reserves of oil significantly contribute to the volatility of the area. Moreover, it is the hotbed of Islamic fundamentalism, the most destabilizing force in the Muslim world in recent years.

Although Moscow's interest in the Gulf region was apparent in Soviet-German relations in the early period of World War II, this interest was not manifested directly until the early 1970s. The British withdrawal "East of Suez," the emergence of the Indian Ocean as a strategic area, the Shah of Iran's regional ambitions, and the intensified world demand for oil then served to draw the USSR into the region.[1]

Soviet interests in the Gulf are not necessarily attributed to Moscow's need for Gulf oil *per se*, but to its desire to control the source of oil and to use it to pressure the West. The USSR currently possesses abundant energy reserves and remains a net exporter of oil. Consequently, geopolitical considerations, rather than the energy factor, must be examined to explain Soviet behavior in the area.[2]

In the absence of definitive knowledge of the deliberations of the Soviet leadership, Moscow can reasonably be depicted as having several broad objectives in the Gulf: (1) reducing Western influence, (2) expanding Soviet influence, (3) obtaining some degree of access to the oil of the region, and (4) ensuring its security

* The views expressed in this article are the author's and do not necessarily reflect the views of the U.S. Government or any of its departments or agencies.

interests.[3] It seems clear that the Soviet leadership is concerned with denying or restricting military access to the area by the West, especially the US, to make it more difficult to protect Western interests, and, conversely, with facilitating Moscow's exploitation of new opportunities as they arise.[4]

Moscow could attempt to achieve its goals by seeking control over the Gulf by direct invasion, influence over the region by indirect intervention, and interference with the flow of oil to the West. All of these options may be viewed as threats to the vital interests of the US.

Assessments of the likelihood of each of the above Soviet policy options vary considerably. Where they diverge most notably is over Moscow's interest in controlling the Gulf. One view sees the Soviets as motivated geopolitically, and perhaps ideologically, in extending their control over the broad Southwest Asian area and reaching to the Indian Ocean with the traditional aim of acquiring "warm water ports." A modification of this position sees a Soviet commitment at least to acquire influence over this entire region.

An opposite view depicts the USSR as concerned pragmatically with maintaining a defensive perimeter along its southern border in Southwest Asia, especially in the "Northern Tier" of Turkey, Iran, and Pakistan. This view sees Moscow as predisposed to extend its influence in the Gulf only opportunistically as suitable situations develop which can be exploited.[5]

Proponents of both the "programmatic" and the "pragmatic" interpretations have argued their cases cogently, but both views are limited in their interpretation of regional political diplomatic events as a guide to future Soviet actions. For example, the invasion of Afghanistan, the provision of arms to selected clients, and the signing of friendship treaties are subject to varying interpretations, and do not necessarily provide definitive guides to Soviet motivations or future policies.[6]

At the same time, the pattern of Soviet activities in the Gulf over the past several decades obviously reflects something of the USSR's interests in the region. For Moscow, the objectives of its policy in the Gulf to a large extent can be viewed in terms of its global superpower rivalry with the US. In using a variety of means — arms shipments, economic and technical assistance, diplomatic contacts and trade — to promote its interests, Moscow has patiently bided its time, thus far content to win largely incremental gains in the region.[7]

The Soviets have skillfully promoted their interests by supporting Arab political positions, particularly *vis-a-vis* the Arab-Israeli conflict and Washington's support of Israel. Soviet diatribes against US policy and US interest in military facilities in the area have fallen on somewhat receptive ears among the Gulf Arabs. At the same time, the effectiveness of the Soviet propaganda campaign has been circumscribed by the Soviet invasion of Afghanistan, which has infuriated much of the Arab world, particularly the governments of the Gulf states.

In their dealings with Gulf countries, the Soviets have concentrated on bilateral government-to-government relations. Moscow has not used indigenous Communist Parties, or "national liberation fronts," such as the South Yemen-based Popular Front for the Liberation of Oman (PFLO), in its undertakings. The Soviets have denied significant support to such organizations, presumably to maintain a clean slate in their relations with the Gulf states, as well as to obviate any excuse by the West for intervention.[8]

By the early 1970s, the Gulf had come into sharp focus as an area of superpower competition. As the source of a critical share of the West's energy needs, the region came under intensified Soviet political and military pressure, peaking with the invasion of Afghanistan in December 1979. As the 1980s began, Western military capabilities and political presence in the Gulf area were widely perceived in Arab quarters as diminishing, while Soviet interests and capabilities were viewed as increasing.[9]

The trend began in 1977 when a massive airlift of Soviet arms to Ethiopia and the introduction of Cuban forces there demonstrated Moscow's determination and capability to aid a client state, as well as to maintain a military presence on the periphery of the Arabian Peninsula. A Soviet naval buildup thereupon followed in the Indian Ocean, with Moscow also jockeying for position in the 1979 confrontation between North and South Yemen.[10] Concomitantly, the overthrow of the Shah and the Soviet invasion of Afghanistan, along with Soviet gains in Ethiopia and South Yemen, raised fears in the West and among the Arab Gulf states of a carefully orchestrated Soviet strategy of encirclement, aimed ultimately at subverting the Gulf region.

But aside from South Yemen, where the Soviets earlier had made strong inroads, Moscow was unable to capitalize fully on possible opportunities. Perhaps Moscow was overly cautious, or the apparent opportunities simply may have been proven illusory — created by local conditions and similarly foreclosed by local factors. The Saudis and other Gulf states still refused to establish diplomatic relations with the USSR, and the oil embargo was lifted, contrary to Moscow's urgings. The "oil weapon" also proved to be a two-edged sword. While destabilizing Western economies and providing the Gulf Arab states with a huge infusion of cash to buy Soviet arms, it also enabled moderate Arab regimes to purchase large amounts of modern weaponry and technical assistance from Western arms suppliers, thus counteracting potential Soviet influence in the Gulf.[11]

During the late 1970s, the Soviet Union in fact lost ground in key areas of the Middle East. The Soviets were expelled from Egypt, the Sudan, and subsequently Somalia when Moscow changed sides in the Somali-Ethiopian confrontation. The huge increase in Arab oil revenues resulted in the Arabs turning essentially to the West for their development and modernization programs; Soviet technology was almost entirely ignored in the process. Then, the December 1979 Soviet invasion of Afghanistan alienated much of the Islamic world. A United Nations resolution condemning the action was opposed among the Arab states only by Syria and South Yemen. As the decade ended, Soviet fortunes in the Middle East and the Gulf region seemed to drop dramatically in Moscow's eyes.

Ironically, the position of the US and the West in the Middle East at the time was not much improved at the USSR's expense. In fact, new opportunities for Moscow arose following the Camp David accords and the resulting ostracization of Egypt by most of the Arab world. The Soviets also demonstrated their increased willingness and capability to support a client regime against external threats through the military assistance provided to Ethiopia in the late 1970s. This action underscored Soviet intentions of being a key player in the Red Sea/Horn of Africa region.

Concomitantly, the Soviets' very success in the Horn prevented gains that might have been made among the Gulf states as a consequence of Sadat's accommodation with Israel. The Saudis were unhappy with Soviet intervention in the Horn, and their concerns were compounded when the more radical wing of the South Yemeni regime took control of the government in 1978.[12]

While events in Ethiopia and South Yemen in the late 1970s weakened the West's position considerably, Moscow's position in the Gulf had not changed appreciably over the decade. The overthrow of the Shah in 1979 replaced a strong anti-Soviet force in the Gulf with a force that held the potential for destabilizing neighboring countries, but which did not enhance Moscow's position *per se*.

The Soviet invasion of Afghanistan, however, placed Soviet forces in closer proximity to the oil fields of the Gulf and threatened to make the Gulf states more tractable to Soviet interests.

IRAN

As mentioned above, the USSR traditionally has been interested in the Gulf. As the Soviets assumed more and more trappings of a superpower, their interest in increasing the security of their southern periphery grew apace. In this regard, Iran has long been of major importance in the Soviet calculus, not only because of its contiguous land border (one of the USSR's longest), but also because Iran occupies the northern shore of the Gulf and partially controls the Gulf's outlet to the Indian Ocean.[13]

Historically, Moscow has been acutely sensitive to developments on its borders. To traditional Soviet concerns of encirclement and vulnerability have been added the motivations of a superpower — an expansive view of security and an assumed right of predominance in nearby areas. With a contiguous border of 1,250 miles, Iran has traditionally been a neighbor of special interest. Moreover, as a primary link in the "Northern Tier" of Western defensive strategy for some two decades, first as a member of the Baghdad Pact and then of the Central Treaty Organization (CENTO), Iran had assumed a special concern in Soviet eyes.

Besides preventing Iran from being a Western military ally on the Soviet border, Moscow has other important interests in the country, not the least of which is oil. As one of the world's largest oil exporters with an estimated ten per cent of the world's proven oil reserves, Iran looms as a valuable supplementary source of oil and natural gas for either future Soviet needs or the needs of the East European states, which Moscow has been increasingly reluctant or unable to satisfy from its own production. Moscow's interest in the energy market doubtless has made Iran loom increasingly attractive to the Soviets.[14]

While Moscow's policy toward Iran over the years has fluctuated because of shifting Soviet perspectives and changing Iranian political orientations, the basic Soviet goal was constant: to sever Iran's Western alignment and to increase Soviet influence in the country. Moscow carefully nurtured economic ties with the Shah throughout the 1960s.

To say that Moscow thus welcomed the fall of the Shah in 1979 is an understatement. The emergence of the Khomeini regime abruptly ended many years of US and Western predominance and a strong, pro-Western government in Tehran. Interestingly, however, the Shah had established a substantial cooperative relationship with Moscow in the economic and military supply spheres, before the Khomeini revolution disrupted the existing regional equilibrium. Moscow did garner some immediate gains from the overthrow of the Shah, with the new regime appearing to offer substantial opportunities for the expansion of Soviet influence far beyond the limited cooperation established with the Shah. Nevertheless, the promise of early Soviet gains was diluted by Iranian enmity over the Soviet invasion of Afghanistan, Soviet support for Iraq, and Moscow's support of Iran's Communist Tudeh Party.[15]

Following the consolidation of power by the Khomeini regime, Moscow discovered that it faced new problems with the successor government in Tehran. The latter regime seemed to adopt a principle of "negative equilibrium" in its relations with both superpowers, whereby Tehran sought to prevent both the US and the USSR from acquiring influence in Iran.[16] This policy obviously limited the normalization of relations between the two states.

This is not to say that Moscow's strategic gains following the revolution were negligible. To begin with, the US presence and influence in Iran were eradicated. Tehran's foreign policy stance shifted from pro-Western to neutralist and then anti-Western, contributing to the collapse of the already moribund CENTO alliance. The Islamic Republic drastically curtailed foreign arms procurement, in particular cancelling all weapons contracts with the US, and rejected the role as policeman of the Gulf. Tehran joined the anti-imperialist, anti-US grouping of radical Arab states, a development that served to complicate US moves to mobilize support for the Camp David approach toward a Middle East settlement.[17]

Despite the Soviet disillusionment caused by Tehran's forsaking a close relationship with Moscow, the Soviets continued to court Khomeini in search of some measure of influence in Iran. While posturing as a defender of the Iranian revolution, Moscow also tried to encourage anti-Western, and especially anti-US, sentiments in Iran, and attempted to dissuade Tehran from normalizing relations with the West. Moscow simultaneously warned that "any interference ... in the affairs of Iran ... would be regarded by the Soviet Union as matters affecting its security interests."[18]

At the 26th Congress of the Soviet Communist Party in February 1981, Brezhnev referred to the Iranian revolution in favorable but cautious terms. While noting "its complications and contradictions," Brezhnev characterized the revolution as "anti-imperialist," even though "internal and foreign reaction is striving to change its nature." He held out the prospect of Soviet cooperation on the basis of "equality and reciprocity."[19] Brezhnev thus played up the Soviet view of the progressivism of the Islamic Revolution, while playing down the contradictions between Islam and Marxism.

While Moscow took much satisfaction from the fall of the Shah and the demise of the US position in Iran, two subsequent major events had a negative impact on the Soviet position in the Gulf: Moscow's invasion of Afghanistan and the Iran-Iraq war. Whatever the merits or the justification of the invasion of Afghanistan from Moscow's perspective, it had an adverse impact on the Soviet diplomatic position in the eyes of most of the Arab world. The Soviets were stymied in their efforts to foster an anti-Camp David grouping of Arab states. Moreover, the Gulf states turned increasingly to Washington as a counterbalance to Moscow, despite Camp David.[20]

The outbreak of the Iran-Iraq war in September 1980 complicated the Soviet position in the Middle East and the Gulf even further. Indeed, in Moscow's eyes, the war was truly the wrong war at the wrong time in the wrong place. When the war broke out, a case could have been made for Moscow to provide aid to either side. The USSR was linked to Iraq by the 1972 Treaty of Friendship and Cooperation and had been Iraq's main provider of arms since 1958. Moreover, Baghdad had been a leading source of opposition to the Camp David accords and, as a state with pretensions to leadership of the Arab world, it could eventually become the focus of anti-Western Arab unity which Moscow had long espoused. Additionally, Soviet aid to Baghdad would serve to underscore Soviet reliability to its allies in time of need.[21]

On the other hand, cogent argument could be made for assistance to Iran. The revolutionary regime, first of all, had removed Iran from the US sphere of influence, particularly damaging the US position in the Gulf. Furthermore, the possibility of replacing US arms offered the attractive option of solidifying Soviet influence in a key border state which also bordered Soviet-occupied Afghanistan. As in the Iraqi case, there also was the economic dimension, with the promise of resumed Iranian natural gas deliveries to the Soviet Transcaucasus area.[22]

The Soviets were not long in realizing that, regardless of which way the war went, they could gain little and lose much of their presence and influence in the region. Iran's defeat could result in the Khomeini regime's replacement by a more pro-Western government, whereas if the war went badly for Iraq, Baghdad could also turn more to the West for assistance. From the beginning of the conflict, therefore, Moscow has called for a negotiated end to the fighting, arguing that neither Iraq nor Iran would gain from the war.[23]

Moscow's dilemma here was that it required a good relationship with both sides and could not afford to antagonize either. As a consequence, the USSR remained neutral during the first year or so of the conflict.

At a state dinner in October 1980, Brezhnev blamed "imperialism" for causing the war and warned that:

Neither Iraq nor Iran will gain anything from mutual destruction and bloodshed ... It is only the third side, i.e. the US ... which stands to gain. As far as the Soviet Union is concerned, we are for Iran and Iraq settling disputable issues between themselves at the table of negotiations.[24]

During this period, the Soviets tried to cultivate Iran, by treating the Iranian revolution positively in their media and by offering substantial technical assistance, but Tehran evinced little interest. Moscow, however, has not been particularly adept at handling conflicts among its client states, as exemplified by Soviet experience in 1977-1978 with Somalia and Ethiopia.[25]

In an attempt to cultivate good relations with Tehran, the Soviets initially lauded the Khomeini revolution as "objectively progressive" and restrained their negative reaction to such issues as Iranian natural gas pricing. At the same time, the Soviets sought to protect the Marxist Tudeh Party in Iran from the ravages of anti-leftist purges in 1979 and 1980. Moscow accordingly was not long in discovering the frustrations and difficulties inherent in trying to deal positively with the Khomeini regime.[26]

As Soviet overtures and blandishments to Iran failed to produce any significant warming in Tehran's attitude toward Moscow, the Soviets began to tilt toward Iraq a year or so after the conflict began. In March 1980, for example, *Pravda* featured an authoritative assessment of relations with Iran, reflecting Soviet displeasure with Tehran's antagonistic behavior. The article complained of the reduction in the size of the Soviet diplomatic mission in Iran, the closing of Soviet cultural centers, the cessation of Iranian-Soviet banking activities, Tehran's anti-Soviet propaganda campaign, and the fundamentalist regime's inclination to equate Soviet motives with US motives *vis-a-vis* Iran. *Pravda* asserted continuing Soviet support for the Iranian revolution, but disavowed its anti-Soviet aspects.[27]

Despite the semblance of a pro-Iraqi tilt, Moscow remained officially neutral in the war. Moreover, it continued to view the prospects of strategic gains as being greater in Iran than in Iraq, since it still smarted over Baghdad's recent commercial and military contacts with the West. The Soviets nevertheless maintained a balancing act, not wishing to sacrifice their longstanding relationship with Baghdad. As the war continued, Iranian battlefield successes — combined with political frustrations with the Khomeini regime — impelled Moscow to resume arms shipments to Iraq to strengthen Iraqi capabilities. Seeing a decisive victory by either side as inimical to its interests, Moscow by this time apparently abandoned hope for Iranian reasonableness in terminating the war and saw little prospect for improved ties with Tehran over the near term.[28]

In February 1983, Khomeini responded to Moscow's tilt toward Iraq by dissolving the Tudeh Party and accusing Moscow of interfering in Iranian affairs. The Tudeh leadership was arrested, while 18 Soviet diplomats were expelled. Moscow, in turn, condemned the Iranian regime's fanaticism.[29]

The Soviet-Iranian relationship since then has blown hot and cold, or at least lukewarm and cool. In mid-1984, as a light warming trend occurred temporarily in Soviet-Iranian ties, possibly reflecting Iraq's improved ties with the US, Tehran apparently tried to induce Moscow to cut back on aid to Iraq. Delegations were exchanged and talks were held on improving trade and economic relations.[30]

In December 1986, Moscow and Tehran concluded an economic cooperation agreement in the wake of the Iranian decision to resume natural gas shipments to the Soviet Union. The accord embraced commerce, banking, transportation, fisheries, and construction of steel plants and power stations in Iran, and indicated Soviet agreement with Iran in returning technicians who were withdrawn in 1985 over "war dangers."[31]

Despite this apparent warming in economic relations, a December 1986 article in *Izvestiya* constituted one of the sharpest Soviet media attacks on Iran in months, and cast a new chill on the relationship. The article underscored Moscow's longstanding demands for Iranian political concessions prior to any improvement in bilateral relations.[32] As a prerequisite for better ties, the Soviets continued to demand that Tehran (1) cease anti-Soviet propaganda, (2) stop supporting the Afghan rebels, (3) stop its suppression of the Tudeh Party, and (4) agree to cease-fire negotiations in the war. In the face of Tehran's intransigence on these points, no enduring thaw in Soviet-Iranian relations appears imminent.

IRAQ

Iraq's relationship with the USSR, dating from 1958, reached its zenith with the conclusion of a 20-year Treaty of Friendship and Cooperation in 1972. The Iraqi regime's self-perceived isolation in the Arab world was intensified by its disputes with Iran, Syria and Kuwait, and its perception of internal security threats, exemplified by the festering Kurdish minority problem.

As was the case with Moscow's relations with most Arab countries, the USSR's relationship with Iraq was strained by the hostility between Baghdad's Ba'thist ideology and Communism. Other tendentious issues contributed to cool relations between the two countries, such as Moscow's resale of Iraqi oil — which was used as payment for Soviet arms — for more than the price paid to Iraq. Furthermore in early 1978, the Ba'th regime arrested and executed 21 Iraqi Communist Party members for purported subversion in the armed forces, an act which deeply angered Moscow.[33]

Moscow's invasion of Afghanistan and its support of the Ethiopian regime against the Eritrean Muslim rebels also raised the ire of Baghdad. In July 1978, Iraqi President Saddam Hussein stated in an interview: "The Soviet Union will not be satisfied until the entire world becomes Communist,"[34] rather strong words by a client state about its mentor. Following the Camp David accords, Soviet-Iraqi relations warmed somewhat, but were still not profusely adulatory. In Iraqi President Saddam Hussein's words:

> The Soviets are our best friends .... But we should not fall in love with the Soviet Union if it renounces us. Well, this has never happened, even though our views differ, for example on Eritrea's conflict with Ethiopia.[35]

While the history of the Soviet arms supply relationship with Iraq has been uneven, particularly since the October 1973 war,

Baghdad had been perturbed at Soviet laggardliness in supplying new types and quantities of military equipment, such as advanced interceptor aircraft and missiles. The editor of the Ba'th Party newspaper in Baghdad wrote in January 1980 that "the Soviet Union is neither capable nor ready to respond to the Arabs' needs, not even to those countries capable of paying in cash and hard currency."[36] Finally, confirming publicly what had been Iraqi policy for some time, Baghdad announced in June 1980 that it would seek arms from other countries. Since then, Iraq has purchased a substantial portion of its military equipment from France, in contrast to its virtually exclusive arms reliance on Moscow for the previous two decades.

The cool state of relations with Iraq since 1978 affected Soviet policy when Iraq invaded Iran in September 1980. Although Moscow declared its neutrality at the outbreak of the conflict, the Soviets had been tilting toward Iran in the months immediately prior to the Iraqi invasion.[37]

When the war began, the Soviets were not long in realizing that, in almost any scenario they postulated, they had little to gain. Consequently, Moscow took a neutralist stance and Brezhnev stated in late 1980 that "neither Iraq nor Iran will gain anything from mutual destruction, bloodshed, and the undermining of each other's economy."[38]

The Soviet-Iraqi Friendship Treaty of 1972 notwithstanding, the Soviets embargoed the shipment of major new military equipment to Baghdad at the onset of hostilities. The deliveries of equipment through the Jordanian port of Aqaba in the early weeks of the war apparently were merely a trickle, comprising items already in the pipeline. Successive visits to Moscow by ranking Iraqi officials failed to thaw the Soviet arms freeze.[39]

By mid-1981, however, Moscow, presumably realizing that its arms embargo to Iraq was not producing any positive policy results, decided to resume military deliveries to Baghdad. The Soviet policy shift reportedly occurred when Taha Yassin Ramadan, the Iraqi Deputy Premier, visited Moscow in June following the Israeli bombing raid on the Iraqi nuclear reactor in Baghdad.[40]

As the Iran-Iraq war dragged on, increasing Iranian military successes posed another dilemma for Moscow. The unexpected turn of events demonstrated that the risks of nurturing a new alignment in the region were more hazardous than any benefits to be realized. In this case, a victorious and rejuvenated Iranian regime would offer fewer opportunities for Communist penetration, as well as diminished prospects for Soviet influence. At the same time, an emboldened Tehran would exacerbate security concerns among the Gulf countries, which might then seek an increased US military presence in the Gulf. A defeated Iraq, moreover, with the Soviet arms embargo at a time of crisis vividly in mind, would be inclined to turn even more toward the West for military support and economic assistance.

Soviet policy toward Iraq, therefore, has been far from an unblemished success. Moscow has found Baghdad's position to be intractable on a number of issues of importance to it, including Afghanistan, the war, and the status of the Iraqi Communist Party. Moscow has endeavored to draw the Iraqis back into the radical Steadfastness Front of Arab anti-imperialist states, but Iraq has refrained from doing so. Iraqi relations with Syria, Moscow's primary client state in the region, have remained hostile. Consequently, rather than weakening Western influence in the region, Iraqi policy has contributed to increasing Western involvement in the area at the expense of the Soviet Union, thus constituting another of Moscow's current policy dilemmas in the Gulf.

SAUDI ARABIA

The most important state in the lower Gulf from Moscow's perspective is Saudi Arabia. Moscow has had no diplomatic relations with the Saudis since the 1930s, nor is there any immediate likelihood that formal relations will be re-established soon. The Saudi ruling regime is a staunchly conservative Muslim monarchy, which is strongly opposed to Communism. The Saudis have banned the local Communist Party, thereby denying Moscow possible entrée afforded by the party as an instrument of political penetration. Given the nature of the ruling House of Saʿud, the Saudis are acutely concerned over revolutionary movements, be they of a secular or religious character.[41]

Although one of the hallmarks of Saudi foreign policy has been nonalignment, the Saudis have no diplomatic relations with any Communist country. Interestingly enough, the Soviet Union was among the first countries to recognize King ʿAbd al-ʿAziz Al Saʿud and to extend diplomatic relations in the 1930s. Since then, however, Soviet-Saudi bilateral relations have been extremely limited. Other than a small amount of trade, relations between the two countries have been limited to official statements and media commentary. At the same time, the current absence of Saudi ties with Communist countries is not due to a dearth of Soviet overtures.

Soviet commentary on the Saudi regime has alternated between hostile statements on how the monarchy serves US imperialism and is opposed by the downtrodden working classes, and friendly statements promulgating the advantages of Saudi-Soviet cooperation and advocating the establishment of diplomatic relations. Saudi commentary on the Soviet Union on the other hand has been generally negative, since Riyadh has consistently viewed Moscow and Communism as antithetical to Islamic society and the Saudi monarchy.[42]

By the mid-1970s, the security situation in the southern part of the Arabian Peninsula had improved, to the relief of the Saudis, with the defeat of the South Yemeni-supported rebels in Oman. The radical South Yemeni regime established diplomatic relations with several Gulf countries, including Saudi Arabia, in 1975-1976. While the Soviets and the Saudis did not entirely cease their mutual polemics, Riyadh did issue some conciliatory statements, such as one by then-Crown Prince Fahd, stating that the Saudis wanted good relations with both East and West and that Riyadh might "settle" its relations with Moscow. The Soviets welcomed such statements but evinced disappointment over the Saudi desire to have friendship "without embassies."[43]

When Saudi-US relations took a turn for the worse following the Camp David accords of September 1978, Moscow tried to derive advantage from the situation. A January 1979 article in the Soviet journal, *Literaturnaya Gazeta*, blamed the US for the negative Saudi image of the USSR and called for an improvement in Soviet-Saudi relations. The article saw "no implacable conflicts" existing between Moscow and Riyadh. Radio Moscow shortly thereafter promulgated the novel proposition that Communism and Islam were not really incompatible.[44]

The Saudis, for their part, responded in like manner. The Saudi foreign minister noted the positive role of Moscow in the region, while Crown Prince Fahd postulated the exchange of ambassadors at some point. This round of friendly statements abruptly ended with the Soviet invasion of Afghanistan in December 1979. Saudi Arabia was one of the chief organizers of the Islamic summit conference which convened in January 1980 and condemned the Soviet invasion.[45]

Moscow thereupon resumed its criticism of the Saudi monarchy. It concomitantly blamed Washington for provoking Saudi fears of the "Soviet threat" and claimed that the US was the real threat to the Saudis. In early 1983, Moscow's commentary became especially vituperative when TASS accused the Saudis of torturing their domestic opponents. The Soviets were particularly annoyed over Riyadh's use of Afghanistan as an "excuse" for not establishing diplomatic relations with Moscow.[46]

The Saudis have remained adamant in regarding Afghanistan as a critical impediment to friendly relations with the Soviet Union. Saudi officials have from time to time alluded to the possibility of friendship with Moscow, but only if Moscow meets the conditions of (1) Soviet withdrawal from Afghanistan, (2) the reduction of the military presence in South Yemen and Ethiopia, (3) the cessation of all hostile Soviet propaganda toward Saudi Arabia, and (4) greater religious freedom for Soviet Muslims.[47]

In the context of Soviet long-term goals, a Saudi official added another concern for Riyadh: "The answer is simple: our oil .... We do not expect the Soviets to use their power to maneuver themselves into a position to make arrangements for a guaranteed oil supply."[48]

In August 1985, speculation in Arab circles over a possible Saudi overture toward the USSR increased when a Saudi soccer team headed by the King's son, Prince Faisal, visited Moscow. The Soviet media highlighted the visit, which included protocol meetings with the Soviet deputy foreign minister. Despite Moscow's interest in improving ties, the Saudis remained non-committal. In Gulf circles, moreover, Prince Faisal is not regarded as particularly influential. Accordingly, the Soviet attention lavished on the Prince may have reflected Soviet naïveté regarding Saudi relationships.[49]

In an interview in December 1985, Saudi Defense Minister Prince Sultan went so far as to rule out any imminent establishment of ties with Moscow. He repeated as preconditions "a non-belligerent Soviet attitude towards Islam" and "the extent of the Soviet leadership's response to Islamic causes in Afghanistan or elsewhere."[50] Since the Saudis foresee little likelihood of Moscow meeting these conditions, they probably have little realistic expectation of establishing close relations with the Soviets any time soon.

Nevertheless, the January 1987 visit to Moscow by the new Saudi oil minister, Hisham Nazir, occasioned further speculation in diplomatic circles of a Saudi tilt toward the USSR. The announced purpose of the visit was to discuss oil production and prices, and Moscow did announce a 7.5 percent cut in oil exports in solidarity with OPEC policy. Nazir's visit, one of the first such public visits by a senior Saudi official, and his meetings with high-level Soviet officials, were highly publicized in the tightly-controlled Saudi press. Another Saudi official commented that the Saudis "are talking more and more with the Soviets. I think that Saudi Arabia will establish relations with the Soviet Union within three years."[51] Such gestures, however, have arisen in the past and thus far have had no significant, lasting impact on the firming of Soviet-Saudi ties.

The Soviet ambassador to the UAE similarly predicted in February 1987 that the USSR would soon establish diplomatic relations with Saudi Arabia. "I am certain that in the future there will be normal relations between our two countries and this will not be far off," Ambassador F.N. Fedotov told an Arab newspaper. "We will have an embassy in our country."[52]

The pattern of Soviet-Saudi interaction, limited as it has been to date, seems to indicate that the key obstacle to friendly relations between the two governments remains overall Soviet policy in the Southwest Asian region.[53] While Moscow desires closer relations with Riyadh, the Soviet leadership apparently does not regard this goal in itself as important enough to warrant significant changes in its regional policies.

KUWAIT

Kuwait, which has maintained diplomatic relations with the Soviet Union since 1963, has had a unique relationship with Moscow since that time. Going beyond the exchange of ambassadors, the Soviet-Kuwaiti relationship has resulted in Kuwait's purchase of Soviet arms, joint statements critical of the US on numerous policy issues, and Kuwaiti endorsement of Soviet Middle East peace proposals. While not agreeing on all policy issues, the Kuwaitis — unlike the other Gulf Cooperation Council (GCC) member countries which cite Soviet policy actions as reasons for non-cooperation with the USSR — have played down policy differences with Moscow in the interest of friendly relations.

Moscow highly regards its ties with Kuwait as a successful demonstration of "peaceful coexistence" between a socialist state and an Arab monarchy, and more importantly, as a model for emulation by other Gulf states. The Soviets lose no opportunity to re-broadcast Kuwaiti government and newspaper statements that criticize the US and praise the USSR. Moscow no doubt regards such pro-Soviet statements from Kuwait as having more propaganda impact than similar issuances from Soviet Third World client states, since Kuwait has no obligation to make them at all.[54]

Kuwait established diplomatic relations with the USSR in an effort to create a "more balanced relationship with the two superpowers," as one Arab diplomat put it.[55] Kuwait also desired to neutralize leftist opposition groups in the country and to gain favor with Iraq and other regional states with Soviet links. The Kuwaitis calculated that close ties with Moscow would serve as insurance in causing the Soviets to restrain the activities of domestic opposition groups in the country. Also, the Kuwaitis hoped that close relations with Moscow would lead the Soviets to discourage Iraq's prior territorial designs on Kuwaiti territory. By being friendly with the Soviets, the Kuwaitis hoped to induce Moscow to foreswear cooperation with their internal or external opponents, and indeed, none of Kuwait's current security threats appear to come from groups supported by Moscow.[56]

To further nurture a close relationship with Moscow, the Kuwaitis, beginning in 1974, sought to purchase Soviet arms. Initially, Moscow declined to sell military equipment, probably because of concern over affecting relations with neighboring Iraq. The Kuwaitis successfully persisted, however, even while insisting that no Soviet military advisers should accompany the delivery of equipment, nor that any Kuwaiti military personnel should go to the USSR for training, fearing Communist subversion within the Kuwaiti armed forces. In a departure from arms aid packages concluded with other developing countries, the Soviets agreed to the Kuwaiti proviso, and by late 1976, an arms package, reportedly valued at $400 million, was prepared for implementation. When the agreement was actually signed in March 1977, however, the Kuwaitis scaled back the accord to $50-million-worth of equipment, largely embracing SA-7 man-portable surface-to-air missiles and field artillery.[57]

In February 1980, Moscow concluded an additional $200 million arms package with Kuwait, which included 100 SA-6 and additional SA-7 air defense missiles, as well as a number of FROG-7 tactical rockets. Kuwait still kept its Soviet military supply relationship limited while it continued to buy the bulk of its arms from the US, Britain, and France.[58]

By the summer of 1984, Soviet-Kuwaiti military cooperation increased further. After Kuwait's request for Stinger surface-to-air missiles was rejected by Washington, the Kuwaitis again turned to the USSR, which agreed to sell Kuwait the air defense equipment it wanted in an agreement worth over $300 million. This time, however, according to the Kuwaiti press, Soviet military instructors were to be sent to Kuwait, and Kuwaiti personnel would be sent to the USSR for training.[59]

The Kuwaitis' interest in procuring arms from the Soviets probably stemmed from their desire to enhance their external security with the weapons, as well as to solidify their relationship with Moscow and strengthen Kuwait's credentials as a nonaligned state. The Soviets probably saw their weapon sales to Kuwait as yet another inducement for persuading the Gulf monarchies that they too could benefit from closer relations with Moscow.

In the economic sphere, Kuwaiti relations with the USSR were reinforced by a protocol on economic cooperation concluded during the February 1986 visit to Moscow by Kuwaiti Oil Minister Shaykh 'Ali al-Khalifa Al Sabah. The protocol included provisions for joint oil prospecting in both countries, along with oil marketing and banking cooperation. Of special attraction to the Soviets was the offer of Kuwaiti expertise in developing offshore oil, a service of considerable utility to Moscow.[60] Then, on the heels of a renewed bilateral trade agreement, a consortium of nine Kuwaiti banks and financial institutions in February 1987 extended a $150 million syndicated loan to the Soviet Union. The loan, the first such arrangement by the Kuwaitis for the Soviet Union, was hailed by both countries as "a new milestone" in bilateral financial cooperation and in setting the stage for Kuwaiti investment in the Soviet Union and Eastern Europe.[61]

In a further example of unprecedented arrangements with Moscow, the Kuwaitis in early 1987 were discussing the leasing of oil tankers from the Soviet Union as well as the US, and the possible provision of US and Soviet military escorts for Kuwaiti tankers in the Gulf, as the Iran-Iraq war military threat to neutral shipping intensified. Soviet and Kuwaiti spokesmen referred to such an arrangement as "a commercial deal," but the naval escorts allowed under such an agreement would in effect enhance the Soviet and the Western military presence in the Gulf.[62]

Besides an arms sales relationship and a limited amount of bilateral trade, Kuwait also maintains a semblance of cultural and technical links with the USSR. Neither side derives much in the way of material benefits from the relationship, but the political value is significant. Moscow regards its 140-member embassy in Kuwait,[63] a large staff by Gulf standards, as a useful listening post in the Gulf and an important channel to Saudi Arabia and the lower Gulf states.[64]

Of all the areas of cooperative bilateral relations between the two countries, Moscow probably values the foreign policy aspect most highly. Kuwait alone of the GCC countries welcomed Brezhnev's December 1980 proposals for Gulf security, which called for a ban on all outside forces and military bases in the area. The Kuwaitis feel that the presence of one superpower in the Gulf will lead to the other's presence as well. Kuwait accordingly believes that if the US refrains from a military buildup in the region, the USSR will do likewise. Kuwait also has urged the other members of the GCC to normalize ties with Moscow, in the belief that friendly GCC gestures toward the USSR will be reciprocated by Moscow.[65]

While Kuwait's government remains conservative and anti-Communist, in effect Kuwait has become pro-Soviet in its foreign-policy rhetoric. Moscow consequently has come to value its relationship with Kuwait. Although Moscow no doubt would welcome the establishment of a more radical regime in Kuwait, the Soviets probably realize that any semblance of support for potential opposition forces in the country would likely cause the current government to end its friendship with Moscow. The Soviets accordingly are likely to continue friendly cooperative ties with Kuwait, given the considerable foreign policy and propaganda benefits accruing from the relationship.

THE OTHER LOWER GULF STATES

Soviet efforts to establish diplomatic relations with other Gulf states have borne fruit in the cases of Oman and the United Arab Emirates. On September 26, 195, Oman unexpectedly announced its establishment of diplomatic relations with the Soviet Union, following a meeting in New York between Soviet Foreign Minister Eduard Shevardnadze and Omani Minister of State for Foreign Affairs Yusuf bin 'Alawi 'Abdullah. This was a surprising development, first because Oman's Sultan Qaboos had been a dedicated anti-Communist ruler, and second, as an important site of Western military facilities, Oman had appeared to be an unlikely prospect for a Soviet presence.[66]

The decision by Sultan Qaboos to open diplomatic relations may indicate that fear of Iranian fundamentalism has replaced fear or distrust of the Soviet Union and its client state, South Yemen, in the eyes of the Gulf states. In this regard, the end of the South Yemeni-supported Dhufar rebellion in Oman in the mid-1970s and a more normalized relationship between Oman and neighboring South Yemen seem to have been important factors contributing to Oman's decision. Oman probably felt that development of closer ties with the Soviet Union would help to preclude any disposition on the part of Aden to renew support for future insurrectionist groups in Oman.[67]

The Omani minister of state for foreign affairs expressed his country's conviction that Moscow would take steps to help ease tensions in the Arabian Peninsula and work to improve stability. Although he specified no particular countries, undoubtedly he was referring to South Yemen and its improving relationship with Oman.[68] Sultan Qaboos assured both Washington and London that his decision to establish ties with Moscow implied no "change of heart" on his part but emphasized Oman's "non-aligned status".[69] The Omanis desired to maintain close relations with the US and Britain, and indicated that the Soviets were to have no resident ambassador in Oman for some time. Instead, the current Soviet ambassador to Jordan would be accredited to Oman as well.[70]

On November 14, 1985, the UAE became the third GCC state to establish relations with the Soviet Union. Just as Kuwait and Oman had preceded the UAE in establishing ties with China, the UAE followed the two Gulf states in opening links with Moscow, but for somewhat different reasons. While the Omani decision was related to improved relations with South Yemen, the UAE's decision was apparently linked to its election to the UN Security Council in October 1985, to be effective in January 1986.[71] Elected to fill one of five vacancies for non-permanent council members, the UAE may have thought that its non-aligned status would be usefully served by diplomatic relations with both superpowers.

Of particular consequence for the Western countries, especially the US, the decisions of Oman and the UAE to establish relations with Moscow also sent clear political signals of probable displeasure with certain Western policies, especially close US-Israeli ties. Whether these two countries made their overtures to Moscow with or without Saudi Arabia's blessing is uncertain. In any case, the two states frequently have taken their lead in foreign policy from the

Saudis, who at least may have regarded the moves as a signal worth sending to the West to not take the GCC countries for granted.

Moscow cannot help but have been buoyed by the establishment of relations with the two Gulf states, and no doubt hopes that these developments eventually will lead to ties with Saudi Arabia and the remaining Gulf states. The Soviets probably have no illusions over the prospects for displacing the West on the Arabian Peninsula, but they presumably view the diplomatic exchanges with Oman and the UAE as enhancing Moscow's aura of respectability, which may prove to be an increasingly valuable political asset for Moscow in the Gulf in the long run.

SOVIET PROSPECTS IN THE GULF

The USSR's formidable military capabilities in the Southwest Asian region have not been translated into political influence in the Gulf area. Although Soviet military intervention remains a possibility in a crisis situation, Moscow has been pursuing a policy of moderation in striving for normal relations with the Gulf states, while trying to undermine Western influence and prevent the expansion of a US military presence. It has pushed for an agreement with the West and China to prohibit foreign military bases and the use of force in the Gulf, as part of a demilitarized "zone of peace" in the Indian Ocean. Moscow has implied that it will not intervene in the Gulf, as long as Washington is excluded from the region. At the same time, formidable impediments to improved Soviet relations with the Gulf states exist in the way of Moscow's continuing occupation of Afghanistan and the war there, its close ties with the radical South Yemeni regime and other radical "national liberation" groups in the area, and the conservative Arab states' profound aversion to Communism, strengthened by Islamic nationalism.[72]

Soviet prospects in the Gulf are heavily dependent on local events and conditions over which Moscow has little control. Of central importance is the course of the Gulf war and the future policies of the combatants. The Iran-Iraq war has proven to be much more of a problem to Moscow than an opportunity. The Soviets would no doubt prefer to be an ally of both warring states, rather than having to choose between them. From Moscow's perspective, the least desired outcome would be a clear-cut victory by either side, inasmuch as the victorious state presumably would be less dependent on Moscow's largesse and thus less susceptible to Soviet influence.

Despite its history of frictions with the Iraqis, Moscow would not be happy with a fundamentalist Shi'a regime in Baghdad. A dominant Iran would be even less appealing to the Soviets, particularly given the prospect of Iranian hegemony over the lower Gulf states. While the Soviets would not be averse to a weakening or overthrow of the conservative Gulf monarchies, one possible effect of Iranian expansionism would be to push the Gulf states further under a protective US umbrella. The prospect of fundamentalist Islamic governments in the Gulf countries would also be unappealing to Moscow. As a desired outcome, Moscow would likely favor a negotiated settlement of the Gulf war, with itself as a key mediator.

The Soviet military occupation of Afghanistan notwithstanding, the Gulf regimes have played down fears of a direct Soviet incursion in the Gulf and have focused instead on the possible prospect of Soviet-supported subversion in the area. To offset that possibility, several Gulf states have followed the lead of Kuwait in establishing diplomatic ties with Moscow, in the hope that such a relationship might offer some leverage with the Soviets. In any case, the Soviet invasion of Afghanistan no doubt suggested to the Gulf Arabs that the Soviets constitute a force to be reckoned with in the area, leading the Gulf rulers to conclude that it may be preferable to hedge their bets, rather than rely solely on the West for diplomatic and military support.[73]

The Gulf rulers do not wish to see their region become a center of superpower confrontation, much less a battleground. Unable to defend themselves adequately against any major power intervention, the Gulf states must try to ensure that neither superpower has an excuse to act. At least some elements in Gulf ruling circles see an advantage in playing off Moscow against Washington, so that neither side will feel impelled to move into the region without serious provocation.[74]

As for the Soviet interest in Gulf oil, as time goes on, Moscow will probably find itself increasingly concerned with this commodity. With the Gulf states having taken control of the Western oil companies, the Soviets can no longer harp on one of their favorite themes of support for "the struggle against oil monopolies." The USSR, moreover, has been largely excluded from the ongoing economic development process in the Gulf, and it does not have the technology to make iself a desired partner.[75] A crucial question then arises for consideration by the Gulf states and the

81

West as to whether the Soviet Union eventually will become a net importer of oil. Given the current Soviet shortage of hard currency, will the Gulf states then be exposed to Soviet action more drastic than economic bargaining?

The Soviets have been obliged to concentrate on attempting to convince the Gulf states of their benign intent, while concomitantly espousing a Gulf security arrangement. The 1980 Brezhnev proposal to ban foreign military bases and the use of force in the Gulf foundered, however, on the rock of the Afghanistan invasion. Another problem to be overcome by Moscow has been its involvement in local conflicts, such as the Horn of Africa and the Yemens. Such involvement has aroused concerns on the part of the Gulf states. Similarly, the USSR's identification with national liberation movements (including close ties with the radical South Yemeni regime) also has exacerbated Soviet difficulties in normalizing relations with the lower Gulf states.[76]

At least or the immediate future, Moscow is likely to continue its moderate, gradualist policy of politically supporting the Gulf states while exploiting their security concerns. Their intention is to establish what the Soviets refer to as "mutually beneficial relations" which may evolve into long-term relationships. The Soviets also will continue to seek and exploit regional instabilities that have the potential of weakening pro-Western elements in the various Gulf states.[77] Within the above constraints, the Soviets will most likely concentrate on doing their utmost to prevent expansion of the US military presence in the Gulf. They will attempt to accomplish this by playing on the fears of the Gulf states *vis-a-vis* possible US designs on the oil fields, on Arab resentment over US support for Israel, and on the hope that the USSR will stay out of the Gulf if the US does.

At the same time, the Soviets probably will concentrate on nurturing bilateral state relations in the Gulf in the absence of any opportunities for a more dramatic breakthrough. Moscow's support for national liberation movements or local Communist parties as a consequence will likely remain muted, at least for the time being. The Soviets accordingly will support or pressure the Gulf states, as their actions dictate, while continuing to underscore the theme that the USSR stands ready to improve relations.[78]

Finally, Moscow seems to have come to terms with the contradictions of Third World politics. Reconciled to dilemmas, accepting the continuation of local conflicts it cannot resolve, and prepared to commit substantial resources in situations where desired outcomes are far from certain, the Soviets have aspired to local gains more to undermine the US and the West than to achieve local Communist influence.[79] Moscow thus appears to have favored a tactical approach offering incremental gains in the Gulf, rather than relying on a broadly structured policy to achieve regional goals.

NOTES

1. David L. Prior, *Soviet Relations in the Gulf* (Washington: Center for Strategic and International Studies, for the US Department of Defense, Office of Net Assessment, 1983), p.1.

2. Atef A. Gawad, "Moscow's Arms for Oil Diplomacy," *Foreign Policy*, No. 63 (Summer 1986), p. 147.

3. Roger Kanet, *Soviet Strategy in Southwest Asia and the Persian Gulf Region* (Urbana, Illinois: University of Illinois Press, March 1985), p. 7.

4. Stephen Page, "Moscow and the Arabian Peninsula," *American-Arab Affairs*, No. 8 (Spring 1984), p. 90.

5. An example of this approach is cited in Kanet, p. 6.

6. Lenore Martin, *The Unstable Gulf* (Lexington, Mass: Lexington Books, 1984), p. 118.

7. Page, p. 89.

8. Ibid., p. 90.

9. Michael Dixon, *The Soviet Union in the Third World, 1980-82: An Imperial Burden or Political Asset? The Soviet Union and the Middle East* (Washington: Library of Congress, Congressional Research Service, December 1983), p. 7.

10. Ibid.

11. Page, p. 88.

12. Ibid., p. 86.

13. S. Chubin, "Soviet Policy Towards Iran and the Gulf," in Charles Tripp, ed., *Regional Security in the Middle East* (New York: St. Martin's Press, 1984), p. 125.

14. Ibid., p. 128.

15. Dixon, p. 12.

16. S. Chubin, "The Soviet Union and Iran," *Foreign Affairs*, Vol. 61, No. 4 (Spring 1983), p. 930.

17. Dixon, p. 130.

18. TASS, March 25, 1980.

19. Foreign Broadcast Information Service (FBIS), *Soviet Union Daily Report*, February 24, 1981, pp. 10-11, as cited in Dixon, p. 15.

20. Robert O. Freedman, "Patterns of Soviet Policy toward the Middle East," *Annals of the American Academy of Political Science*, (November 1985), p. 46.

21. Ibid., p. 47.

22. Ibid., p. 48.

23. Karen Dawisha, "Moscow and the Gulf War," *The World Today*, Vol. 43, No. 1 (January 1981), p. 11.

24. TASS, September 30, 1980.

25. A. Becker and F. Fukuyama, "The USSR and the Middle East," in Colin Legum, ed., *Crisis and Conflict in the Middle East* (New York: Holmes and Meier, 1981), p. 83.

26. Ibid., p. 84.

27. Cited in Dixon, p. 17.

28. Ibid., p. 21.

29. Center for Defense Information, *Soviet Geopolitical Momentum: Myth or Menace?* (Washington, 1986), p. 21.

30. Ibid.

31. *Washington Post*, December 13, 1986, p. 14.

32. Cited in FBIS, *Soviet Union Daily Report*, December 3, 1986, p. H1.

33. Edmund Ghareeb, "Iraq: Emergent Gulf Power," in H. Amirsadeghi, ed., *The Security of the Persian Gulf* (New York: St. Martin's Press, 1981) p. 220.

34. Quoted in ibid., p. 221.

35. Ibid.

36. *Al-Thawra*, January 3, 1980, as quoted in Dawisha, p. 9.

37. Ibid., p. 10.

38. *Pravda*, October 9, 1980, as quoted in Dawisha, p. 11.

39. *Washington Post*, March 3, 1981; *Christian Science Monitor*, September 4, 1981.

40. *Financial Times*, July 6, 1981.

41. Kanet, p. 16.

42. Mark Katz, *Russia and Arabia: Soviet Foreign Policy Toward the Arabian Peninsula* (Baltimore: Johns Hopkins University Press, 1986), p. 131.

43. Quoted in ibid., p. 136.

44. William Quandt, "Riyadh between the Superpowers," *Foreign Policy* No. 44, (Fall 1981), p. 50.

45. Katz, pp. 137-138.

46. Katz, p. 138.

47. Katz, pp. 138-139.

48. Quandt, p. 52.

49. Economist Intelligence Unit (EIU), *Quarterly Economic Review — Saudi Arabia*, No. 4 (1985), pp. 5-6.

50. Ibid., No. 1 (1986), p. 5.

51. *Baltimore Sun*, February 1, 1987.

52. *New York Times*, February 7, 1987, p. 3.

53. Katz, p. 139.

54. Katz, p. 157.

55. *Baltimore Sun*, February 1, 1987.

56. Katz, p. 158.

57. Richard Nyrop, ed., *Persian Gulf States: Country Studies* (Washington: USGPO, 1985), p. 139; Katz, p. 164.

58. Ibid.

59. Ibid., p. 165.

60. EIU, *Quarterly Economic Review — Kuwait*, No. 1 (1986) p. 5.

61. Associated Press Wire Service Report, February 15, 1987.

62. *Washington Post*, April 15, 1987.

63. *New York Times*, February 7, 1987, p. 3.

64. Prior, p. 13.

65. Katz, pp. 168-169.

66. *Middle East International*, October 11, 1985.

67. EIU, *Quarterly Economic Review — Oman*, No. 4 (1985), p. 18. See also the chapter by Hermann Eilts elsewhere in this volume.

68. Ibid.

69. Ibid.

70. EIU, *Quarterly Economic Review — Oman*, No. 1 (1986), p. 16.

71. EIU, *Quarterly Economic Review — UAE*, No. 4 (1985), p. 8.

72. Dixon, p. 8.

73. Michael Sterner, "The GCC and Persian Gulf Security," in Thomas Naff, ed., *Gulf Security and the Iran-Iraq War* (Washington: National Defense University Press, 1984), p. 12.

74. John Bullock, *The Gulf* (London: Century, 1984), p. 66.

75. John C. Campbell, "The Gulf Region in the Global Setting," in H. Amirsadeghi, ed., *The Security of the Persian Gulf* (New York: St. Martin's Press), 1981, pp. 21-22.

76. Page, p. 92.

77. Kanet, p. 21.

78. Page, p. 94.

79. Andrew Pierre, *The Politics of International Arms Transfers* (Princeton: Princeton University Press, 1982), p. 82.

Part II:
Significant Issues

Introduction

Part One set forth some of the broad issues affecting the policy decisions of Gulf leaders. This section examines, in greater detail, how such decisions are made in the context of specific regional foreign-policy issues. Perhaps the three most significant issues, weighing most heavily on the minds of regional leaders, and the three having the greatest continuing impact on foreign-policy decisions are: the Iran-Iraq war; the political and economic fortunes of OPEC and the future of their oil; and the rise, spread, and growing regional influence of extremism — social, political, and religious in character — in the Middle East generally and in the Gulf specifically.

The most dangerous enduring conundrum, as Wayne E. White points out, is the Iran-Iraq war. Since its beginning in 1980, the war has split the Gulf asunder, has threatened to engulf the other littoral states, has involved much of the rest of the Middle East and Islamic world, has gained the wary attention of the rest of the world, fearing both economic strangulation from the loss of Gulf oil supplies and the specter of American-Soviet confrontation. In mid-1987, more than ever, it is the issue most on the minds of military and foreign-policy planners in the Gulf states, as well as all of their fellow citizens. The war is the regional issue that the Gulf's leaders most fear for its capability of erupting with little advance notice into a much more serious and extensive conflagration directly involving their nations. At the same time, it is the problem over which these leaders have the least control, despite their repeated efforts to mediate or otherwise influence the outcome.

Will the conflict ever really be resolved, or will it drag on indefinitely? As Wayne White notes, the border between Iran and Iraq is located on a centuries-old geopolitical fault line. The frontier separates two peoples with distinct histories and cultures — the Aryan Persians and the Semitic Arabs. It is a divide between conflicting legacies of glorious empires, separate languages, sectarian differences, and an animosity spanning many generations.

What, then, can we expect to transpire in the years ahead? Will this conflict be another Hundred Years War? Even if the fighting should end, can we expect periodic future clashes along this fault line? In what way do present fears of the regional leaders alter their future expectations and goals, as well as their present and future policies aimed at achieving these goals?

Another kind of challenge has emerged in recent years with the oil glut and the fall in prices from their earlier peak of over $30 a barrel to the level in mid-1987 of less than $20. The strains this economic reality have created within the Organization of Petroleum Exporting Countries (OPEC) add to the foreign-policy dilemmas and pressures.

The chapter by Joseph C. Story discusses the impact of oil on the Arab Gulf countries since the 1973-1974 price explosion, paying particular attention to the impact of the changing international oil market in the 1980s. What internal and external politics will the Gulf oil producers take in the years ahead? In the immediate future, will dwindling financial resources and recurrent budget deficits force Gulf states to disregard OPEC decisions and follow their own interests? Will Saudi Arabia's leadership within OPEC prevail? And, looking down the road, when the balance of power within OPEC increasingly gravitates to the Gulf, will international oil policy be set by the GCC states, instead of by OPEC? Will the world ever return to an era of dominance by OPEC — or any group of producing nations?

Even though the war and the adverse fortunes of oil have the immediate attention of the area's rulers, the greater long-term danger to the region's present order may well be the Islamic revolution in Iran and its strident call for a return to more fundamental tenets of Islam, both as a theology and as a political ideology. Professor Rouhollah K. Ramazani contributes a thought-provoking analysis on this subject. At the same time that the influence of anti-establishment religious leaders is growing, expectations of more popular involvement in the processes of government are also becoming more prevalent. How are the forces similar, and in what ways do they seem to operate at cross purposes?

To what extent does this Islamic revivalism coalesce with socioeconomic deprivations to create a climate for political violence? Will this ferment continue in its hardline manifestation, or will it evolve and soften over time to meet, at some middle juncture, the exigencies and immediacies of modernization in the region? How will the unique social, tribal and religious circumstances of a given country interact with and perhaps alter the influences of the Islamic revolution?

5

The Iran-Iraq War:
A Challenge to the Arab Gulf States

Wayne E. White*

INTRODUCTION

The Iran-Iraq war is the first major conflict to challenge immediately the Arab Gulf states in modern times. Recent developments in the interminable war, which entered its eighth year in late 1987, have intensified this challenge. The seriousness of the threat posed by the war is magnified by the vast differences in military power between the belligerents and the states that comprise the Gulf Cooperation Council (GCC). The continuation of the war clearly is not in the interest of the GCC states. Even during periods of relative stalemate, the potential for dangerous escalation is always present.

On the whole, the GCC states have managed the crisis of the war with considerable skill. They appreciate the extent of their military vulnerability and thus far have carefully avoided a major confrontation with Iran. Yet, they also realize that Iraq is the only significant obstacle to increased Iranian interference in their affairs, and they have risked Tehran's wrath by providing crucial financial and logistical support to Baghdad. Meanwhile, the Gulf states have gradually improved their own military capabilities and enhanced the level of collective cooperation under the aegis of the GCC.

They have turned to the US for only limited assistance. Arab Gulf leaders recognize that US military power remains the ultimate trump card in the GCC deck, but they appear to believe that the US connection is a military asset that must be judiciously managed to minimize potential countervailing liabilities. Kuwait's request for

* The views expressed in this chapter do not necessarily reflect those of the US Department of State.

Map 3: The Iran-Iraq war front

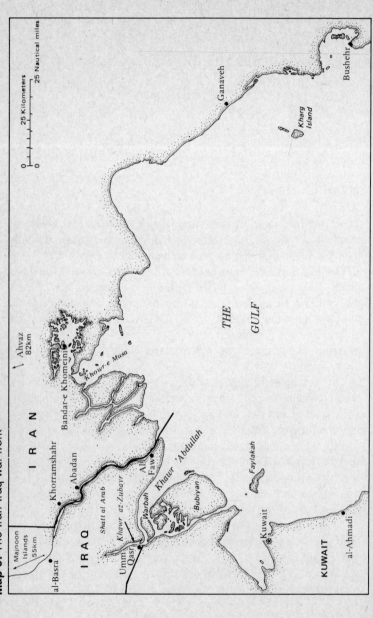

the reflagging of its tankers came after more than six years of war and several years of Iranian attacks on ships serving Kuwait. While, in general, requests for direct US assistance have been restrained, the GCC states undoubtedly benefit collectively from the existence of certain real or imaginary "red lines," the violation of which Tehran fears would bring greater US involvement in the Gulf.

Although the war represents a continuing military and political crisis for the GCC, GCC governments can probably deal with the challenge it poses without resort to extensive outside assistance so long as neither Iraq nor Iran gains the upper hand. The war has increased the military threat from Iran, but it has somewhat lessened the concerns of GCC states with regard to Iraq. The need for a major infusion of external help could become critical only in two extreme scenarios: major Iranian military successes along the battlefront or an Iranian attempt to assault directly one or more GCC states or to close the Strait of Hormuz — moves that would most likely occur in reaction to devastating Iraqi air attacks against Iran's oil industry.

THE EVOLUTION OF THE IRAQI AND IRANIAN THREATS

Iraq

The pre-war Gulf Arab view of Iraq was mixed. There was great relief over the maturation of Iraq's Ba'th Party regime and the resultant Iraqi drift toward a more moderate consensus-oriented stance on both international and regional issues. The slackening Iraqi interest in furthering political interference in the Arab Gulf states through various dissident front organizations was noted with relief. Also, the Iraqi regime steadily deepened its economic ties to the West and increasingly grew concerned over the danger of Soviet interference and expansionism in the area. The crackdown on the Iraqi Communist Party in mid-1978 closely followed the Soviet-backed coup in Afghanistan. The announcement of President Hussein's "Pan-Arab Charter" in January 1980 came on the heels of the Soviet invasion of Afghanistan, and its rejection of the presence of foreign troops on Arab soil was interpreted as being primarily directed at the USSR.

Yet, at the same time, Iraqi military power and political clout was increasing by leaps and bounds. This trend was greeted with some uneasiness by the states having fresh memories of Iraqi political interference and, in the case of Kuwait, being the object of unresolved territorial ambitions. During 1978-1979, Iraq took the lead in marshalling an Arab consensus behind the policy of isolating Egypt. The Non-Aligned Movement, meeting in Havana in September 1979, chose Iraq for the 1982 chairmanship. The Baghdad regime used its burgeoning oil wealth to expand vastly the size of the Iraqi army between 1973 and 1980. Oil earnings enabled Iraq to amass hard currency reserves of over $30 billion by late 1980.

The war dramatically altered this state of affairs. It absorbed and neutralized much of Iraq's ability to flex its muscles militarily, diplomatically and economically outside the immediate arena of its war with Iran. Iraq's voice in inter-Arab affairs diminished greatly. Perhaps of greatest significance to the Arab Gulf states was Iraq's emerging dependency on Arab Gulf logistical and financial support, as a result of the Iranian blockade of Iraqi ports. For a variety of reasons, the onset of the war greatly accelerated the moderation of Iraqi views on a number of issues, bringing, for example, a resumption of diplomatic relations with the US and ties just short of full relations between Baghdad and Cairo.

Iran

The Islamic revolution in Iran posed two challenges for the Gulf: bellicose Persian nationalism and aggressive, radical Shi'i Islam. The first of these threats was not new. The Shah's vigorous program of military growth, particularly the navy, and his 1971 seizure of the disputed islands of Abu Musa and the Tunbs west of the Strait of Hormuz provided ominous indications of Iranian ambitions in the Gulf under virtually any leadership. In mid-1979, the revolutionary regime in Tehran reawakened Iran's territorial ambitions in the Gulf, prompting, for example, renewal of its claim to Bahrain.

An even more potent threat was the Tehran regime's avowed desire to expand the Islamic revolution by toppling the Arab Gulf governments. The Iranian media, as well as the Iranian leadership, began calling openly and repeatedly for citizens of the Arab Gulf states to overthrow their rulers. The response of Shi'a, and even of Sunni, populations along the Gulf's southern littoral to Khomeini's appeals was unknown. However, the Mecca mosque incident of 1979 underscored the potential for trouble from Islamic fundamentalism, be it Shi'i or Sunni.

Nevertheless, pre-war concerns were largely political. The huge military machine painstakingly assembled by the Shah was neglected and thrown into disarray by government purges and the flight of key personnel. The revolutionary regime cut its military ties to the US, making it far more difficult to support its largely US arsenal. The Revolutionary Guard Corps existed before the war, but the guard's combat units that now muster tens of thousands of crack troops along the Iran-Iraq battlefront had not yet evolved into a formidable military force. Finally, Iran's oil exports had dramatically declined, and the Iranian economy was in disarray.

The war added an active military dimension to the threat from Iran. The Iranian military proved far more resilient than many had thought and it may have come close to defeating Iraq in mid-1982. Indeed, during the first two years of the war, the Tehran regime drew increased strength from its crusade to drive Iraqi forces from Iranian soil. For the first time, Iran lashed out militarily at the Arab Gulf states.

Nevertheless, for the most part, Iran has chosen not to take actions that would involve the GCC states directly in the war. Iran has maintained a dialogue with the Arab Gulf states, on occasion sending or receiving envoys. Even in the midst of the tension following the July 31, 1987, incidents in Mecca, Iranian President Khamene'i sent a "special envoy" to discuss "regional developments" with Oman's Sultan Qaboos.[1] This policy is aimed at minimizing the drain on the Iranian military resources which can be put to better use against Iraq.

GCC ATTITUDES TOWARD THE WAR

Gulf Arab leaders do not believe the continuation of the war is in their best interest. Their relatively limited military capabilities give these governments a major stake in regional stability. Regardless of the presence or absence of diplomatic relations between these states and the USSR, all fear that the Soviet Union could gain additional regional influence in the short term as Iran becomes more desperate for heavy arms, or over the longer term, should one of the two belligerents become destabilized.

Moreover, as long as the war continues there will be a risk of major escalation with which the GCC states would have great difficulty coping. The war is dismissed by many observers as a stalemate, but it has cycled through phases in which it easily could have gone through a metamorphosis that would have had grave implications for the GCC.

Iraq appeared close to losing the war on the ground in 1982, a development that might have brought about the fall of Iraq's Ba'th Party regime. In March 1985, Iraq won a narrow and costly victory in a battle which might have given Iranian forces a foothold in Iraq, astride one of the two main roads linking Baghdad and Basra. In August and September 1985, Iraq demonstrated it could do serious damage to Iran's oil-export terminal at Kharg Island, but it apparently chose not to persist to the point of shutting it down.

The 1986 Iranian breakthrough at al-Faw along the Shatt al-'Arab was a particularly frightening example to all the GCC states of the threat posed by the war. Since Iraq's victory east of Basra in July 1982, the ground war had been of concern primarily in the context of the threat it posed to Iraq. But in February 1986, Iranian troops penetrated as far as the Khawr 'Abdullah channel, threatening to bring the battlefront to the borders of the GCC. In January 1987, Iraq fought a bloody defensive battle to halt a determined Iranian attempt to break through to Basra. Finally, the rise in tension in the Gulf in mid-1987 provided another pertinent example of the war's volatility.

A reflection of Arab Gulf attitudes toward the war is found in views concerning Iraqi attacks against Kharg Island. Opinions differ widely, with some wishing to see Iraq press its attacks against Iranian oil facilities. In general, however, this view is more prevalent among exasperated leaders who wish to see something done to undermine Iranian intransigence in an attempt to end the war, or, alternatively, to diminish Iran's war-making capabilities. It does not necessarily represent the ideas of those supporting Iraq.

Others fear that a determined, prolonged and successful Iraqi air campaign against Iranian oil facilities would seriously destabilize the Gulf. This strategy might impel Iran to extend the war beyond its present parameters, forcing the GCC to request US aid and bringing Iran into conflict with the US. In any case, the views of the GCC states concerning Kharg Island probably are moot — there is no evidence that Iraq would alter its military strategy to take into account the wishes of the GCC states.

MILITARY THREATS TO THE GCC

Iran's ground and air forces are largely preoccupied with the war against Iraq, and the Iranian navy is not nearly as strong as it was under the Shah. The air force, which has been used frequently in operations against or near the GCC, has been decimated by the war. Its remaining aircraft are undoubtedly in a poor state of repair due to the lack of regular supplies of spare parts. Nevertheless, there are at least four potentially serious, war-generated threats that the GCC is facing or conceivably might have to face. All four relate to Iran: Iranian air, naval, or missile attacks on GCC targets (other than shipping); Iranian land attacks from southern Iraq; an Iranian attempt to close the Strait of Hormuz (probably less of a threat by mid-1987, given the marked increase in the foreign naval presence in the Gulf); and, lastly, Iranian-backed political subversion. Three of these threats are military.

The possibility of Iranian air or naval attacks is taken very seriously by GCC governments. Iranian aircraft attacked the Kuwaiti town of al-'Abdali along the Iraqi-Kuwaiti border twice in November 1980, and damaged a Kuwaiti oil facility in October 1981; and Iranian Silkworm missiles apparently were launched against Kuwait in September 1987. Since the spring of 1984, Iranian aircraft have regularly retaliated for Iraqi attacks on Kharg Island by hitting merchant vessels bound largely for Kuwait or Saudi Arabia.

Kuwaiti Defense Minister Shaykh Salem Al Sabah told US officials in 1984 that Kuwait was Iran's "first target" in the GCC, and this remains true.[2] Because Kuwait is located at the northern end of the Gulf, only minutes from the battlefront and just across Khawr 'Abdullah from Iranian forces, Iranian aircraft can strike Kuwaiti targets swiftly and without crossing large international sea lanes, thus giving Iran a modicum of deniability. Kuwaiti air defenses are less cohesive than those of Saudi Arabia, making it more difficult for the Kuwaitis to deal with surprise Iranian air attacks.[3] Furthermore, Kuwait, along with Saudi Arabia, has made multi-billion dollar war loans to Iraq and has sold oil on Iraq's account.[4] Finally, a large portion of Iraq's military resupply is received through Kuwaiti ports.[5]

Another militarily vulnerable state is the United Arab Emirates (UAE). The UAE is too far away to receive air defense cover from Saudi Arabia, and, according to a US Senate study, does "not have the early warning or tactical air capability to defeat an attack by

Iran."[6] Yet the UAE, particularly Dubai, is one of Iran's major regional trading partners, and has been financially and logistically less supportive of Iraq, prompting Iran to leave the country largely unmolested.

The other Gulf states, notably Saudi Arabia, are in a better military position. At least in the air, with its sizeable fleet of modern F-15 fighters supported by AWACS radar aircraft, Saudi Arabia is far less vulnerable than Kuwait and the UAE. The ramifications extend beyond the defense of the kingdom. A senior Saudi official told US Senate staffers in 1984 that the kingdom considers the defense of Bahrain to be "the defense of Saudi Arabia."[7] Qatar may be in a similar category. Oman has a small but effective air force, and its ties to the US and Great Britain make it a less attractive target for Iran.

All of the GCC states, including Saudi Arabia, remain vulnerable to the Iranian navy. Although the Iranian navy is somewhat decrepit, it is probably still larger and more sea-capable than the combined naval forces of the GCC. It can be used by the Iranians to lay mines, to shell onshore and offshore targets, or to land commandos and demolition teams as was done during the first year of the war against Iraq's offshore oil export terminals. The Revolutionary Guards can carry out small naval missions as well. Saudi Arabia, for example, has more than 85 offshore oil platforms, any of which would be nearly impossible to defend against a naval attack.[8]

The GCC states, singly or combined, could not hope to resist a major land attack from Iran. However, it is unlikely that such an attack could be delivered across the Gulf because Iran would not have the naval capability to support it and might blunder into a confrontation with Western naval forces. It would have to come by land through southern Iraq. Thus, this threat would not emerge unless at least a portion of southern Iraq had been overrun by Iran. Kuwaiti and Saudi Arabian land forces would have great difficulty stopping an attack by even limited numbers of battle-hardened Iranian troops from southern Iraq. This of course would explain the apparent alarm among the Arab Gulf states that accompanied the Iranian advances in southern Iraq around al-Faw in early 1986 and Iran's effort to menace Basra in its "Karbala 5" operation in early 1987.

Likewise, the military forces of the GCC states would not be able to block an Iranian attempt to close the Strait of Hormuz. Iran probably has the capability to close the strait if Western naval forces do not intervene. If Iran announced it would use force to stop all vessels moving through the strait, backing up the threat with its naval and air forces, it is hard to imagine shippers ignoring this decision. However, beyond occasional threats that it will stop all Gulf oil exports if its own exports are cut off by Iraq, its searches of ships for Iraqi-bound contraband, its recent, sporadic mining of the shipping lanes, and its random attacks against merchant ships, Iran has shown little real interest in closing the strait. Tehran undoubtedly fears that a serious effort to close the strait would bring Western intervention.

THE POLITICAL THREAT TO THE GCC

Perhaps the most difficult threat to assess is the potential for Iranian political subversion among the Shi'a residents of the GCC states. There are significant Shi'a communities in Bahrain, Kuwait, the UAE, and Qatar, and 400,000 Shi'a are concentrated in Saudi Arabia's Eastern Province.[9] Another estimated 300,000 Shi'a of Iranian descent live in Kuwait, Bahrain, Qatar and the UAE.[10] Yet, there have been no major episodes of political strife since the beginning of the war. The Bahraini coup plot, uncovered in early December 1981, evidently involved a relatively small number of conspirators.

The Iranian revolution has considerable appeal for lower and middle class Shi'a — and some Sunnis as well — in the Arab Gulf states because it has openly challenged there forces of non-Muslim cultural and political influence and seeks to overturn established Muslim institutions and governments. Many Shi'a in the Arab Gulf states view themselves as second-class citizens, with less opportunity for political participation through existing government institutions and more limited economic opportunities than those of resident Sunnis. The sympathies of many Shi'a in the GCC states probably are with Iran.

However, the effectiveness of Iran's revolutionary message has been reduced by a variety of factors. There has been a long history of tensions between Arabs and Persians, and even now Iran's aims are a mix of revolutionary and imperialist ideas. In addition, the image of revolutionary Islam in Iran has been tarnished by violence, extremism and political clumsiness in the eyes of middle and upper class Shi'a.[11] Also, many Shi'a in the Arab Gulf states probably realize the risks of challenging Sunni ruling families in states that, with the exception of Bahrain, have Sunni majorities. Moreover, Gulf leaders have utilized traditional peninsular institutions such as the *majlis* to remain in relatively close contact with even their Shi'a communities.[12]

The behavior of the Shi'a in Iraq also may suggest that the threat of wholesale political disaffection among Gulf Shi'a may have been generally overestimated. Much to the surprise of many observers, Iraqi Shi'a do not appear to have caused any serious problems for the Iraqi regime since the onset of the war.[13] This may be partly because of the difficulty of confronting a notably well-organized regime supported by a powerful security apparatus. Yet, the ability of the Iraqi army, with huge numbers of Shi'a cadres, to stand up over a period of years to fanatical frontline assaults in fighting, probably the bloodiest in modern Middle Eastern history, suggests that the Shi'a value their Arab identity over their sectarian identity.

Despite what seems to be a common view that the GCC states are relatively fragile entities, they have shown themselves to be "among the most politically stable societies in the Middle East."[14] With the threat posed by revolutionary Iran since 1979, the stability of these six Gulf states, three of which did not become fully independent until 1971, is quite impressive.

THE EVOLVING STRATEGY OF THE GCC STATES TOWARD THE WAR

The policies of the Arab Gulf states toward the war have gone through some metamorphosis since September 1980, but they generally represent a fairly well-tuned process that balances support for Iraq with a continuing dialogue with Iran, as well as local military capability supplemented by limited outside aid.

The broad outlines of these policies emerged in the first nine months of the war. The Arab Gulf states were from the outset reluctant to express strong public support for Iraq which would alienate Iran. In fact, several days after the outbreak of the conflict, Iraq complained about Arab states, undoubtedly including those in the Gulf, taking "stands of silence".[15]

The Arab Gulf states threw their support behind Iraq in a variety of other ways, however, in the early months of the war. During the first week of the war, Baghdad was permitted to store some of its air force at bases in Saudi Arabia. In the spring of 1981, as Iraq's massive hard currency reserves were bled by the war, Saudi Arabia and Kuwait began making multi-billion-dollar war loans to Iraq. In addition, Saudi Arabia and Kuwait allowed the Iraqis to ship military material through their ports.[16]

These moves supportive of Iraq were meanwhile balanced by diplomatic efforts designed to signal to Iran that the Arab Gulf states wanted an early end to the war. During the first year of the war in particular, Saudi Arabia and the other Arab Gulf states threw their support behind the efforts of the Islamic Conference to mediate an end to the war. Such efforts appear to have become less forceful in recent years only because Iran has repeatedly made clear its lack of interest in a negotiated settlement of the war.

Saudi Arabia also turned to the US for limited assistance in the first weeks of the war. AWACS aircraft were deployed to Riyadh in the fall of 1980 to provide the Saudi air force with improved early warning and command and control capabilities. As a result of the deliveries of US arms to Saudi Arabia, especially the deployment of F-15 fighters, Saudi air capabilities steadily improved.

Probably the most striking development in the first year of the war was the establishment of the GCC on May 25, 1981. The onset of the war clearly played a key role in the decision to form the GCC, but the member states initially tried to avoid actions that would make the organization appear to be an anti-Iranian alliance, emphasizing non-military cooperation and playing down the role of security concerns in the GCC's deliberations.[17]

During much of 1981 and 1982, the course of the war tipped dramatically in Iran's favor. In May 1981, Iran began the process of driving Iraqi forces from Iranian territory by retaking the Allah Akbar Heights northwest of Ahvaz. This effort was largely completed in May 1982, when Iranian forces retook Khorramshahr.

Meanwhile, fueled by Iranian battlefield successes, Tehran's behavior toward the GCC states became noticeably more provocative and Iranian propaganda became more vitriolic. Iranian aircraft attacked and damaged a Kuwaiti gas oil-separation plant on October 1, 1981, in the immediate wake of Iran's success in driving Iraqi forces back across the Karun River near Abadan. Iran sent agitators to disrupt the fall 1981 pilgrimage, accusing the Saudis of mistreating the Iranian pilgrims.[18] King Fahd appealed to Tehran to instruct its pilgrimage leaders not to commit acts that would violate the sanctity of the *hajj*, but to no avail.[19] In December 1981, the Iranian-backed conspiracy was discovered in Bahrain. Iran denied involvement in the Kuwait bombings, and in January 1982,

101

President Khamene'i declared that Iran had not had a role in the Bahraini plot.[20] Little credence was given to these denials.

The aforementioned events significantly increased the level of concern among the GCC states, and in reaction, triggered a marked change in the policies of the member states. Security issues soon began to dominate the deliberations of the GCC. The GCC military chiefs of staff met in September 1981, and in May 1982 an extraordinary GCC foreign ministers' conference was convened, largely to discuss the Iran-Iraq war situation.[21] The Arab Gulf media became considerably more supportive of Iraq and critical of Iran. A Radio Riyadh commentary called the Iranian rulers a "disgrace to Islam" in November 1981 for disrupting the *hajj*.[22] In the wake of Bahrain's discovery of a major conspiracy, Saudi Arabia signed separate mutual-security pacts with Bahrain and Qatar.[23]

Following Iraq's repulse of the Iranian offensive northeast of Basra in July 1982, a period ensued during which the level of general concern among the GCC states over the war subsided. Such major financial backers of Iraq as Saudi Arabia and Kuwait became sufficiently confident of Iraq's ability to withstand further pressure that they scaled back their economic aid to Baghdad, a move made also to ease the financial pinch created by declining oil revenues.[24]

The GCC, however, continued to make progress toward greater military and security cooperation. Summits and ministerial meetings were held during which the organization became an even more routine venue for multilateral cooperation. Four chiefs of staff meetings had been held by November 1983, and in October 1983, a joint military exercise was held in the UAE involving 6,500 troops.

The next crisis period in the war came between October 1983 and June 1984. Iraq for the first time began to take serious measures aimed at crippling Iran's oil exports, and the first major incident of Iranian-backed terrorism took place. In the fall of 1983, the Iraqis apparently took delivery of Super Etendard aircraft from France equipped with Exocet anti-ship missiles. Although these were not used for about six months, reports of their transfer raised the level of concern among the GCC leaders. In December 1983, the US Embassy in Kuwait was badly damaged by a truck bomb, and bombs exploded at other locations including Kuwait International Airport. In the next major development, the Iraqi Super Etendards struck their first blow against Iran's oil lifeline on April 27, 1984, when the tanker "Safina al-'Arab" was struck and damaged by an Iraqi missile. With Iran's May 13 retaliatory attack on the Kuwaiti vessel "Umm Casbah," the so-called "tanker war" was in full swing.

The advent of Iranian attacks on Saudi and Kuwaiti-bound vessels prompted both states to request Stinger surface-to-air missiles from the US. Yet, the most notable response to the Iranian attacks was the Saudi interception in early June 1984 of an Iranian aircraft seeking shipping targets off the Saudi coast. Fortunately, both Riyadh and Tehran acted cautiously in the wake of the shoot-down to avoid a bigger confrontation. The Saudis took care to minimize the significance of the incident in their public statements, and the Iranians shifted their attacks on shipping from the northern to the southern Gulf in order to avoid further encounters with the Saudi air force.

There were more war crises during 1985 and 1986: the failed Iranian offensive in the Hawiza Marsh north of Basra in March 1985, the August-September 1985 Iraqi bombing campaign against Kharg Island, and the February 1986 Iranian offensive along the Shatt al-'Arab. The GCC has continued its mixed response to these crises by maintaining public and diplomatic support of Iraq while keeping the door open to Iran. For example, in May 1985, in the wake of the spring fighting, Saudi Arabia's Foreign Minister, Prince Sa'ud al-Faisal, visited Tehran in an apparent bid to mediate between Iran and Iraq and to continue a dialogue between the GCC and Iran. When Iran stepped up its search and seizure efforts against merchant ships plying the Strait of Hormuz in late 1985, the Omanis judiciously avoided any confrontation with Iran.

The February 1986 crisis was one of the most frightening to date. It marked the first occasion that Iranian troops threatened to reach the borders of a GCC state, and Iraq, for the first time since mid-1982, appeared incapable of repelling a major Iranian thrust into Iraqi territory. The proximity of intense see-saw fighting to Kuwait probably tempted both sides to spread the battlefield to Kuwaiti territory, such as Bubiyan Island, to break the bloody tactical stalemate at al-Faw.

Meanwhile, the Iranian press resumed its calls upon the peoples of the Arab Gulf states to depose their "corrupt kings and sheikhs," and Prime Minister Musavi declared "We cannot allow other countries to sell oil on behalf of our enemy." The Saudi and Kuwaiti foreign ministers rushed to Baghdad to consult with the Iraqis. Later, in an apparent attempt to persuade Syrian leader Hafiz al-Asad to abandon his support for Iran, or indirectly to convince Iran not to expand the war to the GCC states, the Saudi and Kuwaiti foreign ministers visited Syria.[25]

Kuwait came under intense Iranian pressure in early 1986. An Iranian spokesman indicated in late February that while the Kuwaiti government emphasized that it did not want the war to spread to Kuwait, the Kuwaiti press had been pro-Iraqi. The spokesman added that "these contradictions are unbearable for us."[26] Nonetheless, the Kuwaitis evidently decided not to give ground, at least publicly. Kuwaiti Defense Minister Shaykh Salem announced on February 25 that Kuwait's "armed forces stand firm in their resolve to defend the country in the face of Iranian threats."[27]

An interesting footnote to the GCC's reaction to developments in the Iran-Iraq war has been the shift in the behavior of Kuwait and Oman. Kuwait's attempts early in the war to balance support for Iraq with an open door to Iran did not shield Kuwait from Iranian retribution. Several times, Kuwait has been the victim of Iranian military retaliation or Iranian-inspired terrorism. As a result, in its desire to reduce its vulnerability, Kuwait has moved from ambivalence toward the US to a strong desire to improve US-Kuwaiti relations.[28] This process culminated in 1987 with Kuwait's request for the "reflagging" under the US flag of its tankers, which had been targeted — more than those of any other GCC state — by the Iranians.

In contrast, Oman has moved in the opposite direction. Oman increasingly has stressed the need to avoid any direct GCC-Iranian confrontation. Oman is farther from the battlefront and therefore apparently has been able to give more weight to the need to cultivate a long-term relationship with Iran. Consequently, according to a 1984 Senate study, the Omanis are a bit "less comfortable now than they once were" with the US-Omani Facilities Access Agreement. However, it must be borne in mind that this agreement was originally conceived to assist the US in resisting the Soviet threat to the region — not the Iranian threat to the GCC.[29]

PROBLEM SCENARIOS

Two scenarios are cause for deep concern among GCC leaders: an Iranian victory over Iraq, and a decisive Iraqi interdiction campaign against Iranian oil exports. Should Iran prevail over Iraq, or seize control of significant portions of southern Iraq, Iraq no longer would be a territorial buffer between Iran and the GCC. In this scenario, the Iraqi heartland and two GCC states would be directly menaced by Iranian ground forces. Should the Iranians penetrate Kuwaiti or Saudi borders in strength, it is unlikely that either country would be able to do much more than slow or harass the Iranian forces which had proven too much for even the vastly more numerous Iraqi army to stop.

An effective and prolonged Iraqi bombing campaign against Iran's main oil-export terminal at Kharg Island and against smaller Iranian terminals in the lower Gulf could drastically reduce Iran's ability to support the war financially. Some in the GCC might well favor such a development as a way to nudge Iran toward ending the war. However, Iranian leaders such as President Khamene'i and *Majlis* Speaker Rafsanjani have declared on occasion that if Iran is unable to export acceptable amounts of oil, crude exports from elsewhere in the Gulf would be stopped as well.

There is undoubtedly a certain amount of bluster in such statements. However, an Iran pressed to the wall economically by Iraqi air attacks might not be content to sit back and allow states that Iran views as supportive of Iraq to continue exporting. Iran might not act precipitously — such as by trying to close the Strait of Hormuz. Instead, it might initially begin a slow process of squeezing GCC governments by means of stepped-up attacks on shipping, attacks on offshore wells, sporadic air strikes against on-shore targets, or sabotage and political subversion within GCC states with large Shi'a populations, in hopes of intimidating the Arab Gulf states without triggering strong Western intervention. More drastic measures might follow.

It is impossible for the GCC alone to cope effectively with an Iran that is willing to use a much larger measure of its military muscle to confront the GCC states, particularly on land. As a result, these two scenarios might well generate Iranian behavior requiring the GCC states, either individually or collectively, to seek considerable outside military aid from either or both of two sources.

Help from the moderate Arab states

The GCC might turn to the moderate Arab states for assistance. However, probably only two such states — Jordan and Egypt — are near enough and possess sufficient power to make a difference against Iran. So long as the Iranian threat was confined to the air or to the sea, even if it involved commandos or small amphibious landing forces, limited infusions of Jordanian or Egyptian forces could be highly effective.

If the Iranians moved against the GCC by land, however, the picture would be greatly complicated. Tens of thousands of troops would probably be required to stop a large Iranian army emerging from southern Iraq. Egypt and Jordan would have some difficulty fielding a force of such size such a distance from home. In addition, for domestic and political reasons, those governments might also hesitate to send so many of their troops into the Iranian slaughter-house. Indeed, when Iraq faced possible defeat in May 1982, the Egyptian Defense Minister, Muhammad Abu Ghazzala, announced that his government would not send troops to Baghdad.[30]

The superpowers

The GCC leaders undoubtedly know that "the fighter and attack aircraft aboard just one US carrier ... could probably neutralize the Iranian ports and air bases at Bandar Abbas and Bushehr ... in a few hours."[31] However, there are constraints that make the Arab Gulf states somewhat reluctant to call for US assistance. Washington's support for Israel makes heavier reliance on the US a more sensitive political proposition. Also, there seems to be a deep-seated concern that while the US initially might help the GCC, the US commitment might not endure over the long term, eventually leaving these states to face a strong and vengeful Iran relatively alone.[32]

There is probably considerable hope among GCC governments that Iran would fear US intervention enough to be warded off by the mere threat of it; this probably has been and will remain a major factor in Iran's behavior toward the GCC. Requests for US and other Western assistance probably will be balanced by appeals to both superpowers to take measures aimed at ending the Gulf war or preventing its expansion beyond Iran and Iraq, such as the enforcement of UN Security Council Resolution 598. However, despite Kuwait's longstanding relationship with the USSR and recent openings by the UAE and Oman to Moscow, there is a universal fear among the GCC states of greater Soviet involvement in the region.

THE GCC'S CONTINUING STRATEGY

The future strategy of the GCC states, both collectively and individually, will be a mixture of the same elements utilized with considerable effectiveness during the 1980-1987 period. Unless Iran knocks Iraq out of the war militarily, or succeeds in physically separating Iraq from the GCC states, Saudi Arabia and Kuwait will continue their efforts to sustain Iraq as a land buffer between the GCC and Iran. At the same time, however, they probably will continue some measure of dialogue with Iran and will resist any wartime or post-war Iraqi efforts to enter the GCC or to turn it into an anti-Iranian alliance.

Meanwhile, the GCC states will energetically pursue their efforts to improve military defenses. Probably little can be done over the short term to improve significantly the woeful inadequacy of GCC ground forces *vis-a-vis* those of Iran. It will be a long time before the GCC's highly-publicized Rapid Deployment Force is able to face substantial numbers of crack Iranian troops. Yet, the GCC air deterrent against Iran has been, and is likely to continue, improving noticeably against the waning capabilities of the Iranian air force. The June 1984 shoot-down of an Iranian F-4 markedly increased Saudi confidence. Indeed, senior Saudi officials told US Senate staffers in 1984 that they would "retaliate massively" if attacked by Iran.[33] In the absence of an Iranian ground threat, the Saudis probably would strike back in response to serious Iranian air or naval provocations.

The GCC, however, could not cope with an Iranian ground threat or a serious attempt by Iran to close the Strait of Hormuz without outside assistance. The danger of Iran giving greater consideration to such an option, or other efforts to harass the GCC, will increase if Iraq responds to Iranian military pressure along the battlefront by lashing out with even greater determination against Iran's oil industry. With regard to the potential for serious trouble in the strait, GCC governments probably hope the US would step in without a GCC request to keep the sea lanes open, much as the US has responded to the threat of Iranian mines in Gulf sea lanes and anchorages. In 1984 Senate testimony, Assistant Secretary of State Richard Murphy said of the GCC states: "They are trying to protect ... national waters, if you will, and ask us to defend the international waters."[34]

To some degree, similar to what the Iraqis have done through much of the war, the GCC states are playing a waiting game. They are attempting to forestall an Iraqi defeat and avoid a major confrontation with Iran while waiting for Khomeini to pass from the scene. GCC leaders probably do not believe that they are currently in a position to come to a lasting accommodation with Iran. Hence, they will continue to tread water tactically, employing a mixture of political, military, and economic improvisation, in an effort to preserve as much of the status quo in the Gulf as possible until changes in Iran permit the GCC governments to seek a more enduring *modus vivendi* with Tehran.

NOTES

1. "Sultan Meets Iranian President's 'Special Envoy'," Tehran IRNA in English, Foreign Broadcast Information Service (FBIS), *Daily Report: Near East and South Asia*, August 11, 1987, p. J1.

2. US Congress, Senate, Committee on Foreign Relations, *The War in the Gulf* (Washington: USGPO, 1984), p. 30.

3. Ibid., p. 30.

4. Ibid., and Nadav Safran, *Saudi Arabia: The Ceaseless Quest for Security* (Cambridge: The Belknap Press of Harvard University, 1985), p. 372.

5. *The War in the Gulf*, p. 30.

6. Ibid., p. 31.

7. Ibid.

8. Ibid., p. 28.

9. Ibid.

10. James A. Bill, "Resurgent Islam in the Persian Gulf, "*Foreign Affairs*, Vol. 63, No. 1 (Fall 1984), p. 120.

11. Ibid., p. 117.

12. Ibid., p. 122.

13. Michael Sterner, "The Iran-Iraq War", *Foreign Affairs*, Vol. 63, No. 1 (Fall 1984), p. 132.

14. John Duke Anthony, "The Gulf Cooperation Council," in Robert G. Darius, John W. Amos II, and Ralph H. Magnus, eds., *Gulf Security in the 1980s* (Stanford: Hoover Institution Press, 1984), p. 42.

15. Safran, p. 368.

16. Ibid., pp. 369 and 372.

17. Anthony, p. 84. See also the chapter by John Duke Anthony elsewhere in this volume.

18. Robert G. Darius, "Khomeini's Policy Toward the Mideast," in Darius et al., eds., *Gulf Security in the 1980s*, p. 42.

19. Safran, p. 377.

20. "Khamene'i Questioned on Foreign, Domestic Issues," Tehran Domestic Service in Persian, FBIS, *Daily Report: Middle East and Africa*, January 8, 1982, p. I1.

21. Anthony, pp. 82-84.

22. Safran, p. 377.

23. Darius, "Khomeini's Policy," p. 37.

24. Sterner, pp. 130-131.

25. Reuter, "Iran Sends Envoys to Explain War, Oil Price Views," No. 1754 of February 16, 1986; and "More on Kuwaiti, Saudi Ministers in Damascus," Kuwait KUNA in Arabic, FBIS, February 16, 1986.

26. "Iran Calls on Kuwait to 'Correct' Foreign Policy," Tehran IRNA in English, FBIS, No. 181 of February 26, 1986.

27. "Tense Atmosphere Surrounds Kuwaiti Silver Jubilee," Associated Press, No. AP-NY-02-25-86 1825 EST.

28. *War in the Gulf*, p. 20.

29. Ibid., pp. 22, 27 and 32-33.

30. Safran, p. 383.

31. *War in the Gulf*, p. 20.

32. Sterner, p. 141.

33. *War in the Gulf*, p. 28.

34. US Congress, House of Representatives, Committee on Foreign Affairs, *Developments in the Persian Gulf, June 1984* (Washington: USGPO, 1984), pp. 44-45.

6

Gulf Oil Policies in the 1980s

Joseph C. Story

The development of the Gulf Cooperation Council (GCC) since its creation in 1981 has taken place against an economic backdrop set by an organization which the GCC is likely itself to come to dominate: the Organization of Petroleum Exporting Countries (OPEC). Over the late 1980s, as the pendulum swings back to favor oil producers against oil consumers, the power of the GCC within OPEC will grow, to the extent that, by the 1990s, the GCC will be seen as the very heart of OPEC, pumping more than half of the oil traded within the non-communist world.

THE ORIGINS OF THE OIL GLUT

Until the early 1970s, the world scarcely noticed its growing dependence on oil. However, at the beginning of the 1970s, four factors emerged which provided the foundations for radical change. First, the oil-producing states were encouraged to assert more power in an international climate which acknowledged and promoted the interests of Third World countries. Second, the international oil industry had evolved from a structure completely dominated by the majors — the gigantic, multinational "Seven Sisters" — to a more complex arrangement involving many more independent and national oil companies. Third, the "soft" oil market of the 1960s had tightened into a seller's market by the end of the decade. The fourth factor was the emergence of OPEC as a relatively cohesive group of producers who both desired and were increasingly able to act in concert.[1]

The real price of oil had declined modestly during the 1950s and 1960s, encouraging a rapid increase in the use of petroleum products and energy in general. Due to falling real revenues, the producing states sought to set higher prices for internationally traded oil, and insisted upon more direct participation in oil operations. The looming inability of world oil supplies to meet growing consumption gave increasing weight to the demands of the producing states.

The catalyst for the shift in power was the fourth Arab-Israeli war of October 1973. Saudi Arabia and most of the other Arab oil producers were persuaded to institute an oil embargo against the United States and the Netherlands for their perceived support of Israel, as well as against South Africa for its racist domestic policies. The Arab oil producers instituted gradual production cutbacks until their demands were met. As a result, within a few short months, the posted price of crude oil rose from $3.01 a barrel (October 1973) to US$11.65 a barrel (January 1974). Oil-consuming nations around the world faced immediate repercussions ranging from severe economic dislocation, to increased inflation, deepening recession, an increased burden on the Third World, and additional pressure on the already shaky international financial system.

A new price spiral in 1979 gave a second shock to the global economic order. In the five years since the shocks of 1973-1974, a

Figure 6.1: Oil prices reflect international events

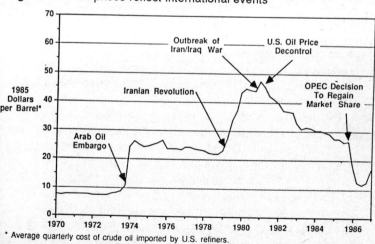

* Average quarterly cost of crude oil imported by U.S. refiners.

Source: US Department of Energy, *Energy Security: A Report to the President of the United States* (Washington: March 1987); p.15

number of structural changes had taken place: the real price of oil had declined; the absorptive capacity of the OPEC countries had grown; and world dependence on OPEC oil continued unabated. It took only a year for the posted price of oil to jump from $18 to $28. However, the price leap was clearly too high to be sustained, and eventually it provoked a worldwide recession and the emergence of new sources of supply around the world, such as the North Sea, Mexico and the North Slope of Alaska.

Within a few years, the tight market had been transformed into an unbalanced situation characterized by reduced demand and excess supply. By the beginning of 1983, OPEC was experiencing great difficulty in maintaining its official price of $34. Nearly all the producers — with the notable exception of Saudi Arabia — were resorting to unofficial discounting. For the first time, an effort was made to introduce production quotas for OPEC members. OPEC production plummeted from a high of nearly 31 million barrels per day (mbd) in 1979 to about 14 mbd four years later. Even the decline in OPEC's market share was not enough to offset falling prices.[2] The world slipped into an oil glut far greater and longer-lived than most observers had anticipated.

THE IMPACT ON THE GCC PRODUCERS

The GCC is sitting on 43 percent of the world's oil reserves, with Saudi Arabia alone controlling a 25 percent share. By contrast, the US has only 4 percent of world reserves. However, actual production fell well below these levels as OPEC's grip on the market declined. In 1980, Saudi Arabia was responsible for 16.62 percent of world crude production; by mid-1985 its share had fallen to just 4.76 percent.

The other GCC states, with the notable exception of Oman, saw their share of a shrinking market fall during the same period, though by a smaller amount. Overall, the GCC witnessed a massive erosion of influence. In 1980, it had provided 23.61 percent of world oil, while in June 1985 it accounted for just 10.34 percent.

The 1981-1985 period saw the first moves between GCC states to present a common front on oil policies. In the wake of the Islamic Revolution in Iran in 1979 and the second round of oil price increases, triggered by the Shah's downfall, Saudi Arabia and the United Arab Emirates (UAE), the grouping's two largest producers, began working together to restore stability to international oil prices. They consistently maintained marker prices $2 below those of Iran and more radical producers, and in the end secured a single pricing structure for all OPEC production. Together with Kuwait, they helped hammer out the various quota arrangements of the mid-1980s, which aimed at ensuring stability in both production and pricing — a policy thwarted by the rapid rise of non-OPEC production and by cheating from other OPEC nations such as Nigeria, Libya and Iran.

Moreover, world demand during this period dropped dramatically. In 1980, a global production level of 59,538,000 barrels per day (bd) was necessary to meet demand; by June 1985, the level was down to 50,824,000 bd, a nadir exceeded only during the spring production shortage of 1983. This decline showed that the conservation efforts of the 1970s and 1980s were far more effective than was at first envisaged. So long as oil prices remained high, continued conservation efforts were encouraged.

THE SAUDI RESPONSE

The overwhelming predominance of Saudi reserves has been the principal reason for the kingdom's weight within OPEC. Its small population, relatively low absorptive capacity, and its history of overproduction for existing needs have combined to make Saudi Arabia the "swing producer" in OPEC. By adjusting production levels, either up or down, the Saudis could keep prices steady and force recalcitrant OPEC members into line. But after 1973, it became increasingly clear that this role was not viable within the context of the prolonged oil glut.[3]

The Saudis became particularly concerned about the situation as the recovery of the oil market they had anticipated failed to materialize. Several factors worried them. The high oil prices established in the wake of the Iranian revolution were seen as a major cause of the world recession of 1981-1983, during which Saudi oil production declined from 9.8 to 5.1 mbd. Although there were some signs in 1984 that the US market might be receptive to increased supplies of Saudi crude because of high economic growth rates, economic prospects for the OECD group as a whole, which consumes three-quarters of the world's oil output, did not look favorable.

After 1984, the Saudis also became concerned at the way in which other fuels were eating into oil's share of the energy market, particularly in Europe and North America. The Soviet Union's Siberian pipeline was a major factor in this, a factor which worried the Saudis for political as well as economic reasons.

The rise of non-OPEC crude presented similar problems. When OPEC appeared to gain control of the market with its first major price increase in 1973, it was producing just under 31 mbd, 55.66 percent of a global total of 55.7 mbd. In 1980, its position had eroded a bit, but at 26.9 mbd it was still accounting for 45.17 percent of world output. By June 1985, however, non-OPEC producers were clearly in the ascendancy: OPEC production was down to 17.3 mbd, just 34.12 percent of global production.

That the expansion of non-OPEC production and revenues should have taken place precisely because the kingdom was attempting to stabilize the market through output and price restraint was especially galling to Saudi leaders. It became clear to Riyadh that the swing-producer approach, with which Oil Minister Ahmad Zaki Yamani was particularly identified, was not achieving the desired results. As a swing producer, Saudi Arabia agreed to adapt its production according to the market in order to stabilize the general OPEC oil production and crude oil prices.

In a shrinking market with increased production from non-OPEC members, as well as several OPEC members who did not respect their quota assignments, Yamani's approach meant that Riyadh had to reduce its production drastically. In 1985, production from non-OPEC countries reached such a level that it became clear to the Saudis the market was not stable and their revenues were being eroded to an unacceptable level.

In June 1985, the Saudis decided to abandon their role as swing producers in OPEC. In the autumn of 1984, the 13 OPEC nations had sought to maintain their weakening grip on the market by reducing their production from 17.6 mbd to 16 mbd, with Saudi Arabia reducing its production from 5.0 mbd to 4.35 mbd. However, as swing producer, this level was seen as the maximum that Saudi Arabia would produce, rather than as an average production level. In short, if Saudi Arabia were to abide by the rules which it played such a great part in formulating, it could expect further drops in its production below this level. How far depended on how much oil needed to be pumped in order to ensure that supply matched demand. The persistent increase in non-OPEC production, coupled with concealed price cuts and production increases by many OPEC states, made Saudi Arabia's position untenable.

Table 6.1: Monthly average Opec crude oil production

(in mbd)	July 1986	January 1987	June 1987
Algeria	0.60	0.60	0.60
Ecuador	0.30	0.27	0.04
Gabon	0.17	0.15	0.15
Indonesia	1.35	1.28	1.30
Iran	2.20	2.20	2.40
Iraq	1.80	1.65	2.00
Kuwait	1.81	1.00	0.95
Libya	1.15	1.00	0.95
Nigeria	1.56	1.24	1.30
Qatar	0.40	0.28	0.35
Saudi Arabia	5.90	3.70	4.00
UAE	1.56	1.20	1.33
Venezuela	1.70	1.65	1.69
OPEC Total	20.49	16.67	17.42

Source: Wharton Econometric Forecasting Associates, *Middle East and Africa Economic Outlook,* Vol. 7, No. 2 (October 1987), p. 2.30.

Only Kuwait, Venezuela, Indonesia, and Qatar joined the kingdom in cutting actual production levels — although the latter three still continued to produce at above the new November 1984 quota levels. Saudi Arabia, Algeria, and Kuwait were thus the only three members actually prepared to produce at, or below, quota level in order to make the system work.

The Saudis believed that eventually consumption would start rising again. It did not. In November 1984, the 21 member nations of the International Energy Agency and France consumed 32,960,000 bd, while in June 1985 the total was down to 30,040,000 bd. On a more accurate basis, consumption by the same 22 countries — effectively the developed Western world — ran at 31,919,000 bd during the first half of 1985, against a comparable level during the first half of 1984 of 32,677,000 bd.

The decision to abandon the swing-producer role was not made easily. It meant challenging the other leading oil producers, whether in or out of OPEC. Riyadh demanded of its partners in OPEC that they adjust their output to allow Saudi Arabia to produce additional crude up to its 4.35 mbd ceiling. Yamani also reiterated that OPEC nations must strictly adhere to official selling prices and agreed production quotas.

115

For the Saudis, faced with a May 1985 production level of 2,590,000 bd and a June 1985 production level of 2,420,000 bd, drastic action was necessary to improve revenues. Saudi exports were running at little more than 1.5 mbd, earning the country around $1.25 billion a month, while the country's budget required oil income of almost $3 billion a month.

Once they decided on a new course of action, the Saudis moved quickly to implement it. In July, four supertankers, with a combined capacity of 8.5 million barrels, were chartered for storage purposes. They joined other tankers, carrying 35 million barrels, and 15 million barrels stocked at dumps on land in Rotterdam and the Caribbean, as stockpiles available for quick sale.

However, the main development was a dramatic shift in pricing policy. The kingdom relinquished its former adherence to contract sales, opting instead for what came to be known as the netback system. According to this arrangement, Saudi Arabia agreed to determine the price of its crude oil as a function of the value at which it was sold when already refined. This meant that crude oil would be sold at a later time than when the contract was actually signed. In a declining oil-price market, this also meant cheaper oil. The benefit for the oil companies was that cheaper oil prices would increase demand and profit. The benefit for the Saudis was an increased demand which, in turn, would allow them to regain their share of the market. The spot market was still avoided.

To begin with, netback deals were arranged with the four former US shareholders in Aramco. Then, various leading European companies secured Saudi oil on netback terms. After that, there were contracts with Japanese and Far Eastern suppliers. Finally, Saudi oil was being supplied by early 1986 to small independent refiners in the US and elsewhere.

The flood of Saudi oil onto the market prompted the dramatic oil-price collapse of 1986. To begin with, the oil entered the market in an orderly fashion, with the majors using it essentially to supply their own regular customers. While Saudi production in August 1985 was only 2,340,000 bd, the lowest monthly total since the post-1973 oil boom began, it was up to 2,980,000 bd in September of the same year, and to 3,910,000 bd in October. In November 1985, it broke the 4 mbd mark, and in the following months Saudi Arabia pumped steadily at between 4 and 5 mbd. On at least one occasion, it tested its production capacity with a brief burst of up to 6 mbd.

THE OTHER GCC PRODUCERS RESPOND

It took six months for most of the other members of OPEC to realize the full impact of the Saudi strategy. The Kuwaitis understood the strategy from the beginning, and appear to have been taken into Saudi confidence at an early stage. The UAE began following a similar strategy at a later date. With Qatar and Bahrain producing much smaller quantities, that left Oman as the only significant GCC producer outside Saudi Arabia's fold, at least so far as oil policy was concerned.

Kuwaiti production dropped to about 1 mbd in early 1986 in support of the Saudi policy, but a few months later domestic economic considerations prompted a 70 percent rise in production, a figure well over the country's OPEC quota. Kuwait's insistence on an enlargement of its quota at the end of the year served as a major obstacle in OPEC deliberations. Qatar, already one of the smallest producers in OPEC, faithfully adhered to the letter of its OPEC commitments and, as a consequence, saw its production drop below 200,000 bd in February and March of 1987, a drastic fall compared to its average production of 400,000 bd in 1984.

The UAE also saw its production slashed by OPEC quotas. The federal nature of the state leaves oil policy in the hands of the individual amirates. The long-standing rivalry between the two principal members, Abu Dhabi and Dubai, ensured that the UAE would not be able to honor its quotas. Abu Dhabi, which historically has produced about three-fourths of the UAE total, was forced to take the brunt of the production cutbacks, due to Dubai's argument that Abu Dhabi had agreed to OPEC quotas in the name of the UAE without consulting Dubai. Throughout 1986, the UAE constantly exceeded its stipulated levels by some 200,000 bd. It took a GCC ministerial delegation in early 1987 to get both amirates to agree to keep the UAE in line — but there was no guarantee that it would last.

The Omanis had very different concerns from those of the other GCC states. Oman only began developing its infrastructure following the palace coup which brought Sultan Qaboos bin Sa'id to power in July 1970. Oil was discovered much later and in much less volume than in the other GCC states. Oman never joined OPEC or OAPEC. For the other GCC members, the years from 1980 to 1985 witnessed the completion of most of their major infrastructure projects. For Oman, however, they witnessed the beginning. While the other states could tolerate revenue reductions due to production level decreases, Oman needed to keep raising oil output. In 1980, Omani oil production was 282,000 bd. The following year it averaged 319,090 bd. In June 1985, production averaged 480,000 bd and for the first time production, on at least one day, had exceeded 500,000 bd.

It took time for the Saudis to persuade Oman to cooperate with their new strategy. As late as 1986, Omani production was still rising rapidly. By the early part of the year, it averaged 540,000 bd,

Table 6.2: Petroleum shipped through the Strait of Hormuz, 1986

Destination:	Saudi Arabia	UAE	Iran	Kuwait	Qatar	Bahrain	TOTAL	
Japan	797	831	214	180	168	36	2226	(37%)
United States	635	44	19	68	13	2	781	(13%)
Italy	364	50	135	151	4	1	705	(12%)
France	321	34	65	22	28	1	471	(8%)
Netherlands	216	14	81	120	6	1	438	(7%)
West Germany	151	4	41	19	—	—	215	(4%)
Spain	114	9	66	20	1	—	210	(4%)
United Kingdom	73	—	10	13	6	—	102	(2%)
Canada	25	—	30	—	—	—	55	(1%)
Other	409	69	111	134	15	5	743	(12%)
TOTAL	3105	1055	772	727	241	46	5946	(100%)
	52%	18%	13%	12%	4%	1%	100%	

Gulf petroleum exported by pipeline	
(in tbd) from Iraq to:	
United States	81
Japan	161
Western Europe	486
Others	218
(in tbd) from Saudi Arabia to:	
United States	50
Western Europe	100

Source: US Congress, House of Representatives, Committee on Armed Services, Defense Policy Panel and Investigations Subcommittee, *National Security Policy Implications of the United States Operations in the Persian Gulf*; Report (Washington: USGPO, 1987) p. 15.

and there were plans to raise production to an average 575,000 bd throughout 1986.

The Saudis understood the need for the Omani production increases, but wanted GCC prices to be broadly similar in order to compete effectively as a block with crude produced elsewhere. In March, with Oman's announcement that it was postponing implementation of its third five-year plan, it appeared that the Omanis were finally receptive to Saudi thoughts on the future of the world oil market. By the spring of 1986, Oman was clearly within the GCC's oil policy fold. As a consequence, Oman agreed in September 1986 to cut back production by 10 percent to show solidarity with OPEC and support for its price-stabilization efforts. That left its production at approximately 550,000 bd. A further cut was announced in early 1987 and a desired level of 530,000 was set for the year.

THE GCC PRICING AND PRODUCTION STRATEGY

Overall, the Saudis believe that the Arab Gulf states are in a better position to fight an oil price war than anyone else. Although oil prices dropped below $10 a barrel in 1986, three of the GCC states — Kuwait, the UAE, and Qatar — still enjoyed a surplus on their current-account balance of payments. Bahrain's economy, being more service-oriented, does not suffer so adversely from oil price clashes as the others, while Saudi Arabia still has some $40-50 billion of very liquid reserves to draw on over the next few years until oil markets stabilize. Only Oman has a need for income from oil revenues at pre-1986 levels, hence the kingdom's tolerance of expanded Omani production.

The Saudi aim was to deliver a sharp shock to the market, so that they would regain market share and then hold it at a satisfactory price level. To the Saudis, and subsequently to the other Gulf states, this contained an implicit acknowledgement that the old contract marker price of $27.60 a barrel for Saudi crude was too high. The issue then was what price was necessary to force the market into shock, and what price was then necessary to ensure a stable market thereafter. The Saudis estimated that if prices went down to a level of $16-18 a barrel, the market should then start coming to its senses, with the producers of more expensive non-OPEC crude more prepared to reach an accommodation with OPEC on prices and/or production levels. The Kuwaitis went along with this, and

119

were prepared to accept a temporary drop to $16 a barrel to restore market stability.

In the event, prices dropped well below these anticipated temporary floors as oil markets overreacted to Saudi Arabia's return to substantial levels of oil production, in a complementary manner to the way they had overreacted in 1979 to the downfall of the Shah. As of July 1986, the market had yet to stabilize properly, and the OPEC ministers had not been able to reach a consensus on new prices and quotas.

The situation remained relatively stable through the remainder of 1986 and the first half of 1987. In August 1986, the GCC producers were able to reach a temporary two-month OPEC agreement with the radicals, led by Iran, to end the eight-month-old price war by reducing total OPEC output from over 20 mbd to 16.8 in September and October. Saudi Arabia agreed to cut its output from 6 mbd to 4.35 mbd, while Kuwait agreed to drop from 1.6 mbd to 900,000. Oil prices immediately jumped some $4-5. The production controls were extended until the end of 1986 after 16 days of haggling in October — the longest OPEC meeting in history. Most members received small quota increases, while Kuwait won approval of a nearly 10 percent rise in production to just under 1 mbd. In the midst of the pricing turmoil and sharply curtailed Saudi income, Oil Minister Ahmad Zaki Yamani was abruptly fired by King Fahd in October. His replacement was Hisham Nazir, a former Yamani deputy and a long-time minister of planning.

Another stormy 10-day OPEC meeting in Geneva in December 1986 resulted in across-the-board acceptance (except for Iraq) of 7 percent production decreases in order to hold overall OPEC production at a level of 15.8 mbd. As a consequence, prices began rising toward the OPEC target of $18 a barrel, and a move toward the scrapping of netback agreements in favor of a return to fixed-price contracts marked the beginning of 1987. The June 1987 OPEC meeting resulted in an accord to raise production slightly (although actual production peaked at about 20 mbd in August, well above the prescribed 16 mbd level), but the membership clearly was moving cautiously in order not to disturb the fragile price equilibrium.

If prices continue to stabilize over the short-term at a level of $18-20 a barrel, this would probably be enough to increase demand for OPEC oil in general, and for Saudi and other GCC oil in particular. In addition, the current state of low oil prices should mean that demand for oil will pick up much earlier than previously antici-

Table 6.3: US imports of crude oil by country of origin

(in tbd)	1960	1970	1973	1977	1980	1985
Organization of petroleum exporting countries:						
Algeria	1	8	136	559	488	187
Indonesia	77	70	213	541	348	314
Nigeria	0	50	459	1143	857	293
Saudi Arabia	84	30	486	1380	1261	168
Venezuela	911	989	1135	690	481	605
Other OPEC (a)	241	197	564	1880	865	264
Arab OPEC (b)	292	196	915	3185	2551	472
Total OPEC (c)	1314	1343	2993	6193	4300	1830
Non-Opec exporting countries:						
Canada	120	766	1325	517	455	770
Mexico	16	42	16	179	533	816
United Kingdom	–	11	15	126	176	310
TOTAL	1815	3419	6256	8807	6909	5067

Notes:
a. Includes Ecuador, Gabon, Iran, Iraq, Kuwait, Libya, Qatar, and the United Arab Emirates.
b. Includes Algeria, Iraq, Kuwait, Libya, Qatar, Saudi Arabia and the United Arab Emirates.
c. Excludes petroleum imported into the United States indirectly from the OPEC countries, primarily from the Caribbean and West European refining areas as petroleum products which were refined from crude oil produced in OPEC countries.

Source:
US Department of Energy, Energy Information Administration, *Annual Energy Review 1986* (Washington, 1987).

pated. Senior US economists have advised Congress of their belief that the United States would again become a major importer of OPEC crude and products in the 1990s, with the Gulf states playing the major production role in OPEC. However, the persistence of low prices at present means that demand will pick up some two or three years earlier than it would have if Saudi Arabia had continued to defend throughout 1986 OPEC's previous price and production policy. In 1985, the Saudis and their GCC colleagues had thought that the period 1990-1992 would be the time when OPEC, and the GCC in particular, would enjoy its second golden age. Now they see the world market balancing and demand picking up as early as 1987-1989.

Table 6.4: US imports by source

(in tbd)	1985 Q1	Q2	Q3	Q4	1986 Q1	Q2	Q3	Q4	1987 Q1
Algeria	9	133	72	96	91	95	85	105	116
(% of total	3.0	3.4	2.0	2.2	2.5	2.1	1.5	2.1	2.5)
Canada	549	591	545	631	608	652	655	742	645
(% of total	18.5	15.1	14.8	14.7	16.5	14.3	11.9	14.7	13.9)
Ecuador	71	68	130	117	99	101	100	117	74
(% of total	2.4	1.7	3.5	2.7	2.7	2.2	1.8	2.3	1.6)
Gabon	8	54	80	60	19	30	33	47	24
(% of total	0.3	1.4	2.2	1.4	0.5	0.6	0.6	0.9	0.5)
Indonesia	233	288	298	329	245	320	375	279	287
(% of total	7.8	7.4	8.1	7.6	6.6	7.0	6.8	5.5	6.4)
Iran	—	28	131	99	86	41	160	52	128
(% of total	—	0.7	3.6	2.3	2.3	0.9	2.9	1.0	2.8)
Iraq	—	80	73	22	21	87	118	91	56
(% of total	—	2.1	2.0	0.5	0.6	1.9	2.1	1.5	1.2)
Kuwait	10	9	7	37	33	72	73	55	45
(% of total	0.3	0.2	0.2	0.9	0.9	1.6	1.3	1.1	1.0)
Mexico	657	769	776	705	588	697	664	629	662
(% of total	22.1	19.7	21.1	16.4	15.9	15.2	12.0	12.5	14.3)
Nigeria	158	305	268	324	239	315	572	454	290
(% of total	5.3	7.8	7.3	7.5	6.5	6.9	10.4	9.0	6.2)
Norway	34	32	16	35	72	30	57	59	90
(% of total	1.1	0.8	0.4	0.8	1.9	0.7	1.0	1.2	1.9)
Saudi Arabia	64	42	11	395	528	604	664	731	658
(% of total	2.2	1.1	0.3	9.2	14.3	13.2	12.0	14.5	14.2)
UAE	31	65	28	13	—	35	65	74	22
(% of total	1.1	1.7	0.8	0.3	—	0.8	1.2	1.5	0.5)
Venezuela	256	366	370	452	328	510	563	540	561
(% of total	8.6	9.4	10.1	10.5	8.9	11.2	10.2	10.7	12.1)
OPEC	921	1,439	1,470	1,945	1,687	2,210	2,852	2,550	2,283
(% of total	31.1	36,8	40.0	45.2	45.7	48.4	51.7	50.6	49.2)

Source: Wharton Econometric Forecasting Associates, *Middle East and Africa Economic Outlook*, Vol. 7, No. 2 (October 1987), p. 2.24.

However, OPEC's return as the world's most influential source of oil will be accompanied by radical changes within that organization. A third of OPEC's members will cease to be important oil exporters over the next eight or nine years. These include Indonesia, Algeria, Gabon and Ecuador. Other OPEC countries, including Nigeria, will face high costs associated with pumping their oil.

However, Saudi Arabia and at least two of its colleagues in the GCC, Kuwait and the UAE, still have the capacity to produce much more than they did in 1987. Saudi Arabia has in the past produced at more than 10 mbd, and the capacity for such a level of production is still in place. This will be of immeasurable benefit, as cutbacks in oil exploration elsewhere in the world, the consequence of falling prices and collapsing oil company earnings, take effect. In four years' time, or perhaps earlier, greater productive capacity will be required.

However, all countries, including most of OPEC, are now cutting back on exploration. As a result, new fields needed to make up for current production may not be in place before four to five years.

This is especially true of the United States and the Soviet Union. The US has seen nationwide exploration and development spending drop by 35-40 percent since the start of 1986. Domestic drilling in the US has fallen by 60 percent since 1985. In the Soviet Union, overproduction of existing fields to ensure that production quotas are maintained is bringing about the possibility of a major decline in oil production by 1990. A decline in Soviet exports is likely to account for almost the whole of this drop, estimated at between 900,000 and 1,300,000 bd between 1986 and 1990.

Declining non-OPEC production is vital to the Saudis. Their case is largely based on the simple economic premise that the cost of pumping wells in the kingdom can be as low as $1 a barrel, while elsewhere normal costs, without taking into account amortisation or repayment of infrastructure costs, is usually $4-7 a barrel, and in some cases can run as high as $15 a barrel. Kuwaiti and UAE production is also cheap.

Indeed, one of the targets of the new Saudi production policy is the Soviet Union. Riyadh was upset by the way Moscow managed to persuade energy users in Western Europe to buy gas pumped from Siberia via the new pipeline built in the late 1970s and the early 1980s, parts of which are still under construction. The Saudis are not that unhappy to see the Soviet Union's largest source of hard currency earnings, revenues from oil and gas, slashed. According to official estimates, the Soviet Union lost 60 percent of its regular foreign-exchange revenues between January and April 1986. In the future, this will not only hurt the Soviet Union's economy, but will also prompt it to hold back on capital spending on future projects designed to export energy. In the wake of the oil price slump and the Chernobyl meltdown, the Soviet Union's energy industry will be looking mainly for customers at home, rather than abroad.

THE OUTLOOK FOR THE 1990s

The outlook for the GCC states in the 1990s looks bright. The collapse in oil prices already appears to be prompting the increase in demand required if oil-producing countries in the GCC are to assume the position of dominance in world markets anticipated for them during that decade.

In the meantime, there will be years of belt-tightening. Saudi Arabia failed to publish its annual budget in March 1986, and delayed announcing it until the end of December. The 1987 budget was also postponed. Publication of the budget on time would have informed the world what prices the Saudis were seeking for their oil. The 1986 budget, when finally published, anticipated a deficit of 30 percent. The kingdom pointed out that its oil revenues had fallen by 80 percent between 1980 and 1986. Kuwait already had produced an austerity budget based on the worst-case scenario of $15 a barrel for the rest of 1986, and its 1987 budget projected an even larger deficit. Meanwhile, the UAE resolved the issue in its time-honored fashion by declining to produce budgets until the years in question were almost finished. Oman announced a budget cut of 10 percent in 1986 and 14 percent in 1987, as well as cutbacks and postponements of its 1986-1990 five-year plan. Bahrain announced austerity measures, while Qatar's reserves effectively meant that the emirate had no real problems apart from the current-accounts situation.

For Saudi Arabia, the UAE and Qatar, the cushion provided by financial reserves will be determined by the length of the glut. Oman and Bahrain have very little in the way of reserves on which to fall back. Only Kuwait, which receives more income from return on investments than from oil, has seen its reserves grow. Despite the temporary hardships, the GCC producers have already achieved some of their objectives. North Sea oil production has reached a plateau. In April 1986, the Saudis claimed their first clear victory. The Norwegian government fell over the issue of how to tackle Norway's oil-price-fall problems, and a Labor government more sympathetic to OPEC came into office. Mexico will not increase production, a development which is particularly significant as, in December 1985, Saudi Arabia overtook Mexico to become, for the first time in four years, the leading supplier of crude oil to the US.

The presence at the 1986 OPEC meeting in Vienna of Malaysia, Mexico, Egypt, Oman, and Angola illustrated the fact that non-OPEC producers now share OPEC's concerns about oil markets.

Table 6.5: Estimated international crude oil and natural gas reserves

Area and Country	Crude Oil (billion barrels)		Natural Gas (trillion cubic feet)	
	1976	1986	1976	1986
Middle East:				
Bahrain	0.3	0.1	3	7
Algeria	6.8	8.8	126	106
Egypt	2.0	3.6	3	9
Libya	25.5	21.3	26	21
Iran	63.0	48.8	330	28
Iraq	34.0	47.1	27	28
Kuwait (a)	70.6	94.5	34	41
Oman	5.8	4.0	2	8
Qatar	5.7	3.2	28	152
Saudi Arabia (a)	113.2	169.2	66	130
Syria	2.2	1.4	1	4
UAE	31.2	33.1	23	105
Total	360.3	435.1	669	639
Other Opec:				
Ecuador	1.7	1.7	12	4
Gabon	2.1	.6	3	1
Indonesia	10.5	8.3	24	49
Nigeria	19.5	16.0	44	47
Venezuela	15.3	25.0	41	59
Total	49.1	51.6	124	160
North America:				
Canada	6.2	6.9	56	100
Mexico	7.0	54.7	12	77
United States	30.9	24.6	216	185
Total	44.1	86.2	284	362
Western Europe:				
Norway	5.7	10.5	19	103
United Kingdom	16.8	9.0	30	33
Eastern Europe & USSR:				
USSR	78.1	59.0	918	1550
Other (b)	3.4	1.9	12	15
Total	81.5	60.9	930	1566
World Total	598.7	697.4	2300	3626

Notes:
a. Includes one-half of Neutral Zone.
b. Also includes Cuba, Mongolia, North Korea and Vietnam.
Source: US Department of Energy, Energy Information Administration, *Annual Energy Review 1986* (Washington: USGPO, 1986).

This concern has yet to be translated into actual cooperation with OPEC, but it is perhaps a portent of things to come. While some other countries, notably Egypt and Oman, have temporarily cut back production, the non-OPEC producers are unlikely to substantially reduce their production until OPEC itself returns to — and observes — an official quota system.

The pressures for such a system, however, will not come mainly from the non-OPEC nations, but from the Saudis and their GCC allies. The GCC states can afford, albeit with some difficulty, to wait for better times. They can — and will — call for workable quota arrangements now. If these fail to materialize, they will not worry too much. After all, in a few years' time, they will be the principal powers within OPEC at a time when the pendulum will have swung back to favor oil producers, rather than consumers.

NOTES

1. Yusif A. Sayigh, *Arab Oil Policies in the 1970s* (London: Croom Helm, 1983), p. 23.

2. "Introduction" in J.E. Peterson, ed., *The Politics of Middle Eastern Oil* (Washington: Middle East Institute, 1983), pp. xv-xvii.

3. Current information on oil developments in the Gulf can be found in the following principal periodicals: *Middle East Economic Digest* (London), *Middle East Economic Survey* (Nicosia, Cyprus), *OAPEC News Bulletin* (Kuwait), *OPEC Bulletin* and *OPEC Review* (Vienna), *Oil and Arab Cooperation* (Kuwait), *Oil and Gas Journal* (Tulsa, Oklahoma), *Petroleum Economist* (London), *Petroleum Intelligence Weekly* (New York), *Platt's Oilgram News* (New York), and *World Oil* (Houston).

7

Socio-political Change in the Gulf: A Climate for Terrorism?

Rouhollah K. Ramazani[*]

In no other region of the world has the onslaught on American life, liberty and property taken a greater toll in recent years than in the Middle East. The region as a whole has become the global hotbed of terrorism. By the end of 1985, the Middle East accounted for 45 percent of the world's terrorist attacks: some of which originated in the area but were completed in Europe.[1] The bulk of terrorist activities within the Middle East has been concentrated in Lebanon and the Gulf region. This essay focuses on the Gulf region, starting with a review of the most serious terrorist incidents since 1983, the majority of which have taken place in Kuwait.

As of 1986, four major incidents had shaken up the tiny shaykhdom and its five partners in the Gulf Cooperation Council (GCC). This regional grouping has viewed the terrorist attacks in Kuwait as attacks on the security and stability of all its member states. Iraq, on the other hand, has made every effort to implicate the Khomeini regime in all these incidents as part and parcel of its war strategy against Iran. I shall outline briefly the principal facts of each incident as a point of departure for the analysis that will follow.

The first major terrorist incident in Kuwait took place on December 12, 1983, when simultaneous bombings at the United States Embassy, the French Embassy, and other targets killed five and wounded 86 persons. As in the truck bombings of the American Marines and the French paratroopers in Lebanon (October 23,

* This study is based primarily on observations made and conversations held during the course of numerous visits to the Gulf starting in 1979 and including a last visit in 1986. Otherwise, I have cited documentary sources of information.

1983), the "Islamic Jihad Organization" claimed responsibility. Quietly, all the GCC regimes blamed Iran, as did Western sources.[2] The 17 Iraqis, out of 25 convicted for the crime, all belonged to the Iraqi underground Shi'a party known as *al-Da'wa*. The demand for the release of these imprisoned terrorists has triggered other acts of terrorism not only in Kuwait, but also in Lebanon where both American and French nationals have been held captive by Shi'a. They have been bargaining chips in efforts to obtain the freedom of fellow Shi'a and, in some cases, relatives.

The second attack verified the dangers confronting a nation choosing to imprison terrorists. On December 4, 1984, a Kuwaiti airliner bound for Karachi (with 155 passengers and 11 crew members) was hijacked by Shi'a terrorists, taken to Tehran and held there for six days. Two Americans were killed and several Kuwaitis wounded before the surviving passengers were freed.[3] Within a year after the sentencing of the terrorists in the embassy bombings by a Kuwaiti court, other Shi'a terrorists had abducted six Americans in Lebanon and the Islamic Jihad had made calls to the effect that if their fellow Shi'a were not released they would execute their captives.

Kuwait was again the target of terrorism when an explosive-laden car rammed into the motorcade of the Amir Shaykh Jabir al-Ahmad Al Sabah on May 25, 1985. Two members of the Amiri Guard and a passerby were killed and 11 others wounded. The Islamic Jihad's spokesman congratulated the amir on his escape and expressed the hope that the message had been clearly understood. Contacting a foreign news agency in Beirut, the spokesman also warned that a new blow would soon be directed against the "reactionary Arab regimes."[4]

The assassination attempt, like the hijacking of the Kuwaiti airliner, seemingly was motivated by the desire to force the release of the 17 prisoners convicted in Kuwait in exchange for American and French hostages held in Beirut. Apparently this was inferred from two facts: the shadowy Islamic Jihad's demand, ten days before the attempted assassination, for the release of the prisoners, and Prime Minister Shaykh Sa'd al-'Abdullah Al Sabah's rejection of the demand immediately after the attack. According to the Kuwaiti daily *al-Anba'*, however, the car bomber was a member of the *al-Da'wa* Party, as had been those convicted for the multiple bombings mentioned before. Generally, the "Islamic Jihad" has been considered as a cover name for a variety of terrorist groups.[5]

More importantly, there was a real fear at the time for the welfare of the embryonic Kuwaiti parliamentary democracy as a result of the shaykhdom's mounting security concerns. Heir Apparent and Prime Minister Shaykh Sa'd warned that the attack on the amir might force Kuwaitis to sacrifice the liberal ways they had become used to in secure times. A tough anti-terrorism bill was approved by the cabinet on June 9, 1985, providing the death penalty for terrorist acts resulting in loss of life. Other penalties were envisaged by the bill for membership in anti-government underground groups — obviously referring to *al-Da'wa* — and for writing and publishing seditious material.[6] Details of the bills are difficult to learn, but as late as nearly a year later there was evidence of some concern among Kuwaiti intellectuals regarding the potential erosion of Kuwaiti democracy. Some expressed concern over the possible suspension of parliamentary life as a result of pressure from the prime minister, while others seemed to believe that the amir was fully committed to the continuation of the assembly and was happy with the outpouring of affection for him by so many Kuwaiti people after the attempt against his life.

A fourth terrorist incident in Kuwait took place on July 11, 1985, when bombs exploded at two popular cafés in the al-Sharq and al-Salmiya areas and killed 11 people and wounded 89.[7] Responsibility for the bomb blasts was claimed by the "Arab Revolutionary Brigades Organization," which had in the past claimed credit for attacks on diplomats from Jordan and the UAE in Europe, India, and the rest of the Gulf region. The Kuwaiti newspaper *al-Ra'i al-'Aam* once again tried to blame Iran for the incident, but lacking reliable information it simply commented on accounts of the forces opposed to the Khomeini regime.[8]

Although these four major terrorist incidents in Kuwait since 1983 constitute the most serious terrorist activities in the Gulf region in recent years, the problem of terrorism in the area has not been confined to Kuwait. A real turning point was the year 1979 when the triple crises of the Iranian seizure of American hostages, the capture of the Grand Mosque in Mecca and the burning of the American Embassy in Islamabad took place. In 1981, the discovery of an abortive coup plot in Bahrain sent shock waves around the Gulf. Other terrorist plots in Qatar, Saudi Arabia, and elsewhere in the Gulf have been attempted. Some have succeeded and some have failed.

This brief sketch of some recent terrorist activities in the Gulf area should be viewed within the context of three broad points.

First, the focus on the Gulf region by no means implies that terrorism is an exclusively Shi'a phenomenon. To be sure, the Gulf region is the world's Shi'a heartland. Most Shi'a Muslims of the world live in the region. Also, to be sure, the largest number of terrorist acts in recent years have been committed by Shi'a inhabitants of Lebanon. Nevertheless, terrorist acts have been committed by Sunnis as well, such as those who killed President Sadat in Egypt. Furthermore, Islamic terrorist factions are active in other parts of the Muslim world, as evidenced by the Moro National Liberation Front in the Philippines and the al-Zulfiqar group in Pakistan.

Second, terrorism is not an exclusively religious phenomenon in the Middle East. The resurgence of terrorism among purportedly religious groups in recent years has overshadowed the terrorist activities of other radical groups that are secular both in ideology and in political orientation, such as the Libyan-backed Abu Nidal group (200-300 members), the Popular Front for the Liberation of Palestine (PFLP), the PFLP-General Command, the Palestinian dissidents led by Abu Musa, and the Syrian-backed al-Sa'iqa group, not to mention such non-Muslim groups as Armenian terrorists, the Jewish Defense League, and the Maronite extremists who massacred innocent refugees in the Palestinian camps of Sabra and Shatila in Lebanon in September 1982.

Third, the large percentage of terrorist incidents in the Middle East in recent years should not obscure the fact that terrorism is a worldwide phenomenon. To cite a few examples, narcoterrorism in Latin America is a new phenomenon, adding to the already mounting terrorist activities by a variety of groups with or without the support of Cuba and Nicaragua, just as Sikh terrorism has surfaced in India in the past couple of years. Besides these examples from the Third World, outside the Middle East and the Muslim world, it is well to remember the notorious West European terrorist groups such as the Red Army Faction, which has attacked American and NATO-related installations in Germany, the Italian Red Brigades and the Basque separatists in Spain.

EXPLAINING TERRORISM

So much for the "what" of terrorism in the Gulf region. But what can be said about the "why" of it? There are, of course, general theories about international terrorism, ranging from the principle of self-determination and "wars of national liberation" at one extreme to international crime at the other. But here we are concerned more specifically with theories about Middle Eastern terrorism. There are several current explanations of terrorism in the Middle East.

First, there is a historical explanation which discovers the roots of today's terrorism in the "character" of Islamic history, particularly in the fact that there existed in the twelfth century an Islamic terrorist sect known as the "Assassins" (*Hashshashin*). Second, there is a school of thought which considers all terrorist acts as intrinsically criminal and hence all terrorists as "thugs" whose frustration and fanaticism are exploited for selfish political ends by such unscrupulous leaders as the "mad dog" of Libya, or by such notorious factional bosses as Abu Nidal, Abu 'Abbas and others. Third, there is the explanation which views terrorism in the Middle East "as a reflection of the age-old frustration born out of the failure to achieve a Palestinian state." Finally, there is a school of thought according to which radical Islamic fundamentalists, who hate Americans more than Russians, simply use terrorist acts to get their way.

The problem with these and similar explanations of terrorism is that they are largely based on speculation about motivation. Furthermore, explanations about Middle Eastern terrorism also share with general theories about international terrorism one other important feature; they are all simplistic because they are monistic. A single motivation is used as a basis for explanation, be it the right of self-determination in general or Palestinian self-determination in particular.

Yet in reality, it is impossible to get at a diagnosis of terrorism simply in terms of motivation of an individual or a group. The principal difficulty is twofold. First, without too much exaggeration, it may be said that there are perhaps as many motivations as there are terrorists. There are terrorists who kill for a cause, for revenge, and even for kicks. Second, it is often impossible to distinguish between a motivation and an excuse for a given terrorist action. The cynics would have us believe that terrorists simply use ideological slogans — for example, Islam, Arabism or Zionism — to cover their greed for power and fame. But, in reality, an ideology may well be both a cause and an excuse for action, although methodologically, it is not always easy to distinguish between the two.

One way of avoiding the pitfalls of monistic or single-causal explanations is to try to relate terrorism to its environment.

I propose to do this not as an excuse for, nor as a justification of, terrorism, but in order to understand it. As conceived here, environment is the aggregate of geographical as well as ideological, social, economic, cultural, psychological and political conditions which influence the life of an individual or community.

An environmental approach to the study of terrorism is based on five major assumptions. First, terrorism is partly a dependent phenomenon because it cannot be totally separated for study from its environmental base. An individual or a group may kill for any motivation, but the act of violence cannot be isolated from its context. Second, terrorism is locational. The phenomenon is said to be "international" either in the ordinary sense that acts of terrorism take place in every region or country of the world, or in the more technical sense that individuals and groups who commit terrorist acts are controlled by sovereign states, commonly called state-sponsored terrorism. In this latter sense "international terrorism" is distinguished from "transnational terrorism" which refers to acts carried out "by basically *autonomous nonstate actors*, whether or not they enjoy some degree of support from sympathetic states.[9] In either case, we still assume that terrorism is locational and thus its study must be placed in the context of a given country, region or other location if it is to be adequately understood. Third, terrorism is situational. That is, besides asking where it takes place, it is necessary to ask *when* it happens. Fourth, being partly a dependent variable, terrorism should be regarded as multi-causal because the environment that influences the behavior of an individual or a group contains many different factors. Fifth, and last, terrorism is dynamic because environmental factors, being interconnected, constantly interact.

As applied to the Gulf region as a whole, one would hope that this broader environmental approach to the study of terrorism will aid in understanding the ideological, social, economic, cultural, psychological and political complexities that underlie the problem. It leads to six major clusters of factors, analytically separable but interacting with one another over time and space to influence individual and group behavior, including the behavior of extremists on the fringes of Gulf societies. The radicals resort to the threat or use of force as their only recourse, regardless of whether their motivation is religious or secular, personal or communal, rational or emotional.

IRAN'S REVOLUTIONARY PARADIGM

Although the impact of the Iranian Revolution on the Muslim world has yet to be studied systematically, there is a consensus among scholars based partly on first-hand observations that its effects have been felt in Muslim communities all the way from Marawi in the Philippines to Manama in Bahrain, and beyond.[10] What is the nature of that impact? Does it diminish or intensify in relationship to the distance of various Muslim or Muslim-inhabited countries from Iran? Whatever the answer to these questions, there is little doubt that in no other region of the world have the effects of the revolution been so pervasive and persistent as in the Gulf. To be sure, Iran is the single largest Shi'a Muslim-inhabited country in the world. It is also the most populous state in the region and the most strategically-located country — abutting both the Soviet Union and the Strait of Hormuz — and putatively still the most powerful state despite the material toll which the revolution and the war with Iraq have exacted. But none of these factors by itself can account for the regional effects of the Iranian Revolution. Rather, it is the combination of these factors with what may be called the Iranian revolutionary paradigm that has over the past eight years simultaneously appealed to and repelled other societies in the Gulf region. In essence, this paradigm consists of both Iranian ideology and practice.

On the "appealing" side of the ledger, four major elements stand out. First, there are those groups and individuals in the Gulf region to whom Khomeini's claim to an all-Islamic and non-sectarian message has a special appeal. For such people, the fact that Shi'a particularism cannot be isolated from his overall ideology does not seem to matter. Nor does the fact that Khomeiniism is the official creed of the Iranian state. Second, the uncompromising insistence of both Khomeini's ideology and Iranian practice on the absolute goal of political independence is widely believed to contain more than mere rhetoric. The overthrow of the perceived pro-American Shah, the taking of American hostages, the defiance of the Soviet Union and the destruction of the pro-Moscow Communist Tudeh Party seem to many Gulf citizens to accord credibility to the Khomeini claim. Equally, the bitterly anti-American and anti-Israeli crusade of the Khomeini regime and its alliance with Libya and Syria have sympathizers among the Gulf Arabs. The Iranian crusade for Jerusalem, and for creating a Palestinian state by destroying Israel, coupled with Arab hatred of Israel, contributes to radical ideological trends in the Gulf region.

The other two aspects of the appeal of the Iranian revolutionary paradigm concern the perceived social and cultural emancipation of Iran. Khomeini's emphasis on the first concern of the "Islamic Revolution" with the economically poor and socially deprived classes, or the *mustaz'afin*, has a populist ring that appeals to Shi'a and Sunni lower classes alike.

In the view of one Bahraini citizen, for example, in no country in the region has the oil wealth been so equitably distributed as it has been in Khomeini's Iran. On the cultural side, the anti-Western, especially anti-American, thrust of Khomeiniism combines with an incessant call for "Islamic self-reliance," a call that stirs the hearts and minds of those who believe that Western cultural penetration has created a crisis of identity and a sense of Islamic inferiority. In this context, the widely-known Iranian slogan of "neither East, nor West" means total emancipation — not simply political non-alignment and economic self-sufficiency — from subservience to the superpowers as a means to the lofty goal of restoring Islamic self-respect.

On the "repellent" side of the ledger, there are also four major ingredients. First, no matter how insistent militant Iranians may be on the all-Islamic character of their ideology, many Arabs believe, probably rightly, that the Khomeini ideology embraces Shi'a particularism. This perception is repugnant to some Islamic groups such as the Kuwaiti *Jami'at al-Islah*, although this group's negative attitude toward the Iranian paradigm may be said to be balanced by the pro-Iranian stance of the *Jami'at al-Saqafa*. The second ingredient, closely related to the first one just mentioned, is the conception and practice of the rule of the clerics in the Iranian political system. Many Gulf Arabs who admire the Khomeini regime for its sustained defiance of the superpowers, reject the model of Iranian governance for their own societies. To be sure, the role of the Arab *ulema* in the political process of some Gulf Arab countries, such as Saudi Arabia, has increased in recent years; but this development does not place them on a par with the Iranian clerics, who had always played a major role in society and even in politics long before they seized the reins of power from the Shah. Even Arab Shi'a are not necessarily impressed by the idea of the guardianship of the jurisprudent, *vilayat-i faqih*, as it is being practiced in Iran.

A third dimension of the Iranian revolutionary paradigm that seems to repel segments of the Gulf Arab citizens, especially the liberal elements, is the perceived souring of the revolution. The magnetic influence of the Iranian revolutionary drama was everywhere to be sensed during 1979-1981, but the disappointment with the Iranian experience has increased since then for two major reasons. Given the support of the masses for the revolution at inception, many Arab intellectuals, like most Iranians, believed that the fruits of the revolution belonged to all strata of the society, including the middle classes. But the suppression of a wide variety of middle-class-based political groups and the ever-increasing dominance of the clerics and their lower-class supporters, such as the Hizbollahis, has diminished the appeal that the revolution enjoyed during its first few years. Furthermore, the large-scale purges, summary executions, involvement of teenagers in the war through the *Basij* (Mobilization Force) and the *Pasdaran* (Revolutionary Guards), the deterioration of the status of women, and the like have dampened the earlier appeal of the revolution.

Fourth, as these negative impressions of the revolutionary paradigm began to spread, the ancient cultural differences between Arabs and Persians and between Sunnis and Shi'a started to surface. The Saddam Hussein regime has tried to exploit the old Arab-Iranian cultural differences in his reference to the battle of al-Qadisiya, when the Arab Muslims defeated the Persian Sassanids in AD 637, in the war with Iran. Unlike the Arab-Persian conflict, however, the Shi'i-Sunni differences are not exploitable by Arab leaders because they could boomerang, given the presence of large Shi'a populations in their societies. Nevertheless, on-site observation suggests clear intensification of sectarian feelings.

Despite the repellent side of the ledger, the appeal of Khomeiniism on the whole continues. Even those Gulf Arabs who are repelled by certain perceived negative aspects of the Iranian example have not been able to avoid an intensified atmosphere of political consciousness. This can play into the hands of demagogues and radical politicians, especially in combination with the other factors discussed below.

SOCIETAL "REJUVENATION"

One of the most important of these factors is what the United Nations calls the problem of "rejuvenation", that is, an increasing percentage of young people among the population. Without this problem, the Gulf Arab communities would probably have been

135

less susceptible to Iranian revolutionary agitation, notwithstanding an intensified sense of political consciousness. The problem of rejuvenation in the Gulf area is more acute than in most other Third World regions because of the additional problem of the large percentage of foreigners in Gulf societies and hence the relatively small size of the citizen populations.

We may recall the 1960s when the effects of the "baby boom" of the earlier decades began to be felt in our own West European societies. The "rebellious young" became the watchword of those days in explaining the social upheaval that accompanied the arrival of a new generation. The Third World now faces this problem acutely. United Nations statistics show that some 60 percent of the populations in the underdeveloped regions of the world are under 20 years of age as compared with about 40 percent in the "more developed regions." Taking the politically most active age group in the Gulf, that is the group between 10 and 34 years of age, about 46 percent of the population of all Gulf countries was between 10 and 34 years old in 1980. Projecting this figure into the year 2000, it will increase to about 48 percent. In the United States, by comparison, Americans of the same age group accounted for about 43 percent of the population in 1980 and will *decrease* to about 35 percent in the year 2000. Among all the Gulf countries, Bahrain had the highest percentage of this age group (51.11 percent) in 1980, while Oman had the lowest (44.10 percent) in the same year.[11]

One of the most striking features of the profile of terrorism in the Gulf region is the involvement of the younger people in acts of political violence. In the Kuwaiti terrorist incident, except for three out of 21 terrorists whose ages are unknown, all were under 30 years of age. More important, out of 21 convicted, 16 were in their twenties.[12] If indeed rejuvenation of the population and social and political extremism go hand in hand, then the trend in the Gulf region is likely to contribute further to an environment of political violence.

Second, to take up the problem of the large numbers of expatriates in the Gulf societies, the problem of rejuvenation is compounded by what may be called the problem of societal perforation because of the large number of expatriates. The intensity of this problem is different from country to country. The UAE ranks the highest among the GCC states. Its foreign population forms more than 80 percent of the total population of a quarter of a million people and hence its citizen population is less than one-third of the total. Qatar and Kuwait rank after the UAE in terms of the percentage of their foreign population, at 73 percent and 61 percent respectively.[13]

The correlation between large numbers of foreign expatriates and an environment favoring terrorism may be inferred from two developments. First, every major terrorist act has involved expatriates of one kind or another.[14] Ever since the Iranian Revolution, a number of Gulf Arab countries have been expelling expatriates. Many of them have been sent home in recent years because of drastically declining oil revenues. Saudi Arabia, for example, plans to have 600,000 fewer by the end of its five-year plan in 1990 and Kuwait also plans to change the ratio of foreign to local population from the current 60-40 percent to 50-50 percent. But many expatriates are also being expelled because of a heightened sense of insecurity. Since the multiple bombings, terrorist-plagued Kuwait has deported many thousands of Iranians and also other nationalities. At least 50,000 expatriates have been deported since the assassination attempt against the life of the Amir took place in May 1985.

SOCIETAL ALIENATION

A third cluster of factors that seems to contribute to an environment of radicalism in the Gulf region is societal alienation. There is a general consensus that alienation of individuals and groups can contribute to social and political violence in both underdeveloped and developed societies. When it comes to considering a particular country or situation, however, there seems to be disagreement about the sources of alienation. For example, many observers have identified "modernization" as the key in the resurgence of Islam and the eruption of the Iranian Revolution. Some emphasize rapid economic change, some the slow pace of economic development, and others the maldistribution of wealth.

The Iranian Revolution, as I have suggested elsewhere, was *at inception* a "revolution of rising alienation," stemming from no single economic, political, moral, or ideological source.[15] Rather, it reflected the cumulative effects of a complex of domestic and foreign policies of the Shah's regime over the decades, perceived to be detrimental to the interests and values of a variety of groups and individuals. To many modernized intellectuals, political oppression and lack of political freedom under the Shah's rule mattered most of all. But the uprooted masses of peasantry, who

137

were not able to recognize rapid urbanization as the source of their misery, bewilderment, "anonymity" or "crisis of identity," became increasingly estranged from the Shah's regime because of the wretched conditions of their lives. Examples may be easily multiplied to show how different individuals and groups perceived the policies of the Shah as harmful to their values and interests, especially the clerics and their bazaari supporters.

It has been argued elsewhere that Iranian-type revolutions are not likely for other Gulf states and I suggested above that, on balance, the main effect of the Iranian revolutionary paradigm has been an intensified political awakening in the Gulf region.[16] Yet, societal alienation is also taking place in varying degrees in the Arab Gulf countries and, as in the case of pre-revolutionary Iran, its causes are multifaceted. There are various groups and individuals who seem to believe that their values and interests have been adversely affected by the domestic and foreign policies of the incumbent-regimes. It is beyond the scope of this study to consider this important subject in detail. But it is necessary to make two additional points that bear on the process of societal alienation.

First, the effects of rapid expansion of mass communications and education have begun to combine with the impact of the processes of rejuvenation and intensified political consciousness. The net result has been the rise of a highly politicized younger generation, particularly among the middle classes. Contrary to the current impression, this expanding political awakening is not expressed exclusively in Islamic terms. Secular nationalism, liberal and conservative, coexists and competes with Islamic fundamentalism, radical and conservative.

In the open society of Kuwait, it is easier to observe that Islamic fundamentalism, both Shi'i and Sunni, is challenged today by secular nationalism. In the 1985 parliamentary elections, nationalist candidates gained unexpectedly, while Muslim fundamentalists lost seats they had won in 1981. In less open societies this same phenomenon is more difficult to observe, but the reassertion of secular nationalism is unmistakable today. One major indicator is the rising demand for a modern type of political participation. Except for those who have been coopted by existing regimes, most of the modern members of the middle classes complain about their closed political systems. Politically aware Bahrainis demand the reopening of their suspended parliament, while their Saudi counterparts complain that they have never had more than the ever-suspended promise of a consultative assembly.

Second, if it was feared a few years ago that rapid modernization, fueled by a massive rise in oil revenues, could trigger societal dislocation, income maldistribution, and lifestyle disruption, today it is feared that economic recession as a result of the drastic fall in oil prices may cause whole new sources of societal alienation and hence an environment of political radicalism. The alarmists may exaggerate the odds, but the new problems caused by an unprecedented recession are here already. Today's oil bust can be as disruptive as yesterday's oil boom. The oil revenues of the Arab Gulf states have dropped by about 50 percent since 1981, and the landmark decisions of OPEC in 1982 and 1983 with respect to prices and production, like all other subsequent OPEC efforts to avert greater losses of oil revenues, have failed so far. Given their varying levels of development and their different needs and lifestyles, the Gulf societies may be affected unevenly but all are suffering. The Saudis now have the world's second largest deficit after the United States and were forced for the first time in March 1986 to defer announcement of their 1986/87 budget until the end of the year.

The scrambling by governments to head off the crisis by cutting back on spending, by abandoning dispensable projects, by withdrawing subsidies — especially of water and electricity — and by other economizing measures is leading already to disgruntlement among various groups and individuals. Some Saudi academics complained in 1986 that they had lost about 30 percent of their income because of paying for things for which they never used to pay. But professors are not the only ones who are hurting; bureaucrats, technocrats, businessmen, bankers and others also complain about the financial squeeze and worry about the overall side-effects of the economic slump. Thus, the potential for widespread societal alienation can be serious. This may be particularly true in the case of already disenchanted elements within the various Shi'a communities in the Gulf.

SHI'A VICTIMIZATION

The Gulf is the Shi'a heartland of the world. Out of an estimated 750 million Muslims, about 11 percent are Shi'a. More than half of these are Twelver or Imami Shi'a who live in the Gulf region, forming majorities of the citizen populations in Bahrain, Iran, and Iraq, as well as minorities in Kuwait, Oman, Qatar, Saudi Arabia, and the UAE. Shi'a rule only in Iran, but not even in Bahrain and Iraq where they constitute the majority of the citizen populations. This does not mean necessarily that most Bahraini and Iraqi Shi'a demand Shi'a rule, but they do want a greater share of power in the Sunni-dominated political process. There are radical Shi'a on the fringes of various societies, most particularly in Iraq, who seek to overthrow Sunni rule by violence.

The Shi'a of Iraq have a regional influence partly because they have the largest demographic base. Iraq has the most Shi'a of any Arab country, who number over 8 million, 60 percent of the population. More importantly, the Shi'a of Iraq are the architects of the oldest and the largest network of any underground Arab Shi'a revolutionary movement and organization in the Gulf region. Underground cells or sympathizers of al-Da'wa may be found as far south in the Gulf as the UAE. According to Ayatollah Sayyid Mahdi al-Hakim, son of the late founder Muhsin al-Hakim, al-Da'wa's beginnings date back to "after the [Iraqi] 'revolution' of 1958. Its aims: establishing an Islamic state."[17]

After the Iranian Revolution and the ascendancy of the Shi'a clerics in the polity, the relationship between al-Da'wa and the Iranians developed further. The government of Saddam Hussein claims that before the outbreak of the Iraq-Iran war the Iranian leadership pushed party members and sympathizers to acts of political violence in Iraq and cites this provocation as the chief reason for the Iraqi invasion of Iran. Whether true or not, the Khomeini regime has fully aided and abetted al-Da'wa since the outbreak of the war. In addition, the regime hosts the Supreme Assembly of the Islamic Revolution in Iraq (SAIRI), an organization of Iraqi Shi'a dissidents in Iran. There are over 350,000 Shi'a from Iraq in Iran today, including those Iranian residents of Iraq who were expelled by the Iraqi regime at the outset of the war. The Iranian government openly uses the Iraqi dissidents in its war against Iraq, one example being the military offensive at Hajj 'Umran in the northern front, in which many Iraqi "warriors" (mujahidin) actually participated. But the government of Iran defiantly denies that it uses al-Da'wa Iraqi revolutionaries to perpetrate acts of terrorism in other Arab countries. As seen above, however, most of the suspected terrorists in Kuwait have been identified as Iraqi nationals belonging to this underground party.

None of the facts cited so far — the large number of Iraqi Shi'a, the organization of al-Da'wa, and the Iranian support for it — accounts, however, for Shi'a-sponsored acts of terrorism in the

Gulf region. Rather, these stem from a deep-felt sense of victimization that poisons the social and political atmosphere in Iraq, as it does in varying degrees in other Gulf Arab countries. Among the Gulf Shiʻa the watchword everywhere is "the deprived" (*mahrumin*), a characterization of the conditions of the Shiʻa that even some Saudi Sunnis use in talking about Saudi Shiʻa. The Shiʻa in the Arab states consider themselves as the underdogs. For example, while Saudi Shiʻa believe they have been historically mistreated, the Iraqi Shiʻa believe they have never shared the power and prosperity of the Sunnis, whether under the Ottomans, the British, the monarchy in the past, or the minority Sunni-Baʻthist regime of the Takriti clan at the present time.

The widespread sense of victimization among Shiʻa has been treated in greater detail elsewhere,[18] but it is important to note here the potential for its deepening under the present deteriorating conditions. Every Gulf Arab regime has made genuine efforts in recent years to upgrade standards of living, especially of poorer classes among the Shiʻa. Those who are well off seldom wish to rock the boat and are easily coopted by the Sunni governments. The material betterment of the poor Shiʻa in recent years has not reduced their doctrinal differences with the Sunnis. Nor has it dimmed their bitter memories of historical mistreatment at the hands of Sunni rulers. It has, however, helped somewhat to alleviate past grievances. Present governments must cut corners in order to cope with the consequences of falling oil revenues, but it would be unwise to cut spending on housing, water, electricity and other amenities enjoyed by the Shiʻa.

This discussion of the Shiʻa as a separate group has been intended to emphasize that the process of alienation, for historical, social, political and doctrinal reasons, has gone much further among the Shiʻa as compared with other disaffected groups, both religious and secular. Hence as a factor influencing the climate of radicalism, Shiʻa alienation should receive more empathetic attention. Such attention may help dissipate the myths that have been spun around the very word "Shiʻa". Especially in the United States, mass ignorance about the Shiʻa people has been replaced by mass prejudice rather than knowledge, as evidenced by the automatic equation of "Shiʻa" with "terrorist," "fanatic," and other pejorative appellations. These new stereotypes have effectively reinforced the already heightened anti-American feeling in the region and contribute materially to the fertile environment for radicalism.

ANTI-AMERICANISM

Anti-American sentiment in the Gulf region arose as part of the anti-imperialist movement sweeping across much of the Third World. But it cannot be adequately understood without considering four particular factors. First, unlike the rest of the Third World, the Middle East in general and the Gulf region in particular have been the object of fierce rivalries between the old and the new, and between the great and the super powers ever since Alexander roamed this strategic bridge between Europe and Africa. During the final stages of the fall of the Persian and Islamic empires, Russian and British imperial rivalries dominated the scene until the French and British chopped up the Arab lands for themselves during and after World War I. The discovery of the world's single largest pool of petroleum only increased the Gulf's ancient strategic value to the rest of the world. Foreign political interference, economic domination and military intervention have often accompanied great and super power rivalries and contributed to anti-imperialist feelings, mistrust of foreign powers, and spurts of xenophobic nationalism and Islamic radicalism.

Second, unlike the rest of the Third World, where the process of decolonization has been followed by the realization of the principle of self-determination of peoples, that principle has been realized in the Middle East by only one of the two peoples claiming Palestine as their homeland, that is, the American-supported people of Israel. Palestinian nationalists continue to demand the fulfillment of that principle. But the United States opposes the establishment of any full-fledged Palestinian state, even in the small area of the Israeli-controlled West Bank and Gaza. As a result, some Palestinians and other Arabs and Palestinians — and, since the revolution, some Iranians as well — have set for themselves the goal of setting things right by destroying Israel. These groups claim that the Jewish state is the imperialist obstacle to their goals of Arab unity and Islamic solidarity. The historical anti-imperialist sentiment of the Arabs and Palestinians against the British has thus been transferred to the Americans since 1948 as was that of most Iranians after 1953 when the CIA supported the overthrow of the nationalist government of Dr. Muhammad Musaddiq.

Third, unlike other parts of the Third World, the United States is committed under the Carter Doctrine to intervene in the Gulf by military means, if necessary, to preserve the uninterrupted flow of Gulf oil supplies to world markets, and it has spent billions of dollars on the US Central Command (CENTCOM) since January 1983 in pursuit of this objective. This US policy is repugnant to the politically aware citizens of the Gulf, who perceive CENTCOM as an "interventionist force". This widespread popular perception partly accounts for the insistence by most Gulf Arab regimes on restricting the American military presence to "over the horizon," on having no foreign bases in the region, and on denying the pre-positioning of American military equipment on their soil, despite their dependence on the United States for military buildup and defense.

Fourth, unlike most other parts of the Third World, the United States today is perceived by various segments of the politicized groups in the Gulf region to be too closely identified with conserv-ative and authoritarian Gulf Arab regimes, as it was in the past with the Shah's dictatorial regime. From such a perspective, forty years of the US security relationship with Saudi Arabia, coupled with President Ronald Reagan's so-called corollary which seems to promise American defense of the House of Sa'ud so that it will not suffer a fate similar to that of the Pahlavi dynasty in Iran, offers sufficient proof of the subservience of Saudi Arabia and its GCC partners to the United States.

The astronomical expenditure of these regimes on arms purchases — still largely from the United States despite the rhetoric of diversification and "Saudization" — seems to irritate even those elements of the modernized intelligentsia who may be considered "pro-Western." It may not be widely known in the region that on a per capita basis the arms expenditure of Gulf Arab states is the world's highest, but it does not make much difference insofar as the perception of American dominance in the area is concerned. The United States is perceived to be dominant, and this perception contributes to an environment for radicalism.

Khomeini's perception of the "Great Satan" as the source of the "twin evils" of Zionism and imperialism complicates the problem of anti-American sentiment for the pro-American moderate regimes. It would be a mistake to continue to believe that the public efforts of these regimes to distance themselves from the United States merely reflect popular resentment over the close American identification with Israel. No matter how true this impression might have been before the Iranian Revolution, it is true no longer. Today the Iranian anti-American stance has a significant bearing on the attitudes of these regimes. The establishment of diplomatic relations with the Soviet Union by Oman and the UAE to a considerable extent reflects the desire of these regimes to put their non-alignment rhetoric into practice. They wish simultaneously to neutralize the effects of the anti-American crusade of the Khomeini regime and to respond to anti-American sentiment of the politically aware Arab Gulf citizens in order to assure the survival of their regimes.

THE EFFECTS OF THE IRAN-IRAQ WAR

Has the Iran-Iraq war contributed to the environment of radicalism in the Gulf region? It would be easy to assume that since the war largely reflects the effects of ideological and political radicalism, it has no place in a discussion of the causes of radicalism in the Gulf region.[19] But that would be unwarranted. Having gone on for seven long and bloody years, the war has acquired a life of its own regardless of its causes, and many continue to fear that it might spread to other Gulf states.

The war has contributed to the radicalization of the Gulf political environment in three principal ways. First, it has helped to entrench the extremist faction of the revolutionary movement in power in Iran. The Iraqi invasion played into the hands of the militant Iranians, helping them to consolidate their political control. They had already used the hostage crisis to that end, but the diplomatic and economic sanctions that it entailed had begun to hurt. In seeking a settlement of the dispute with the United States, an Iranian minister conceded that the hostage crisis had been squeezed dry of its usefulness "like an orange." The Iraqi Ba'th, one may add, handed a fresh orange to the Iranian extremists.

The war issue, like the hostage issue, was used in the struggle for power between President Bani-Sadr and his opponents and in the end his dismissal by Ayatollah Khomeini insured the dominance of the radical religious faction. It was no coincidence that the Iranian military successes followed the fall of Bani-Sadr from power and the consolidation of domestic power by his opponents. The hope for moderate politics in Iran had received its first major blow as a result of the fall of the Bazargan government two days after the militant students took over the American Embassy in Tehran. The fall of Bani-Sadr dealt that hope a final blow. By invading Iran, the Iraqi secular radicals hoped to prevent the Iranian religious radicals from consolidating power, but instead they ensured their success. It is anybody's guess whether the Iranian militants would have been as successful in gathering power to themselves without the help of the war, but the war did strengthen their hand and thus has contributed to the overall environment of radicalism in the Gulf region.

Second, the war has aided the process of radicalization of politics in the Gulf region by giving the militant *al-Da'wa* party a new lease on life. The Ba'thist killing of Ayatollah Sayyid Muhammad Baqir al-Sadr — the most respected Iraqi Shi'a *'alim* (learned religious leader) in April 1980 — played into the hands of *al-Da'wa*, the Ba'thists falsely charging that he had been associated with the party.[20] The twin murder of the Iraqi Ayatollah and his sister stirred anger, resentment, and frustration among many Shi'a communities in the Gulf region. Yet, *al-Da'wa*'s ability to use this tragic incident to stir up terrorist acts against the Ba'th within Iraq was limited, especially in the face of the ruthless suppression of the Shi'a dissidents within Iraq.

The start of the war increased *al-Da'wa*'s capability, making it the single most radical and the best organized underground political group in the Arab Gulf countries. On the one hand, the deportation of thousands of Iraqi Shi'a to Iran and other Gulf countries expanded the social base from which *al-Da'wa* could recruit anti-Ba'thist dissidents for its secret cells in the region. On the other hand, the war made it possible for revolutionary Iranians to support *al-Da'wa* and their terrorist activities within Iraq in the same way that revolutionary Ba'thists have supported the Iranian anti-Khomeini *Mujahidin Khalq* faction, led by Masoud Rajavi, in terrorist acts within Iran. As said before, there is little doubt that most of those who have been convicted of participating in terrorist acts in Kuwait have been Iraqi nationals and members of *al-Da'wa*.

Third, the overreaction of the conservative Arab governments to the nightmare of the spillover effects of the war into their territories is threatening what little chance for liberal politics may exist in the Gulf region. Every major sign of the escalation of the war, like every terrorist incident, has resulted in greater tightening of internal security. Despite the denials of government officials, restrictions on travel, on publications, on information and other avenues of freedom of expression and movement have been imposed in the name of security. The fears of Kuwaiti liberals were realized when the Al Sabah family suspended the Kuwaiti National Assembly in July 1986. Their counterparts in Bahrain believe that the Al Khalifa family may well find security a perfect excuse not to consider seriously the idea of reopening that country's suspended parliament, and Saudi liberals see the prospects of establishing a long-promised consultative assembly growing ever dimmer.

The obsession of the conservative Arab regimes individually, or collectively in the GCC, with containing the spread of the war by building up a military deterrence is also of concern to the Gulf liberals. They view the ever-growing arsenals of their countries as a serious threat to their chances for political freedom. They do not deny the need for individual and collective self-defense. But they are skeptical about the usefulness of such a vast military buildup. They point out the small size of their populations, the perforated nature of their societies, and the sectarian divisions in the Arab Gulf states on the one hand, and on the other their excessive dependence on the West, particularly the United States, the inadequacy of trained indigenous manpower, and the diversity of military equipment as arguments against such a buildup. They also express the fear that, to borrow George Washington's words, "overgrown military establishments [are] inauspicious to liberty."

POLICY IMPLICATIONS

To suggest, as I have, that an analysis of terrorism must take into account the environment regardless of motivation in no way implies that terrorism is excusable or justifiable. It only means that one way of coping with terrorism may be to manage the problems that are posed by its environment. Even those who categorically view as criminal all terrorist acts must admit that prevention of crime — no less than punishment of the criminal — is a widely accepted precept in our own society, and that improving the environment of crime is critical to its prevention. In the society of sovereign states — where nations are judges in their own cause and where the day is far off when all acts of terrorism will be considered as criminal and punishable by enforceable international legal norms — we should at least try to limit terrorism by improving its environment. To be sure, the United Nations has finally adopted a resolution that unequivocally condemns as criminal "all acts, methods, and practices of terrorism. " But until this resolution, with which I concur, becomes an enforceable world law, realistically, all that we can hope for is damage limitation. To this end, this study advances the following implications for United States policy in the Gulf.

1. *The United States should resist the temptation to portray Iran as the Great Satan of the Gulf and Islamic radicalism as the twin of Marxism.* Conflict between Iran and the United States or between Islamic fundamentalism and American values and interests is neither inevitable nor permanent, for three major reasons: first, the early appeal of the Iranian revolutionary paradigm among the Arab Gulf people has been diminishing. We risk making it attractive again by fostering an implacable hostility toward Iran, contrary to George Washington's good advice against "permanent, inveterate antipathies to particular nations." Second, regardless of the Iranian example, the resurgence of Islamic fundamentalism has been increasingly challenged by both liberal and conservative secular nationalism in Arab Gulf societies. Third, Iran's new "open door" policy has begun to show definite signs of pragmatic tendencies.

2. *Judging by demographic projections about the rise of an increasingly younger Gulf population by the year 2000, the United States should brace itself for more social and political ferment in the Gulf during the next decade.* The problem of rejuvenation, added to that of expatriates, even though declining in numbers, points to the rise of even more volatile peoples in the GCC countries. A less ubiquitous presence of American expatriates could help the problem of anti-Americanism but not of security, which is posed primarily by Arab expatriates, as evidenced by terrorist incidents. The cutting edge of the rejuvenation problem is the increasing potential for societal alienation.

3. *The current economic recession resulting from the drastic fall of oil revenues may be viewed as either a blessing in disguise or as a new cause of further societal alienation.* To the extent that expenditure-cutting and belt-tightening may put a brake on ostentatious living, waste, and corruption, it may be cause for comfort. However, in my opinion, such an outcome is highly doubtful and we should anticipate increasing disaffection among the young people, who are spoiled and have no stomach for hardship. Most critical is the dissatisfaction of two groups: the modernized middle classes and the Shi'a activists. So far the largesse of the regimes has benefitted both and kept them relatively satisfied, but the austerity measures currently being considered could trigger widespread alienation if fully implemented. If invited to offer advice on coping with these problems, the United States should emphasize the importance of the equitable distribution of wealth, greater efforts at redressing the grievances of the Shi'a communities, and opening up

the political system according to the promises made to the people by the incumbent leaders themselves.

4. *Although the United States has to learn to live with anti-Americanism, we can avoid intensifying it in various ways*. Diplomacy, rather than the use of force, should become the centerpiece of our Gulf policy. Instead of becoming obsessed with punishing the terrorist, we should find ways of rewarding the moderate majority in Gulf societies. Second, all cultural, educational, and informational programs that can help dissipate the misperceptions of the Gulf people about our intentions and actions should be accorded a higher priority than heretofore. Third, to be sure, the Palestinian problem is not at the root of all causes, but it is an undeniable nationalist movement — despite all its factions and feuds and its exploitation by fellow Arabs. Its legitimate aspirations must be seriously addressed by Washington in the enlightened self-interest of both Israel and the United States.

5. *The United States cannot stop the Iran-Iraq war and thus eliminate its radicalizing effects on the Gulf environment, but it can keep its "tilt" toward Iraq strictly curtailed and thus limit the damage*. Once Iran carried the war into Iraq in July 1982, the American tilt seemed inevitable, but half a decade later this imperative must be weighed against other considerations.[21] Too far a tilt toward Iraq may well discourage Iran's emerging qualms about terrorism as evidenced by its unequivocal condemnation of the mining of the Suez Canal and the Red Sea, its capture of the hijackers of the Kuwaiti airliner, its help in freeing the TWA American hostages, and its punishment of one of the hijackers of the Saudi Arabian plane. We must retain the option of establishing a dialogue with Iran sooner or later. Iran retained such an option for months after the disclosure of its secret arms purchases from the United States. But it was forced to suspend this option after the Reagan Administration increased its military presence in the Gulf.

6. *The United States should continue to aid the GCC states in their efforts to create a credible military deterrence, but it should resist the temptation to embrace the group too closely*. To the Gulf liberals, the deepening dependence on American arms is detrimental not only to the political independence of their countries but to their personal liberty. Every major escalation in the war and every terrorist incident has been followed by tighter restrictions on the freedoms of movement and expression. To the extent that these restrictions choke off peaceful dissent, they are believed to increase

the attraction of political violence as the only recourse for bringing about political change.

There is no easy or quick way to eliminate terrorism, but implementation of the above suggestions may help contain the environment of radicalism in the Gulf region. The majority of the people of the area are moderate; only a minority are radical. Not all radicals are terrorists — but all terrorists are radical. The real challenge ahead is how to prevent today's moderates from becoming tomorrow's radicals.

NOTES

1. See US Department of State, Bureau of Public Affairs, *International Terrorism*, Selected Documents, No. 24 (Washington, n.d.).

2. The other targets included the headquarters of American Raytheon Company and the apartment building housing the company's employees, the airport control tower, the Ministry of Electricity and Water building, the Passport Office, and a major petrochemical and refining complex. A Kuwaiti court tried 25 defendants on March 27, 1984. Five were acquitted of involvement in the bombings; six were sentenced to death, three of whom were tried in absentia; seven to life imprisonment, four of whom were tried in absentia; four to 15 years; one to 10 years; and two to 5 years. None of the accused was Iranian. Out of a group of 25, 17 were Iraqis, three were Lebanese, three were Kuwaiti, and two were stateless.

3. Confronted by an Iranian fighter plane upon entering Iranian airspace, the pilot of the Kuwaiti plane claimed that he was running out of fuel, and he was permitted to land at Tehran airport. Iranian officials condemned the hijacking and the killing of two Americans on board the plane and eventually Iranian troops stormed the plane, captured the hijackers and freed the remaining passengers. Iranian judicial authorities promised to put the hijackers on trial and punish them for their crimes.

4. US *Foreign Broadcast Information Service — Daily Report: Middle East and Africa*, Vol. V, No. 102, 28 May 1985 (hereafter, FBIS-MEA-V). Kuwaiti security authorities said on May 26 that they had identified the Iraqi perpetrator of the attack after "assembling pieces of his fingers and examining his fingerprints." Ibid., No. 103, May 29, 1985. The Iraqi ambassador to Kuwait, when confronted with the reports that the culprit was a member of the Iraqi *al-Da'wa* Party, stated flatly that "the party to which the criminal belongs is an Iranian party 100 per cent." Ibid. Speaking "frankly," the newspaper *al-Ra'i al-'Aam* hinted that the "criminal act" against the amir represented the peak of Iranian terror. With some irony, it also reported that the Iranian chargé d'affaires had denounced the incident, sent a bouquet of flowers to the amir, and extended "congratulations" to him on his escape. It then added that this "stand by Iran and its supporters cannot deceive anybody." Ibid. It was subsequently reported that the Kuwaiti security authorities had arrested 20 persons

accused of being connected with the attack and that three of them had admitted their guilt.

5. This consensus refers to the activities of the organization only outside of Egypt, where there is an Islamic faction by the same name. The respected *Middle East Economic Digest*, for example, seems to consider the Islamic Jihad and *al-Da'wa* as two different organizations. It said at the time of the incident that the latter's "aims are broadly similar to those of Islamic Jihad and it is believed there may be some organizational links between the two groups." *Middle East Economic Digest (MEED), June 1, 1985.*

6. Ibid., June 15, 1985.

7. It was also believed that the victims of the incident were from a variety of nations, including 18 Kuwaitis, 1 citizen from the United Arab Emirates (UAE), 1 Iranian, 2 Egyptians, 2 Iraqis, and others of undetermined national origins. Among the Kuwaiti casualties was a senior Interior Ministry official.

8. The newspaper said in part that "the documents [of the anti-Khomeini Iranian national resistance movement] frankly refer to an Iranian scheme with regard to the GCC countries and frankly provide for the declaration of something resembling war on these countries." FBIS-MEA-V, No. 134, July 12, 1985.

9. Emphasis in the original. William Regis Farrell, *The US Government Response to Terrorism: In Search of an Effective Strategy* (Boulder, Colorado: Westview Press, 1982), p. 12.

10. See R.K. Ramazani, "Iran's Islamic Revolution and the Persian Gulf," *Current History*, No. 498 (January 1985), pp. 5-8 and 40-41.

11. Computed on the basis of data in United Nations, Department of International Economic and Social Affairs, *Demographic Indicators of Countries: Estimates and Projections as Assessed in 1980*, ST/ESA/SER.A/82 (New York: United Nations, 1982), pp. 60-61, 250-251, 304-305, 316-317, 320-321, 324-325 and 328-337.

12. FBIS-MEA-V, No. 030, 13 February 1984.

13. See Table 7 in R.K. Ramazani, *Revolutionary Iran: Challenge and Response in the Middle East* (Baltimore: Johns Hopkins University Press, 1986), p. 26.

14. The plotters of the aborted coup in Bahrain included four different nationalities. Out of a total of 73 arrested, there were 60 Bahrainis, 11 Saudis, one Omani and one Kuwaiti. In the case of the multiple bombings in Kuwait, most of the 25 terrorists convicted were Iraqi nationals. At least 13 were known to be Iraqi, three Lebanese, and three Kuwaiti, while the nationalities of the suspects at large were not established.

15. See R.K. Ramazani, "Iran's Revolution in Perspective", Z. Michael Szaz, project director, *The Impact of the Iranian Events upon Persian Gulf & United States Security* (Washington: American Foreign Policy Institute, 1979) pp. 19-37; idem, "Iran's Foreign Policy: Perspectives and Projections," in US Congress, Joint Economic Committee, *Economic Consequences of the Revolution in Iran; A Compendium of Papers* (Washington: USGPO, 1979), pp. 65-97; and a slightly modified version with the same title in Enver M. Koury and Charles G. MacDonald, *Revolution in Iran: A Reappraisal* (Hyattsville, MD: Institute of Middle

Eastern and North African Affairs, 1982), pp. 9-41; idem, "Iran's Revolution: Patterns, Problems and Prospects," *International Affairs* (London), Vol. 56, No. 3 (Summer 1980), pp. 443-457; idem, *The United States and Iran: The Patterns of Influence* (New York: Praeger, 1982); and idem, *Revolutionary Iran: Challenge and Response in the Middle East* (Baltimore: The Johns Hopkins University Press, 1986).

16. Over the years I have been struck, during various visits to the Gulf, by the intense interest of the Arabs in the Iranian Revolution. For example, on my last visit to the Gulf in 1986, I was asked for interviews by two major Kuwaiti publications. For the text of these interviews, see *al-Anba'*, February 15, 1986, and *al-Mujtam'a* magazine, March 11, 1986, pp. 29-33. On the theme of no spread of Iranian-type revolutions in the rest of the Gulf, see also R.K. Ramazani, "America and the Gulf: Beyond Peace and Security," *Middle East Insight*, (January/February, 1982), pp. 2-9.

17. See R.K. Ramazani, "Shi'ism in the Persian Gulf," in Juan R.I. Cole and Nikki R. Keddie, eds., *Shi'ism and Social Protest* (New Haven: Yale University Press, 1986), pp. 30-54.

18. Ibid.

19. See the source Table 7 of Ramazani, *Revolutionary Iran*, p. 26.

20. See H. Batatu, "Iraq's Underground Shi'a Movements: Characteristics, Causes and Prospects," *Middle East Journal*, Vol. 35, No. 4 (Autumn 1981), pp. 578-594.

21. These other considerations are discussed in detail in R.K. Ramazani, "Iran: Burying the Hatchet," *Foreign Policy*, No. 60 (Fall 1985), pp. 52-74.

Part III:
Gulf States in Transition

Introduction

At the root of foreign policy and its formulation are the individual players, local influences, and domestic national politics of the nation-state. Indeed, one can argue that the foreign policy of any particular Gulf state often, depending on the issue at stake, is the international expression of internal and local interests.

The three country studies in this section are illustrative of the political realities, influences, and imperatives which guide those whose task is the governance of Gulf polities. The first is the Sultanate of Oman, examined by Professor Dale F. Eickelman. Set off from the rest of the Gulf and the Arabian Peninsula by topography, geography, and a distinctive historical experience, Oman has developed a divergent and unique perspective. Its mountain fastness gave refuge to the small sect of Ibadi Islam, and the interior long remained closed to outsiders. At the same time, its people are heirs to a long and proud seafaring tradition, and their ancestors ventured not only north into the Gulf, but also south toward Africa and east toward the Asian subcontinent and points farther east.

For this reason, Oman is perhaps the Gulf state with the greatest cosmopolitan experience and history. How does its distinct character affect its perception of its regional role? How will Sultan Qaboos's push toward modernity change the country and its people? As a comparative political study, how do the leaders in the urban capital of Muscat interact with the tribal shaykhs and the villagers of the less-developed interior? And, most importantly, where is Oman's leadership likely to guide it in the years ahead, and how will the direction chosen affect the country's foreign policy?

If Oman has looked outward for much of its history, the Kingdom of Saudi Arabia has drawn its sustenance and identity from its own internal fundamental traditions. Saudi Arabia serves as the guardian of Islam's two holiest shrines in Mecca and Medina. As Dr. David E. Long points out, this responsibility has led Saudi leaders to view themselves as the anointed protectors not only of the holy places, but also of Islam and its traditions. The Saudis have come to feel that their country has a special duty of leadership within the Islamic community, as well as to foster and strive for greater present-day Arab unity.

Dr. Long also notes the traditional insularity of the Saudis and its continuing impact on Saudi politics. By religious and tribal tradition, the Saudi leadership seeks to make decisions by consensus. This is clearly shown in domestic policy-making, but the absence of a clear-cut policy toward their smaller Gulf neighbors in the Gulf often results in an imperious attitude, and sometimes simply paternalism.

By dint of Saudi Arabia's economic and political clout, Saudi perceptions and attitudes will play a preponderant role in shaping regional decisions and actions in the years ahead, particularly in the deliberations of the Gulf Cooperation Council. In assessing the probable Saudi reaction to a specific problem, analysts will need to take into account the Saudi penchant to stand above or to one side of an issue, unless forced by circumstances to take a direct role.

When a crisis arises or a decision must be made, will the Saudis take the initiative, or leave it to others to take the first step? To what extent will they utilize their still-significant economic power to resolve regional issues? Will they be willing to take quick action when confronted by a dangerous situation, as in future developments associated with the Iran-Iraq war, or will they seek to build a consensus before acting, and thereby effectively block a timely response? Will Saudi policy formulation continue to be bound by tradition, and, if so, for how long? How extensive will the influence of younger generations of Western-educated technocrats be?

Finally, Dr. J.E. Peterson takes a close look at the United Arab Emirates (UAE), which in some ways is the quintessential example of the push toward modernity in the Gulf. The UAE's federal structure, and the problems and issues inherent in any federalist experiment, mirrors in many respects the larger movement toward regional cooperation in the GCC. Economically, the UAE displays a broad spectrum from oil-rich Abu Dhabi, to the relatively poor and uninfluential member states of al-Fujayra, 'Ajman, and Umm al-Qaywayn. Politically, the UAE remains precariously balanced between deepening federal integration and the jealously guarded sovereignty of its seven members. It has perhaps advanced further and faster than any other Gulf country in fewer years, transformed from somnolent villages to a modern nation-state.

Using the UAE as a case study, then, how has the Gulf changed in recent years, and in what new directions can we expect its nascent nation-states to go? What will be the effect of the passing of the torch from the older generation of traditional shaykhs to the younger technocratic leaders of today and tomorrow? How will the inevitable tensions between the desire to retain traditional roots and the march forward to economic development and political transformation be played out? And how will these tensions and conflicts affect the federal experiments, both at the national level in the UAE and at the regional level in the GCC?

The Gulf region has changed drastically and significantly in the last few decades. An inevitable and gradual evolution seems likely to continue and Gulf leaders will find it necessary to adapt policies in response to the various shifting tides and fortunes, both from within and from outside, that affect the region. In the internal political structures of these three countries and in their formulation of foreign-policy processes, the forces, influences and players shaping the Gulf of tomorrow can be discerned at work today.

Map 4: Oman

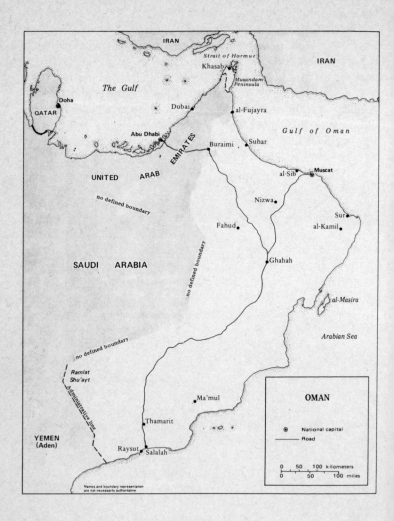

8

Oman's Next Generation: Challenges and Prospects

Dale F. Eickelman

November 1985 marked the fifteenth anniversary of the coming to power of Sultan Qaboos bin Sa'id. Oman's "new era," as the period of Qaboos's reign is known, is just past the midway point to the twenty-first century. This is an appropriate time to assess the accomplishments to date and to estimate how the delicate balance of domestic, regional, and global concerns will shape Oman's critical choices and probable trajectory into the next century.

A decade and a half is not an unusually long time span for those interested in the intersection of policy and disciplines such as social anthropology. The educational changes implemented in the early 1970s are only now beginning to have a major social and political impact. Similarly, current decisions affecting the military, the bureaucracy, and economic development, not to mention the other forms of social and political development that cannot be readily elaborated in five-year plans, will have their sharpest impact at a point beyond the shorter-term horizon appropriate to economic planners. Long-term shifts in political expectations are often just over the horizon of politicians and policy analysts, but they are nonetheless just as real as the need for improved schooling and communications. Such shifts are difficult to define and identify, especially when there is no setting for unofficial public political expression, but the main contours of such shifts are nonetheless discernible. This essay explores how present trends can be assessed to delineate Oman's likely main challenges over the coming two decades.

To use a phrase from an ill-timed toast offered in late 1977 to the head of state of a neighboring Gulf country, Oman can be thought of as "an island of stability in a turbulent corner of the world."[1] The fact that one can focus upon long-term trends and prospects and not upon immediate internal or external threats is in itself an implicit credit to the country's overall effective management and, of course, to good fortune. Like the state to which the 1977 toast alluded, Oman's major challenges over the next fifteen years will most likely be internal rather than external. The principal challenge is that of changing popular political expectations, especially among the rapidly growing cadres of youth who have gone through the civilian educational system or its military counterpart. The first waves of youth who began their studies entirely in the "new era" only entered the secondary school cycle in 1979-80.[2] For Oman's educated youth, as well as for many of the younger cadres in both the military and civilian government employment, the hardships of the pre-1970 era so vivid to their elders are at best a dim memory. The younger generation's changing expectations have been accelerated by the ruler's firm commitment to education for all citizens.

Oman's rapidly growing population forms a backdrop against which political and social trends must be interpreted. No census has yet been conducted in the sultanate, but the best estimates are that its population has more than doubled from 450,000 in 1971 to at least 1,008,000 in 1985, of which 20.7 percent or 219,000 are foreign, a low proportion for the labor-hungry Gulf.[3] Oman's population will likely double again by the turn of the century.[4] At least half the citizen population is under the age of fifteen and thus are fully the children of the new era.

These population estimates have no direct political correlations in themselves, except to demonstrate that Oman shares the demographic characteristics of most Third World countries. Unlike many countries, however, Oman also has considerable natural resources. Yet even if revenues from these resources continue to be applied substantially to infrastructural development, education, health and welfare, spending cannot in itself guarantee political and social stability. Only the continued responsiveness of Oman's political elite to the changing expectations of key elements of Omani society will do so.

Oman's stability to date is the direct result of sustained and responsible political effort. In July 1970, the present ruler drew his country back from the precipice of political and military collapse. Sultan Qaboos and his key advisers, both in and out of government, have on the whole admirably managed the country through a period of regional instability and dizzying economic and demographic growth, factors which in themselves have proved to be highly destabilizing elsewhere. The first phase of the "new era" is now nearing an end. Most of the bridges, roads, hospitals, schools, and even flyovers have been built or are nearing completion, and the infrastructure for a modern military is also in place. The $700-million Sultan Qaboos University opened in September 1986.

The fifteenth anniversary of the new era brought with it panegyrics that were not always specific in content. The genuine accomplishments of the Sultan and the sultanate become much more apparent when the record of achievement is seen in full light of the rough edges and occasional near-misses experienced by Oman and the other states of the region. The following unorthodox account of the new era and of the events leading to it offers more concrete grounds for optimism toward the decades ahead.

THE FIRST FIFTEEN YEARS

The challenges that Oman has had to face in recent decades have in many ways been more serious than those confronted by most of its immediate neighbors. In 1957, British assistance was requested to suppress a rebellion in the country's northern interior.[5] Although the military threat there virtually ceased by 1962, a separate and ultimately more threatening insurgency began in the southern province of Dhufar in 1965. It seriously escalated after the collapse of British rule in Aden in 1967 provided rebels with cross-border sanctuary and support. By mid-1970, sultanate authority in the south barely extended beyond Salala's barbed wire enclosure, and rebel attacks had also begun in the north. The sultanate's security forces faced a rapidly deteriorating situation. Although revenues from oil exports had begun in 1967 and plans were underway for development, the former ruler was perceived as moving much too slowly to satisfy changing Omani expectations of what a ruler should do. This perception of inertia was a major contributing factor in his downfall. Tribal leaders, the merchant community, migrant Omani workers elsewhere in the Gulf and key members of the royal family had either entered into opposition or had ceased to offer active support.

Immediately after Qaboos's accession, bold plans for reform, the development of infrastructure, education and health services were announced and enthusiastically received. Omanis recognized immediately that a major change was underway. On the military front, the declaration of an amnesty for surrendered enemy personnel set a tone for reconciliation that shaped the difficult campaigns of the next five years. Complementary to the counter-insurgency campaign, development funds were poured into the south and several talented ex-rebels were given progressively more significant positions of responsibility. The prolonged stays of the sultan in Dhufar and his own Dhufari origins — the queen mother is from the Bayt Ma'ashani section of the Qara tribe — reaffirm Dhufar's integral role in Oman. Dhufaris are hard to please politically; winning their confidence is one of Qaboos's major personal achievements. Dhufaris not infrequently point out that no other member of the royal family has managed to win their confidence.

The sultan declared the war over in December 1975. Subsequently, only minor skirmishes occasionally tested Omani resolve, such as the brief incursions into Oman by South Yemeni forces and foreign oil survey teams on three occasions in 1981.[6] Soon the major problem became sporadic feuding among units of the irregular tribal forces (*firqat*) that had rallied to Qaboos. Through military skill, a delicate management of regional alliances and careful attention to domestic politics, Oman became one of the few countries of the world to defeat a major Communist-backed insurgency.

Oman's successes in the 1970s were hard won. Military coups, including palace coups, are inherently destabilizing, as comparative experience elsewhere repeatedly has demonstrated. Even as the armed forces underwent major expansion — growing from a mere 2,500 at the time of the coup to 12,500 by mid-1974 and 24,000 by 1984,[7] there was no major political dissent. Massive and rapid economic modernization, especially when accompanied by rapid population growth, has an equal potential for destabilization. Oman's population rapidly swelled in the early 1970s as Omani workers and students returned from other Gulf states and from former Omani possessions in East Africa. The ebullient early years of the new era saw strikes — of oil workers, dockers, and others — and an abortive plot against the government in late 1971. From the start, a decision was made to use the police instead of the military in curbing potential domestic unrest, a policy of moderation which set a positive tone for the new era.[8] Indeed, as one senior official recalled with some pride, one of the first labor strikes ever in the Arab Gulf was in former Sultan Sa'id's Customs Department in 1949, instigated by students who had returned from studies in Iraq.[9] In the main, through restraint, skill, and no small element of luck, these threats were competently managed and the energies of the country were channeled primarily toward its rapid development.

As in any country engaged in massive and rapid development, expenditures were hard to control in the early years, leading a US military mission in the early 1970s to note, in classic Washington obliquity, "that enormous expenditures for luxury items made it difficult to ask the Saudis to underwrite 'war' deficits."[10] Problems in subsequent years included near bankruptcy in 1975 due to a lack of sound fiscal control over the authorization and management of government projects and expenditures, and a decline in revenue.[11] By 1981, a growing perception of financial irregularities among certain officials and advisers reached an evident peak and occasioned comment both among civilians and the military.[12] In part as a result of modern education and more extensive inter-regional contacts than had existed in earlier years, knowledge of such activities was more widespread than in the past.

Corrective action was taken, indicating recognition of the problem at the highest level of government. If efforts to eliminate problems through a stroke of the legislative pen proved futile, at least the difficulty of balancing the need to retain a talented senior cadre in government with allowing them the same commercial opportunities available to those outside government without arousing widespread resentment was firmly recognized.[13] In mid-December 1985, a senior official was abruptly dismissed because his evident abuse of authority in the name of the palace caused sustained civilian complaints and concern among junior officers that the official, nominally a military officer, was tarnishing the reputation of the military. The dismissal suggests that the channels of communication from ordinary Omanis to the very top remain intact.[14] Once again, a signal appropriate to the changed expectations of the "new era" was sent to government officials and those holding high office.

To put matters in perspective, growing concern with fraud in US defense contracting, and the mundane but lucrative contracting activities of officials and party leaders in New York City documented in 1986 and 1987 serve as reminders that problems of abuse of office are not unique to Oman. It is the changing popular threshold of perceived unjust privilege or use of influence that is at issue, especially on the part of students and young officers imbued with the formal statements of civic responsibility embodied in their education and training, and in their interpretations of religious obligation.[15]

Planning and development

A problem common to Oman and to all developing countries is the disparity in development between the capital area and outlying regions. Numerous measures, both large and appropriately small, have incrementally changed the fabric of rural Omani society in recent years. For those who have observed the Omani interior at first hand, transformations in communications, health facilities, schooling, and the provision of multiple other services have been impressive. For the most part these transformations have constructively involved persons from the local communities themselves and have provided employment and small-scale commercial opportunities. Such modest measures as improved supplies of drinking water and regular refuse collection may seem minimal in importance, but sustained efforts on such modest scales have substantially improved the conditions of life in the small towns and oases of the Omani interior as much as the impressive tarmac roads built by multinational firms.

Similarly, many ministries have made significant efforts in decentralizing key functions, in part due to recommendations offered by the State Consultative Council. This decentralization, however tentative to date, checks the growth of a bureaucratic encephalitis, in which all decisions must be negotiated in the capital and at the top. Presumably the establishment in January 1985 of a new Ministry of Regional Municipalities, headed by an activist military officer, is another indication of an intensified concern for regional development.

For the most inaccessible areas, including the strategically significant Musandam province and the region around Buraimi, special government organizations were established when it became apparent that the logistics of development were for the moment beyond the capacity of the existing administrative apparatus. The consulting and management firm involved in these sensitive tasks has proven to be a quick understudy. Even Omanis who resent a strong foreign presence grudgingly acknowledge its achievements in the face of arduous circumstances. A few false steps in local governmental relations in the early 1980s, in some cases due to inherited existing projects, were rapidly corrected. The ability of the Omani government to manage major developmental and administrative innovation without creating local political disruption is a major indicator of continued political health.

The Third Five-Year Plan (1986-1990) marks a major transition for Oman. In managerial terms, the major "turnkey" infrastructural projects of prior years are in some respects easier to undertake than projects having a direct impact upon the livelihoods of large numbers of persons. The emphasis appears geared to long-term strategies to develop non-oil resources upon which the country can rely when oil runs out. Hence studies and projects are increasingly oriented to agriculture, fisheries, water resources, and light industry. Some 60 per cent of the national workforce remains in the inefficient, rapidly declining "traditional" agricultural sector, upon which a large part of the population still depends for its livelihood. Any effort to deal with this sector of the population requires not outside specialists, who can do little more than prepare ethnographic studies to facilitate local efforts, but highly trained local teams with the support both of the government and the local population.

In 1975, manufacturing accounted for only 0.3 per cent of the GDP; in 1985 its share had risen to 3.03 per cent. Significant increases have been registered in fishing (which by 1985 accounted for 40 per cent of non-oil exports), copper (exported since 1983), and flour.[16] Of even more significance, long-term surveys are underway of water resources, so that long-term agricultural policy can be formulated that is both ecologically sound and economically feasible.[17] For business and commerce, a recent analysis of Oman's commercial law suggests that stable and effective mechanisms for the resolution of commercial disputes have developed over the last decade, providing a firm basis for private foreign participation in the economy.[18]

In a recent interview, an Omani minister optimistically claimed that Oman will not experience the uncontrolled growth of its capital and the expense of depopulating outlying regions. Because of improvements in rural regions, "migration from the interior had already been checked."[19] If so, then Oman is the only country in the world where such population movements have been effectively checked. As long-term planning shifts to projects involving Oman's hinterlands, it is increasingly important that an accurate census be taken and widely disseminated in order to facilitate development and the allocation of available resources. The difficulties in realistic planning stemming from the lack of such data have been noted already in prior economic studies.[20] Detailed studies of Musandam and Buraimi have been carried out, as has an economic census of al-Hamra, an oasis of the northern interior.[21]

Plans are now underway for the first nationwide census. The dissemination of its results on a timely and unrestricted basis will facilitate realistic planning and the ability to respond quickly to the reorientations that will inevitably be generated by shifting economic conditions and altered social aspirations.

Oman's growth and stability depend for the foreseeable future upon oil revenues. Hydrocarbons accounted for at least 46 per cent of GDP in 1984, down from 67 per cent in 1975, but remain the single most important source of government revenues. In the late 1970s, estimates were that Oman's oil would run out in the late 1990s. Since then, however, proven reserves have doubled to 4 billion barrels. To compensate for declining oil prices, Oman's oil production, limited to 400,000 bd in spring 1983, has increased gradually to nearly 600,000 bd, a figure reached in 1987 and which most likely will be held constant throughout the Third Five-Year Plan, or until Oman's hydrocarbon infrastructure can be modified to accommodate increased production.[22] For the time being, an uncontrolled economic decline is unlikely. More than other states in the region, Oman appears to have shown restraint in its spending patterns since the start of the current oil price wars and since mid-1985 has made significant cutbacks in government spending and commitments in all sectors, including defense. It also has aggressively increased its market share to avoid budget shortfalls. Both the private and public sectors in Oman continue to have a reputation among businessmen and bankers for paying bills on time. In spite of heavy spending cutbacks, it appears likely that the economic expectations of the population will continue to be met, albeit on a more modest scale.

Foreign policy and regional security

From a condition of almost total regional and international isolation in 1971, Oman has skillfully emerged as an effective voice for moderate Arab states. It has also managed quietly to settle or table border disputes with several of its neighbors, including the United Arab Emirates, where "boundary" issues are for all practical purposes resolved primarily on the basis of the allegiance of groups rather than demarcated territory, an accepted local procedure admittedly complicated by the need to delineate specific boundaries for the purposes of inland and offshore oil exploration.[23] Oman has played an active role in the Gulf Cooperation Council. It also has openly and consistently supported Egypt and the United States in seeking a peace settlement in the Middle East, and has shared US concern over the potential threat of Soviet intervention in the Gulf.

Yet even prior to the fall of the Shah, Oman's policy was to avoid close identification with US military concerns, a policy acknowledged by at least some elements of the US diplomatic and security establishment to be in Oman's long-term interests. Ever since the negotiations over American use of facilities in Oman in 1980, some elements of the US government have sought an expanded US presence and control. These initiatives have been firmly deflected by Omani policy-makers, sensitive as are some of their American counterparts to the long-term negative political consequences of a heightened American presence.

The process of rapprochement with the People's Democratic Republic of Yemen (PDRY), initiated in November 1982 with an agreement to resolve the border dispute between the two countries, gathered pace with the official designation of non-resident ambassadors in September 1985 and the July 1986 agreement in principle to exchange resident ambassadors, together with Oman's offer to assist PDRY in economic development. These moves appear to formalize a carefully negotiated regional detente. PDRY's "international good neighbor" policy was immediately reaffirmed by the "collective leadership" which assumed authority following the bloody factional struggle of January 1986.[24]

In general, the PDRY suggests an alternate course that Dhufar might have followed had Sultan Qaboos's policies of ending the Dhufar rebellion in the early 1970s not been successful. An incisive analysis of political, social, and administrative problems in the Arab world's only avowedly Marxist government suggests an internal situation remarkably similar to Dhufar until recent years: a weak administrative structure of uncertain scope and a pervasive tribal structure and leadership capable of blunting or opposing undesired governmental initiatives.[25] Writing before the recent bloody confrontations in PDRY, one observer suggests that the large presence of Soviet-bloc advisers in the PDRY administration may have added "more fuel to government measures for social change," an inference confirmed in part by heavy damage to the Soviet Embassy complex by troops loyal to the ousted president.[26] Whether the number of Soviet advisers is 5,000, of whom 25 per cent are in military functions, together with 16,000 Soviet bloc personnel, including Cubans, a seemingly inflated figure attributed to

Omani and British intelligence sources,[27] or only 1,000 Soviet military advisers together with 500 Cubans and security specialists from East Germany,[28] Yemeni popular and elite sensitivity to perceived foreign "management" unquestionably rivals that of its neighbor to the north.

Omani recognition of the Soviet Union after two years of high-level contacts is in many ways less important than the timing of the initiative, formally announced on September 26, 1985. Saudi Arabia had just announced a major order for aircraft from the United Kingdom, an agreement unimpeded by the domestic political constraints which hampered American efforts to secure the contract. Likewise, the American administration's efforts to supply aircraft to Jordan continued to be blocked by Congress. The perception has grown among Gulf Arab states that the American foreign-policy establishment is capable of dealing only with one Middle Eastern issue at a time, usually the Arab-Israeli dispute, although the Gulf states were equally concerned with developing an effective "peace process" for the Iran-Iraq war.

Recognition of the Soviet Union reaffirmed that Oman, while retaining its ties with the United States, was able to pursue an independent policy. Although the countries of the region do not necessarily assume that the Soviet Union has changed its long-term aims, the Omani move was based in part upon the assessment that current Soviet policy no longer supports destabilization of the countries of the region and that the Soviet Union had encouraged states allied with it, notably the PDRY, to adopt moderate policies toward neighboring states.[29] Diplomatic ties with the Soviet Union, not currently linked to an exchange of resident ambassadors, firmly signaled Oman's ability to pursue an independent policy. Coming at the opening of the UN General Assembly and just shortly before the GCC summit, the move made Oman a country to be reckoned with in terms of regional politics. Like other Arab moderate states, Oman feels that the Soviets may have a constructive role to play in securing regional stability, particularly in resolving the Iran-Iraq war. Oman has made a point, and perhaps its diplomatic moves will now be read by the United States and other Western states with more consummate care. Available evidence suggests that the move has been welcomed with enthusiasm by younger, educated Omanis, the emerging domestic lobby which sultanate leadership is beginning to take into account.

THE NEXT TWENTY YEARS

Key internal developments that will significantly influence the sultanate over the next two decades in large part can be read from developments already underway in the spheres of education, the military, commerce, and leadership at the top.

Education

Oman's record of education is impressive. For all practical purposes, education prior to 1970 was confined to a narrow band of the elite both for advanced religious education in the interior[30] and a limited "modern" schooling available in Salala and Muscat, including technical training offered by Petroleum Development (Oman). From 25,000 students at all levels in government schools in 1972-1973, there were 142,000 in 1982-1983 and 195,000 in 1984-1985. In 1975-1976, a mere thirty-two students completed the full cycle of secondary education. By the 1983-1984 academic year, 1,088 students had done so. In 1976-1977 only 509 Omani students were studying abroad. There were 2,315 by the 1984-1985 academic year.[31]

Numbers alone do not indicate the significant qualitative change that has occurred. Until 1982-1983, the majority of students to complete higher education were from the capital area. Many had begun the educational cycle prior to 1970 or outside of Oman. As of 1982-1983, the first large numbers of graduating secondary school students from all economic levels and regions of the country began to receive higher educations abroad. These students are returning in increasingly large numbers. It is not clear how they will be absorbed into meaningful public sector employment, which to date has accommodated most returning graduates. The private sector, for its part, continues to prefer foreign managerial and technical talent.

Students from rural areas and from less wealthy families tend to have different perceptions of government and of religiosity than do those from the capital area. By and large, narrow sectarian identity among these youth has eroded in favor of a more general commitment to Islamic principles. Conflict is now much more likely to be generational than sectarian. Nonetheless, the new generation in Oman, as elsewhere in the Arab world, may find new forms of sectarian identity attractive if these are seen to be useful in securing a

167

political voice. As in other Muslim countries, the new generation of Omani youth responds less readily to government-appointed religious scholars than to their own ability to interpret religious texts. After all, the writings of Sayyid Qutb are more readily available in Austin, Columbus, Edinburgh, Exeter, and Tempe, than in Baghdad, Damascus, and Riyadh.

Many of these students would like to see their understanding of Islamic principles applied to the conduct of government affairs. Such a commitment to Islamic identity can be a powerful force in building modern Oman and can be a potentially constructive force. This issue is not merely one of manpower planning, but one of a changing attitude toward state authority.[32]

The military

The best guide to understanding the organizational consequences of Omanization and the emergence of a younger, educated generation for the Omani polity is the Sultan's Armed Forces (SAF), Oman's oldest and largest employer. Even before 1970, the army introduced basic literacy courses for recruits, a program which expanded significantly in subsequent years. For young men in many remote villages, the army's outstanding basic literacy program, staffed primarily by Omani teachers unlike the civilian schools, continues to be a significant means of acquiring literacy. Graduates of this program are often the first literate persons in their villages. In spite of the youth of these recruits, they often assume a leading role in representing their villages to the government and in demanding expanded services such as schools and roads. They also appear to take the army's citizenship lessons seriously, often commenting pointedly upon the ostentatious life styles of some senior officials when local officials plead the lack of resources to provide each village with schools or with transport to them.

Omanization of the armed forces began in earnest in the early 1980s (see Table 8.1), thus bringing to an end dissatisfaction among junior officers with a perceived continued control by foreign officers. The combined figures for Omanization of the three branches of the military do not at first appear dramatic: 51 per cent of officers were Omani in 1980, 57 per cent by 1982, 62 per cent by 1985. If the army is taken by itself, however, the figure approaches 85 per cent, and British advisers claim that the process would have been more rapid had the army not undergone a major re-equipment over the last few years.

Because of in-service training programs, the army possesses a number of officers from the country's interior and from all economic classes, and promotion is tied closely to ability and merit.[33] Foreign and Omani officers acknowledge that the objective, competitive evaluation of subordinates was a difficult skill to inculcate, given Omani cultural values and the preference to avoid direct competition. Omani officers, especially the younger ones who have generally benefited more from higher standards of education and training than their seniors, have proven to be remarkably quick understudies. One officer trained at the British Army's Armoured School at Bobington was given the unusual honor of being invited back as an instructor; an Omani naval officer has taken the "full" course of instruction at Greenwich instead of the abbreviated course generally offered to foreign officer candidates.

The commander of the Land Forces is an Omani from Nizwa, as are the commanders of every regiment, including technical ones such as armor, training, and engineers. Omanization, in other words, is not ornamental and is proceeding apace in staff appointments. The skills needed to evaluate order of battle, threat perception, and the strengths and limitations of equipment and formations of Omani forces and of potential adversaries appear to be readily acquired. Within the next two years, the process of Omanization should be nearly complete except for technical appointments in the army. Omanization of the air force, navy, and civilian appointments in the Ministry of Defense should likewise soon accelerate.

At the beginning of the process of Omanization, some military observers asserted that Omanis had a limited capacity to absorb technical training and managerial skills. It is useful to recall that a similar "wisdom" prevailed prior to nationalization of the Suez Canal. Received European opinion was that Egyptians could not match their European predecessors in quality and skill. Egyptians did so rapidly. In the case of Oman, appropriate credit must be given to the high caliber of seconded British officers, especially in the army, who have facilitated this task, and to the policy guidelines set by key Omanis, especially the sultan, who have facilitated Omanization. The same process has been initiated in many civilian ministries, although Omanization of the Ministry of Education, the largest employer of civilian government personnel, remains a formidable challenge. Likewise in the private sector, 70 per cent of the work force continues to be foreign and the proportion is not

Table 8.1: Nationality of Sultan's armed forces officers, 1980-1985

Year	Omani	Per cent	British (a)	Per cent	Total
1980	482	51%	461	49%	943
1982	636	57%	475	43%	1,111
1985	1,153	62%	713	38%	1,866

Note:
a. Includes a small number of other foreign officers, primarily in logistics (Pakistani) and medical (Indian) capacities.

Sources: Anthony H. Cordesman, *The Gulf and the Search for Strategic Stability* (Boulder: Westview Press, 1984), table 15.6; J.E. Peterson, "American Policy in the Gulf and the Sultanate of Oman,"*American-Arab Affairs*, No. 8 (Spring 1984), pp. 124-25; interviews in Oman and London.

diminishing despite the non-renewal of the contracts of many foreign workers due to recent restrictions upon government spending.

The experience of the army also points to a new notion of government service that may increasingly constitute a break from Oman's recent past. Serving officers do not have the private commercial opportunities enjoyed by some senior civilian officials. Many key government officials and advisers, or members of their immediate family, maintain their business interests. Some thirty key families each enjoy a net worth of over $25 million apiece. It is unrealistic to expect that government officials derived from this category will readily divest themselves of their commercial opportunities.

Hence a main challenge for the Omani polity is to steer a middle course between the efficacious use of existing cadres and a growing perception among younger Omanis of a vastly unequal distribution of income and commercial opportunity. Nonetheless, as in other countries, stability can be enhanced by creating increased openings for a new generation. One Arab monarchy managed this problem in the early 1970s by creating private sector opportunities for senior officers and civilian officials, opening paths for the promotion of more junior cadres in government service. The timing is different for Oman, but most of the senior officials in civilian ministries have been in place since the early 1970s.

Commerce, ethnicity, sect and region

Oman is a complex society in terms of its ethnic, sectarian, linguistic, and regional diversity. To mention only the major divisions: 50-55 per cent of the population is Ibadi Muslim, although a properly interpreted accurate census might suggest that this figure should be adjusted downward; 40-45 per cent is Sunni Muslim; and no more than 3 per cent is Shi'a. Much of the population is Arab, although many Omanis are also of Baluch, Indian, and Iranian origin. Because Oman's domains once included Zanzibar and the East African littoral and emigration from there only began in earnest in the 1960s, many Omani citizens were born in East Africa. Especially since the early 1970s, many talented Omanis of East African origin have been assimilated in Oman, a process that is still underway. In parts of the northern Oman interior, Swahili remains a viable second language, just as Sindi, Baluchi, Farsi and Urdu can be heard regularly in the major towns of the coast, and Mahri and Jabali in Dhufar.[34]

These ethnic, sectarian, and linguistic distinctions are significant, but do not constitute major political "fault lines" for Oman, even if they are occasionally represented as such in earlier literature. Similarly, the stereotyped assertion that Oman's northern interior is xenophobic and inward-looking in contrast to the cosmopolitan, outward-looking trading communities of the coast is difficult to maintain in light of the interior's sustained contact with East Africa and other regions of the Gulf even prior to the advent of the oil economy. For younger Omanis, modern schooling, especially at the secondary and post-secondary levels, has reduced the distance between the various sectarian groupings, just as it has shifted the political perspective from short-term to long-term political concerns and expectations.[35] The integration of all these elements into Omani society is not without its rough edges, especially when it was thought in the late 1970s that Omani East Africans, who in general were more highly educated than their local counterparts, were taking over key governmental positions. Administrative action was taken to equalize opportunities, which in any case will be more equitably distributed throughout the population once more Omanis acquire the appropriate educational and organizational skills.

A particularly salient indication that the potential "fault line" between region and sect has diminished can be seen in overall patterns of business activity. Until completion of a surfaced road between Dhufar and northern Oman in the early 1980s, communications between the country's north and south were expensive and difficult, and interaction between the two parts of the country was minimal. Now civil servants are regularly posted between the two regions, and, of greater significance, businessmen from the south are investing and settling in the capital. Modest entrepreneurs have found opportunities such as transporting fish caught in the south to points in the northern interior, just as Baluch traders sell cloth directly to women in the small oases of the interior.[36] The fact that such inter-regional enterprises can take place without local hostility is one of the most concrete signs of the "new era."

If attention is focused solely upon the major business concerns, especially among the top thirty or so families, it would be easy to conclude that minority sectarian groupings, including the Shi'i Liwati, the Baharina, and the Baluch remain commercially important despite the rise to prominence in recent years of merchant families from the northern interior, of East African Ibadi origin, and from Dhufar. In part, the continued prominence of merchant families from smaller sects is due to the major role they played in the commerce of the country prior to 1970. They were poised from the start to adapt their skills and experience rapidly to expanded commercial opportunities.

Yet within these groups there is a significantly changed comportment and a deliberate effort to make substantial links with other groups. The Liwatiya of Matrah, for example, all had a choice between Indian and Omani citizenship at India's independence in 1947. They chose Omani citizenship, and over the years began to shift to the use of Arabic in their homes in recognition of altered political circumstances. Intermarriage between leading families of different sectarian groups now occurs. More important are the "vertical partnerships," in which key minority families enhance their commercial opportunities in the interior by providing credit facilities and capital to local entrepreneurs and merchants. Such complex, diffuse linkages are especially common in automobile distributorships, food, textiles, hardware, and construction materials.

These vertical commercial and intersectarian linkages are often built upon older, existing credit and trading arrangements and in general appear to work smoothly. The creation of small-scale, local economic opportunities tied to larger commercial interests (a process in part made possible by government policy but also by locally initiated entrepreneurial activities and the Omanization of branch banking) has also served to knit together Oman's constitutive communities. Some key merchants, of course, continue to regard Oman as a pond from which capital can be drawn for investment in Europe, the United States, and the Far East. Many others, however, see their opportunities primarily linked to Oman itself, even if local activities are balanced by transnational ones.

Consultation

One of Oman's best-kept secrets is a long-standing tradition of consultation in local and tribal matters. The tradition is especially strong in the Ibadi interior of northern Oman, where mutual consultation (*shura*) acquires a profound religious significance and shapes the expected style in interpersonal relations, including the functioning of government offices. Deeply ingrained in informal social norms, consultation has since 1979 become an integral part of formal political life.

In April 1979, a twelve-person Council of Agriculture, Fisheries, and Industry was appointed, whose members met monthly to discuss economic policy options and draft recommendations. This was replaced in October 1981 by the State Consultative Council (SCC) (*al-majlis al-istishari lil-dawla*). The name has not gone unnoticed in Oman. *Istishara* in Arabic means "to ask for advice," not to engage in mutual consultation, and the decree establishing this 44-member body, expanded in late 1983 to 55 appointed members, is remarkably cautious. Officially the constituency of the delegates is all of Oman, and technically their deliberations and recommendations are secret. Beginning in 1982, some of these strictures were relaxed. Members took their responsibilities seriously, and learned to work together to study policy issues, make realistic reports, and develop constructive relationships with various ministries.

In December 1985, a third set of appointments was made to the SCC. As with earlier appointments, the same rough ethnic, regional, commercial, and governmental balance was maintained. Regional appointments of this secondary élite show an interesting pattern of attention to local tribal and family rivalries, providing a serial equality: if a notable representing one tribal or local faction was appointed in 1983, the 1985 appointment went to a counterpart notable, thus ensuring a judicious long-term equity and affording a broad spectrum of notables the training and experience which come with membership. As a non-parliament, it is easy to dismiss the SCC as decorative in function. Nonetheless, it serves as an effective device to initiate Omani notables to the complexities of policy-making and to accustom government officials to explaining their decisions in public. The SCC has shown itself to be highly responsible in its deliberations and recommendations; it is reasonable to assume that its responsibilities will gradually be expanded.[37]

Another of Oman's well-kept secrets is its municipal councils. One existed in Muscat since the 1940s. By the late 1970s, every major town possessed such a council. All leading citizens, including young merchants and officials, seem to get an opportunity to serve, and the municipal councils of the larger communities already have become viable institutions for the management of local services. Some produce their own newsletters, and like the SCC, municipal councils give citizens a taste of the complexities of formulating and implementing sound policy decisions.[38]

Municipal councils and other forms of committee work have become a quiet means of involving citizens in the conduct of government affairs. Responsible participation in such councils augurs well for a continued widening of civic responsibilities and participation in governmental processes. It is hoped that these initiatives will form the base upon which citizen energies can add to initiatives taken largely by a perceived inner circle of advisers. Open public channels of communication will enhance the state, not act as a threat to it. Participation need not necessarily take the form of formal democracy. If the term "tribe" is regarded with hostility in sub-Saharan Africa, it conveys a very different, positive meaning in Oman and elsewhere in the Arabian Peninsula.[39] Oman is capable of drawing upon its living, shared traditions and using them to shape the present. There are strong alternative institutions already existing in Oman upon which broader political participation can be elaborated and made to match the substantial progress made in other fields.

Succession

The issue of succession has been raised by various observers, both Omani and foreign.[40] Focus upon the narrow issue of succession is perhaps inappropriate for Oman. Indeed, the ageing of senior members of the United Arab Emirates' government gives more cause for concern in the decade to come. In Oman, after all, there are talented members of the royal family both at the senior and junior levels. Appointment of an heir apparent would be an empty gesture unless there is a clear and present need. As Sultan Qaboos has commented, "I know that this question has been raised, but not by people who know our traditions."[41] The more immediate issue in an absolute monarchy is what the monarch has in mind for the next step. Those who know Qaboos regard him as "charming, quiet, reflective, thoughtful, and intelligent." The public record of words and deeds is the appropriate place to look for an indication of what is to come. The monarch's self-image is that of a leader who has brought his people into the twentieth century, without wrenching them away from their religion and social values. State occasions and affairs of state are well managed. If there is a penchant for monumental projects — stadiums, a university infrastructure built to standards no longer envisaged in any First World construction project, roads, mosques, and a variety of prestige projects — these might be seen as monuments to what has been accomplished over the last fifteen years.

Since Qaboos first came to the throne, he has been aware that the issue of succession is inherently bound up with the question of Oman's future shape. One possibility is to make no plans and to presume, in the accepted wisdom of some of the nation's élite and foreign advisers, that "the Arab" prefers monarchic rule. It is unnecessary to dwell at length upon whether this principle of rule is shared by the educated and religious youth, who nonetheless retain a profound respect for Qaboos and his achievements. A visionary alternative is what might be called the "Juan Carlos" option, in which the ruler embarks upon a calculated self-transformation. Qaboos I, in this hypothetical self-image, is the leader who led his nation from darkness into light, and who possessed the fiscal resources to do so at a pace that no subsequent ruler will be likely to emulate. Qaboos II, who may emerge in the coming decade, is the visionary with the skill to self-transform Oman's existing political forms, building upon existing Omani traditions.

As for the emerging internal political forces of the coming decade, the comments of a skilled diplomatic observer of a monarchy at the other end of the Arab world are useful. The monarch, said the observer, claims that "he has a stethoscope constantly connected to his people and knows when they are sick and when they are well. This is pretty fatuous, because he suffers from the isolation common to all leaders, made even worse in his case by a servile press and court, with none of his advisers being willing to contradict him."[42]

When the private enterprises of advisers are closely related to their positions and their prestige upon their access to the ruler, the possibilities for corruption of the systems of information and limits upon the range of offered advice can be acute. Deliberate efforts must be sustained to extend political antennae beyond the circle of immediate advisers, all of whom are of unquestioned loyalty, and some of whom are highly skilled, but most of whom have been in place since the beginning of the new era. All concerned must be willing to focus upon events just over the present political horizon or to extrapolate likely trends, especially those based upon the changing expectations of Omanis now at the periphery of political participation.

In sum, there are three key issues to consider with respect to Oman's internal political development over the coming two decades. First is the growing impact of educated youth and changing popular expectations. In the 1960s, educated young were known in security circles as the "new threat." They need not be perceived as such. Oman's educated youth form an invaluable, enthusiastic, and talented cadre that can be involved willingly in building a strong, proud Oman, despite the economic challenge of declining oil prices and the likelihood that political conflict involving the Arabian Peninsula will increase, should it become the principal remaining source for world oil by the end of the century or when other supplies become exhausted.

Second, there must be a continued balance between Oman's domestic security and the technical military requirements of US strategic interests. Oman will be strongest internally, and of most value to its allies, if it continues to sustain its present policy of avoiding direct involvement with US security interests. In this respect, Oman has received the support of at least part of the American security establishment. An intensification of direct American involvement must be carefully weighed against its potential for destabilization.

The final choice is one which can only be faced by Omanis themselves. Should internal political difficulties emerge in the coming years, especially among the educated youth, there may be a temptation to rely increasingly upon the internal security apparatus for quick solutions instead of increasing reliance upon the willing engagement of a new, if occasionally fractious, generation of Omanis in running the affairs of the country.

Oman has an impressive basis upon which to build. Long-term economic planning has for the most part been comprehensive and realistic, recognizing the needs to diversify away from oil and to give priority to stopping the decline of the agricultural and fishing sectors and to preserve natural water resources. The need to absorb the rapidly increasing numbers of Omanis with post-secondary educations into the economy and polity is recognized, together with the recognition that there were no ready solutions available even before the present straitened economic circumstances.

His Majesty himself set the tone for the next two decades when he said after the 1985 Gulf Cooperation Council summit in Muscat: "We no longer are sensitive about differences of opinion. At one time we thought a difference of opinion was the end of the world, but now we are prepared to listen to all opinions."[43] Although the ruler was commenting upon the relations among heads of state in the region, his remark can be applied equally to Omani society itself. As one key adviser recently commented, Oman's success to date is not only a question of the ruler having received good advice, but of a willingness to listen and to take action.

NOTES

1. President Carter's toast to the Shah of Iran, at a state dinner in Tehran. Cited in Gary Sick, *All Fall Down: America's Tragic Encounter with Iran* (New York: Random House, 1983), p. 30.

2. Sultanate of Oman, Development Council, Technical Secretariat, Directorate General of National Statistics, *Statistical Year Book*, Twelfth Issue (Muscat: Development Council, 1984), p. 15.

3. John Townsend, *Oman: The Making of the Modern State* (London: Croom Helm, 1977), p. 18; I. Serageldin, J. Socknat, J.S. Birks and C. Sinclair, "Some Issues Related to Labor Migration in the Middle East and North Africa," *Middle East Journal*, Vol. 38, No. 4 (Autumn 1984), p. 632.

4. World Bank, *World Development Report 1984* (New York: Oxford University Press, 1984), p. 193.

5. See Dale F. Eickelman, "From Theocracy to Monarchy: Authority and Legitimacy in Inner Oman, 1935-1957," *International Journal of Middle East Studies*, Vol. 17, No. 1 (February 1985), pp. 3-24, for an account of the changed political circumstances and expectations leading to this event.

6. Anthony H. Cordesman, "Oman: The Guardian of the Eastern Gulf," *Armed Forces Journal*, June 1983, p. 27.

7. Anthony H. Cordesman , *The Gulf and the Search for Strategic Stability* (Boulder: Westview, 1984), pp. 436 and 518.

8. J.D.C. Graham, "The Sultan's Armed Forces, March 1970 to September 1972 (Part 3)," *The Sultan's Armed Forces Association Newsletter*, No. 33 (June 1984).

9. Interview with the author, Muscat, November 1, 1982. The first recorded strike appears to have been at the BAPCO refinery in Bahrain in 1938. For a thoughtful appraisal of the social changes brought about by the oil economy and how Gulf Arabs, including Omanis, reflect upon those changes, see J.P. Bannerman, "The Impact of the Oil Industry on Society in the Arabian Peninsula," in R.I. Lawless, ed., *The Gulf in the Early 20th Century: Foreign Institutions and Local Responses* (Durham: University of Durham, Centre for Middle Eastern and Islamic Studies, 1986; Occasional Papers Series No. 31), pp. 76-90.

10. US Congress, Senate, Committee on International Relations, 95th Congress, *United States Arms Policies in the Persian Gulf and Red Sea Areas: Past, Present, and Future* (Washington: USGPO, 1977), p. 58.

11. Townsend, *Oman*, pp. 122-65.

12. Judith Miller and Jeff Gerth, "U.S. Is Said to Develop Oman as its Major Ally in the Gulf," *New York Times*, March 26, 1985, p. A8.

13. See Royal Decree 39/82 (May 22, 1982), especially Articles 2 and 4. This decree was suspended pending further "interpretation" by a ministerial circular from the Office of the Deputy Prime Minister for Legal Affairs, dated September 15, 1982.

14. The dismissal was noted by Royal Decree 85/95, dated December 12, 1985, which named a replacement.

15. See John Waterbury, "Corruption, Political Stability and Development: Comparative Evidence from Egypt and Morocco," *Government and Opposition*, Vol. 11 (1976), pp. 426-45.

16. "Oman: Retrenchment Follows Oil Price Cut," *Middle East Economic Digest* (MEED), February 22, 1986, pp. 51-52; Permanent Mission of Oman to the United Nations, *Newsletter*, No. 41, March 19, 1986.

17. See, for example, Public Authority for Water Resources, "The Hydrology of the Sultanate of Oman," PAWR 83-1 (Muscat: Public Authority for Water Resources, February 1984).

18. J.H.A. McHugo, "The Practice of Law by Foreign Lawyers in the Sultanate of Oman," *The Michigan Yearbook of International Legal Studies*, Vol. 17 (1985), pp. 89-101. For a related earlier article, see Thomas W. Hill, Jr., "The Commercial Legal System of the Sultanate of Oman," *International Lawyer*, Vol. 17, No. 3 (Summer 1983), pp. 507-534.

19. Cited in Jim Bogdener, "Oman Development Plan Shapes Up," *MEED*, September 14, 1985, p. 30.

20. See World Bank, *Technical Assistance and Special Studies Division, Assessment of the Manpower Implications of the Second Five-Year Development Plan* (Washington: World Bank, November 1981), pp. 201-208, and the argument for the public dissemination of such studies on p. xii.

21. Dale F. Eickelman, "The Oasis of al-Hamra: A Socioeconomic Survey," *Arabian Studies*, Vol. 8.

22. Bogdener, "Oman Development Plan," p. 30; *MEED*, October 19, 1985, p. 31; "Oman: Retrenchment," *MEED*, February 22, 1986, pp. 51-52; J.E. Peterson, personal communication, June 11, 1986.

23. J.C. Wilkinson, "Traditional Concepts of Territory in South East Arabia," *Geographical Journal*, Vol. 149, No. 3 (November 1983), pp. 301-315.

24. Permanent Mission of Oman to the United Nations, *Newsletter*, No. 15, February 4, 1986; John Kifner, "Southern Yemen Offers a Good Neighbor Policy," *New York Times*, February 1, 1986, p. A3; "Sayyid Haitham Talks of Oman's Foreign Policy," *Times of Oman* (Muscat), July 17, 1986, p. 6.

25. Norman Cigar, "State and Society in South Yemen," *Problems of Communism*, Vol. 34, No. 3 (May-June 1985), pp. 44 and 54.

26. Ibid., p. 57; John Kifner, "Battle for South Yemen: How the Fury Began," *New York Times*, January 30, 1986, p. A4.

27. Cordesman, "Oman: The Guardian," p. 30.

28. Norman Cigar, "South Yemen and the USSR: Prospects for the Relationship," *Middle East Journal*, Vol. 39, No. 4 (Autumn 1985), p. 778.

29. Interview by the author with Yusuf bin 'Alawi 'Abdullah, Minister of State for Foreign Affairs, New York, October 17, 1985; see also Riyad Najib al-Rayyis, "al-qissa al-kamila li-'alaqat al-'Umaniya — as-Sufiyatiya" [The Complete Story on Omani-Soviet Ties], *al-Mustaqbal al-'Arabi*, No. 454 (November 2, 1985), pp. 16-18; and Stephen Fidler, "Oman's Ties with Moscow Unlikely to Alter Links with West," Reuter Dispatch UKS241, Muscat, October 9, 1986.

30. Dale F. Eickelman, "Religious Knowledge in Inner Oman," *Journal of Oman Studies*, Vol. 6 (1983), pp. 163-72.

31. Idem, "Ibadism and the Sectarian Perspective," in Brian R. Pridham, ed., *Aspects of Oman* (London: Croom Helm, 1987), pp. 40-42.

32. It should be noted that the structure of Sultan Qaboos University for the moment lacks most of the social sciences and the humanities, disciplines considered by most scholars to be essential components of higher education. Perhaps the intent of the planners, as with early Ottoman reformers, is to ensure an "essential" training unencumbered by foreign ideas (*afkar mustawrada*) or political influences. The stress upon engineering and health sciences is laudable, but it might be pointed out that the most radical faculties in most Muslim countries, including Egypt, Tunisia, Morocco, and Algeria, have been the technical ones, not those in the social and human sciences. Oman may not need dozens of indigenous social scientists, but an infusion of training in these two disciplines among undergraduates might do much to encourage Oman's budding young engineers, accountants, agricultural experts and medical students to think creatively about how to "Omanize" their knowledge and apply it to the problems of Oman's regions and outlying areas.

33. A salient, if extreme, indicator of meritocracy is the role of ex-slaves (*akhdam*) in the army and security services in the early 1970s. At the outset of the "new era," the limited available evidence (Eickelman, "The Oasis of al-Hamra") suggests that ex-slaves were twice as likely as members of the general population to sign up for military service, where talented recruits received in-service training and were promoted in accord

with their abilities. In later years, recruitment became more evenly distributed as all Omani youth saw the advantages of careers in the military and security services.

34. See Dale F. Eickelman, "Religious Tradition, Economic Domination, and Political Domination," *Revue de l'Occident Musulman et de la Méditerranée*, Vol. 29, No. 1 (1980), pp. 21-22; and Fredrik Barth, *Sohar: Culture and Society in an Omani Town* (Baltimore: Johns Hopkins University Press, 1983), pp. 37-52.

35. See Eickelman, "Ibadism and the Sectarian Perspective."

36. Christine Eickelman, *Women and Community in Oman* (New York: New York University Press, 1984), p. 46.

37. See Dale F. Eickelman, "Kings and People: Oman's State Consultative Council," *Middle East Journal*, Vol. 38, No. 1 (Winter 1984), pp. 51-71.

38. For more information on the activities of these councils, see the Sultanate of Oman, Ministry of Land Affairs and Municipalities, *Usbu' al-baladiyat* (Ruwi: National Press, 1984).

39. Yusuf al-'Alawi 'Abdullah, interview by the author, New York, October 17, 1986.

40. For example, US Congress, House of Representatives, Committee on Foreign Affairs, *U.S. Security Interests in the Persian Gulf* (Washington: USGPO, 1981), p. 17; and Calvin H. Allen, Jr., "The Sultanate of Oman and American Security Interests in the Arabian Gulf," in Robert W. Stookey, ed., *The Arabian Peninsula: Zone of Ferment* (Stanford: Hoover Institution Press, 1984), pp. 9-10.

41. Ahmed Jarallah, "Oman Opens Its Doors — With Caution" (interview), *Arab Times* (Kuwait), December 10, 1985, p. 4.

42. Richard B. Parker, *North Africa: Regional Tensions and Strategic Concerns* (New York: Praeger, 1984), p. 33.

43. In Jarallah, "Oman Opens Its Doors," p.4.

9

Saudi Arabia and its Neighbors: Preoccupied Paternalism

David E. Long

Saudi attitudes toward the Arab states of the Gulf have never been explainable entirely, or even primarily, in terms of contemporary strategic, political or economic interests, no matter how important or compelling those interests may be. Hence, a standard Western-styled analysis of strategic, economic and political factors comprising Saudi relations with its neighbors does not convey adequately the complexities and subtleties of the symbiotic relationship between the countries sharing the Arabian Peninsula and the western shores of the Gulf.

The geographic, ethnic, tribal, historical, cultural and religious ties between Saudi Arabia and the other members of the Gulf Cooperation Council — Kuwait, Bahrain, Qatar, the United Arab Emirates (UAE) and Oman — are so closely entwined as to have created a very special kind of relationship among them. As with most "special relationships," the one between Saudi Arabia and the other Arab states on the Gulf is complex, and given to a great deal of misunderstanding by those observing it from a distance.

Saudi Arabia has often been characterized as an "imperial" power in the Gulf. With such a strong preponderance in size, wealth and power, it is hard to visualize Saudi relations toward the GCC states as anything short of imperialism. This characterization, however, is not borne out in actual Saudi behavior toward its neighbors. For one thing, Saudi policy in the Gulf is too ill-defined to be considered an imperial policy. Saudi policy toward the Yemens, for example, has always been better articulated and better organized, coming more or less under the direct scrutiny of the most senior members of the royal family, especially Prince Sultan bin 'Abd al-'Aziz, brother of the king and minister of defense and aviation.

Map 5: Saudi Arabia

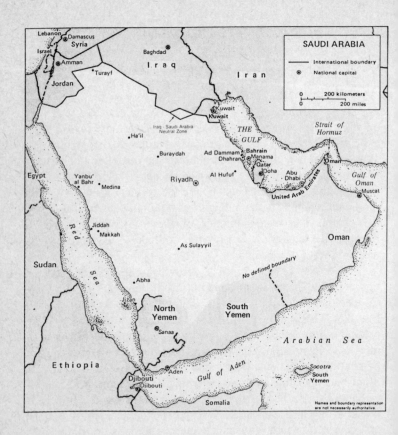

Saudi preoccupation with the Yemens is understandable, given the large Yemeni work force in the kingdom, the ideological threat posed by the Marxist regime in Aden and the strategic location of the two countries at the southern end of the Red Sea. Yet, one could argue that with the bulk of the free world's oil supplies found in the Gulf, the close proximity of the Soviet Union and a long history of challenges to its interests — the Buraimi Oasis territorial dispute in the 1950s, the Dhufar rebellion in the 1960s and 1970s, the energy crisis in the 1970s, and the growing threat of fundamentalist Iran in the 1980s — Saudi Arabia should pay an even greater degree of attention to the GCC states.

Saudi concern with Gulf politics indeed has increased steadily in the last few years, and its political and military cooperation with the GCC has expanded exponentially since the outbreak of the Iran-Iraq war in 1980 and Saudi anxiety over the direct military threat of Iran to the kingdom and its neighbors. Nevertheless, Saudi policy toward the Gulf never has been able to compete over a sustained period with Saudi preoccupations elsewhere. In addition to the Yemens, these include the Arab-Israeli problem, inter-Arab politics, Lebanon, the threat to the Muslim and free worlds from international Communism, and Saudi relations with the United States. The Iran-Iraq war certainly has become a major Saudi policy preoccupation and it has given far more cohesion to the GCC on a multilateral basis, but it has not appreciably upgraded Saudi foreign-policy priorities in their bilateral relations with the GCC member states.

Perhaps the closest analogy in the West to the special relationship between Saudi Arabia and the Gulf states is that of the United States and the other states of the Western Hemisphere. The United States is by far the strongest member of the Organization of American States (OAS), adopting policies towards the hemisphere that are at times paternalistic, such as the Monroe Doctrine; at times fraternal and idealistic, such as the Alliance for Progress; at times high-handed, such as "gunboat" and "dollar" diplomacy. All of the above have been punctuated by long periods of benign neglect. Not surprisingly, the other members of the OAS have developed a "love-hate" relationship with the United States and see it as the "Colossus of the North."

This analogy is not a perfect mirror of the situation in the Gulf, however. Although the United States and Saudi Arabia are each a colossus in comparison to the other members of the OAS and the GCC respectively, and, although both organizations are joined by geography and a common desire to exclude external powers from exerting influence in the region (this was more particularly so in the Western Hemisphere in the nineteenth century), the OAS is far more heterogeneous. Its members are separated by different languages, cultures and, to a lesser degree, by different religious experiences.

In the Gulf, these differences exist on a much smaller scale. Each Gulf state, including Saudi Arabia, has a significant Shi'a community; in Bahrain, the Shi'a represent a slight majority of the population. In none of the GCC states, however, do the Shi'a hold a preponderance of political power. All the GCC states are dominated by Sunni Muslims with the exception of Oman. A small majority of Omanis are members of the Ibadi sect of Islam, an offshoot of the Khariji movement which dates back to the earliest days of Islam.

The Shi'a communities do contribute a degree of heterogeneity to the local populations of the Gulf. Political differences between the Shi'a and Sunnis, moreover, have been greatly exacerbated by the creation of the revolutionary Shi'a regime in Tehran, which transmits a daily diet of invective in Arabic over Radio Tehran and Radio Ahvaz, aimed at furthering the political disaffection of local Shi'a communities on the Arab side of the Gulf. Nevertheless, the existence of a significant sectarian minority, politically if not in actual numbers, creates a shared ethnic and political experience in the Gulf which curiously contributes to a degree of homogeneity among the GCC states. The "Shi'a problem" is a problem common to all except Oman, which does not have a significant Shi'a community.

The factor which contributes most to the very special and close relationship among the GCC states, however, is not religious ties but the sense of common identity based on blood ties. Throughout the Arabian Peninsula (and extending into the desert areas of Jordan, Syria and Iraq), a sense of Arabness exists, which is not merely acquired through a common historical, religious and ethnic experience. It is, rather, something with which one is born. The common heritage of Arab history, the Arabic language, and the religion of Islam, all originated in the Arabian Peninsula among tribes whose descendants still live there today. This bond of blood transcends all other factors and has helped to shape a unique pattern of relationships between Saudi Arabia and its Arab Gulf neighbors. The geographic, ethnic and spiritual heartland of most Gulf

Arabs is Najd, or central Arabia, which is also the political, as well as geographic, ethnic and spiritual heartland of Saudi Arabia itself.

From the perspective of the smaller Gulf states, their relationship with Saudi Arabia can best be characterized as a complex amalgam of love and hate, of respect and resentment, and of independence and acquiescence. As the largest, wealthiest, and strongest of the GCC states, Saudi Arabia is unquestionably the leader. Although the others tend to follow Saudi Arabia's lead, they are extremely sensitive about being patronized on the one hand, or being ignored on the other.

From the Saudi perspective, the relationship with the Gulf states is one of brotherhood and precedence. The GCC states, by virtue of their proximity and their noble Arabian origins, are accorded a special consideration by Saudi Arabia that is given to no other state. Gulf citizens, for example, have not been required to obtain visas for the *hajj* (Mecca pilgrimage), and for that purpose have the same status as Saudi citizens.

In return, the Saudis expect other Gulf Arabs to accord them the status of *primus inter pares* within the GCC. The Saudis can act in quite an imperious manner when they believe that their status has not been properly regarded, and, in their preoccupation with other foreign policy concerns, they can evince a lack of sensitivity for their neighbors' aspirations.

This behavior still does not add up to an imperial design. It would be far more accurate to call it preoccupied paternalism. Even this, however, does not constitute a formal policy but is more of a "prepolicy." That is to say, the Saudis have the makings of a Gulf policy but have never quite developed it to the point of a fully integrated set of goals and strategies. This prepolicy is based on a convergence of interests from a variety of sources and with a varying degree of priority which have caused the Saudis over the years, and especially the last few years, to focus on the Gulf. The development of these policy interests can best be seen in historical perspective.

THE 1970s: THE BEGINNINGS OF GULF COOPERATION

Prior to Great Britain's relatively precipitate departure from the Gulf in 1971, the region received a low priority in Saudi foreign-policy considerations. Oil matters were negotiated directly with the oil-producing companies, and strategic concerns were left to the

British who maintained a protective status over the states in the lower Gulf.

Britain's announcement in 1968 that it intended to end this status within three years came as a shock to the Saudis and the lower Gulf shaykhdoms. Between 1968 and 1971, the Saudis closely monitored British efforts to leave behind a stable Gulf. Riyadh was particularly gratified with the resolution of a number of outstanding territorial disputes, particularly the renunciation of Iran's claim to Bahrain. In the interests of regional stability, the Saudis remained passive as the Shah took over three small islands in the lower Gulf — the two Tunbs, also claimed by Ra's al-Khayma, and Abu Musa, also claimed by Sharjah — but they supported and continue to support the Arab claims.

Despite heightened concern over Gulf security following the British withdrawal, neither the Saudis nor the other Arab Gulf states actively sought to create regional security arrangements. Each of the states unilaterally pursued its own security interests. With greatly increased oil revenue at their disposal, they greatly expanded their military establishments; this was particularly true of Saudi Arabia. However, the few efforts to encourage regional security bore no fruit.

Overall cooperation in the Gulf did increase, however. In 1974, Saudi Arabia and Abu Dhabi worked together to end the century-old territorial dispute over Buraimi Oasis. A Saudi force to re-establish the kingdom's claim to Buraimi had been expelled in the 1950s and the dispute had smoldered on, remaining a stumbling block to further cooperation. Another obstacle to cooperation was removed at the same time when Saudi Arabia ceased to support the claims by the Imam of Oman to an independent inner Oman. The Imam had lived in exile in Saudi Arabia after being ousted by British forces in the name of the Omani government in 1955. The resolution of these two points of contention went far toward creating an atmosphere of amity among the Gulf states which ultimately opened the way to the creation of the Gulf Cooperation Council.

Another factor enhancing Gulf cooperation was Oman's breaking out of a long period of almost total political isolation following a palace coup in 1970 in which Sultan Sa'id bin Taymur was driven from the throne and succeeded by his British-educated son, Qaboos bin Sa'id. Sultan Qaboos abandoned his father's isolationist policies and began to steer Oman away from its almost total reliance on Great Britain for defense and security . At the same time, the sultanate edged toward the political mainstream, pursuing closer political association with the Arabian Peninsula states and the rest of the Arab world in general.

These moves toward more cooperation took time, however, since it was necessary to overcome decades of mutual suspicion. For example, in the course of fighting a major, Marxist insurgency in Dhufar province, Oman accepted the Shah's offer to send 3,000 Iranian troops. While concerned about the rebels, the Saudis nevertheless had considerable qualms over the appearance of non-Arab troops on Arabian soil.

The energy crisis of the 1970s also provided new avenues for cooperation by Saudi Arabia and the other oil-producing countries of the Gulf. The emerging sellers' market of the early 1970s enabled the oil-producing countries of the Gulf and elsewhere to gain control over their own oil resources, and enabled OPEC to set price and production levels. It also brought the Gulf into world focus. Collectively, the Gulf oil producers constituted the single most powerful group within OPEC; Saudi Arabia alone became the most important oil-producing state, not only in OPEC but in the entire free world.

During the 1970s a great deal of cooperation and policy coordination was established among the Arabian Peninsula oil producers. Not only did these states display geographical, ethnic and political affinity, but for the most part their economic situations were similar: small populations, high per capita incomes and a relatively low capacity to absorb capital. As a result, all could be categorized as price moderates placing a great deal of stress on conservation.

As with political cooperation, however, there were also limits on oil-policy coordination among the Gulf states. The predominant position of Saudi Arabia in world oil affairs had led it to a somewhat broader view of its oil interests than its neighbors. Saudi oil policy in the 1970s, and continuing to this day, was geared more toward OPEC as a whole and world market conditions in general than toward Gulf regional interests in particular.

In sum, the 1970s was a period in which many of the elements which impeded Saudi cooperation with the Gulf states were removed. These impediments included the territorial dispute over Buraimi oasis and historically strained relations with Oman. In addition, elements of common interest and concern further enhanced cooperation. They included the common concerns of the Gulf oil producers and growing apprehension over regional security following the withdrawal of the British in 1971. With the departure of the British, it became incumbent on the Saudis to seek cooperation with the newly independent states of Bahrain, Qatar and the UAE, as well as with Kuwait and Oman.

Despite this strong beginning, however, Saudi Arabia still did not rank the Gulf first in order of priority among issues of concern to it in the 1970s. Perhaps most important was the Arab-Israeli issue, which highlighted Saudi Arabia due to the so-called "oil weapon." The energy crisis not only propelled Saudi Arabia into world attention, but it made it a leader in the Arab world through its enormous oil and financial resources. Thus, the kingdom became a major player in the events proceeding from Sadat's historic visit to Jerusalem through the Camp David peace process. In addition, the Communist threat overshadowed nearly all other political considerations, directing the course of US-Saudi relations and, closer to home, preoccupying the Saudis with the Marxist threat in South Yemen.

THE 1980s: THE MATURING OF GULF COOPERATION

As the Gulf entered the decade of the 1980s, cooperative Saudi relations with its Arab Gulf neighbors matured appreciably. Three events in particular played a major role in this process: the oil glut, the Iranian revolution, and the Iran-Iraq war.

The oil glut

Saudi Arabia emerged from the energy crisis as the price-setter in OPEC. Throughout the 1970s, Saudi Arabia, as a price moderate, used its tremendous production capacity to keep the price of oil from climbing even higher. It is not that the Saudis were against increased oil revenues *per se*, but rather that they believed that they could maximize their revenues better through price stabilization than through precipitous price hikes which threatened world oil-market stability. Saudi policies were not always supported by the other Gulf states (except by Abu Dhabi).

As the oil shortage of the 1970s turned into the oil glut of the 1980s, the Saudis continued to pursue a policy of price stability, only now it became necessary to cut production to prevent a collapse of the market. No other country was willing to share the load with OPEC, and production discipline broke down. Many producers had incurred financial obligations they could no longer meet due to declining oil revenues. Consequently, they sought to increase production beyond OPEC quotas in order to maintain income levels. Non-OPEC producers benefited greatly from OPEC-supported prices. They faced no production quotas and took advantage of the situation to increase their production. Without the immense Saudi production cutback, the market would have collapsed. The cost to Saudi Arabia, however, was a drastic decline in revenues.

Finally, the Saudis abandoned their price stabilization role in 1986. With their production down to one-fifth of capacity — from around 10 mbd to under 2 mbd in the summer of 1985 — the kingdom could no longer bear the economic burden. In early 1986, it increased production, collapsing the price to as low as $8 per barrel. In constant 1973 dollars, this was roughly equivalent to $3 per barrel, the price prevailing at that earlier time.

Since oil prices bottomed out in 1986, they have slowly been recovering. It will be at least several years, however, before the market fully recovers from the glut. In the meantime, Saudi Arabia and the Gulf states have had to adjust to some new realities. With substantially reduced revenues, they have had to reduce their annual budgets, shrink their development plans, and stretch out financial commitments. This is probably an overall plus, to the degree that it forces a higher standard of fiscal responsibility. It has also encouraged a higher degree of economic cooperation, to weed out redundant development projects that can no longer be afforded.

On the political side, there has been much speculation that reduced revenues would encourage disaffection with the regimes as opportunities for personal enrichment are greatly reduced. This has not been the case. All of the GCC states have traditional, tribally oriented societies, and blood rather than material wealth is the primary factor affecting political stability. Moreover, as most of the unemployed labor force was foreign labor to begin with, it can easily be sent home.

A more subtle influence of the oil glut on Gulf politics has been the substantial decrease in Western attention given to the region compared to the days when the survival of the free-world economy appeared to depend on Gulf oil. One result of the diminished economic influence of the Gulf states has been the perceived need to expand their political influence. After both houses of the US Congress defeated the administration's proposed arms-sale package to Saudi Arabia in May 1986, the Saudis and their fellow

GCC members became determined to increase their political influence as a group.

The perception by the West of the Gulf's diminished importance also increased the GCC's anxiety over the Western commitment to protect them from external attack. The US decision in the summer of 1987 to escort re-registered Kuwaiti oil tankers through the Gulf has for the moment assuaged that anxiety. Nevertheless, it still remains a potent consideration in Gulf relations with the West. It has also reinforced the jointly perceived need for more cooperation within the context of the GCC. Whatever one can say about the origins of the anxiety, the resulting cooperation has been all to the good.

The Iranian Revolution

In order to understand fully the impact of the Iranian revolution and the Iran-Iraq war on Saudi and Gulf security concerns, one should look at Saudi perceptions of the world around them. As is common with insular peoples, the ruling Najdi tribesmen, surrounded by a sea of sand, long ago developed an "encirclement syndrome" — that is, the conviction that they were surrounded by enemies constantly threatening to annihilate them. The list of enemies has changed over time, of course. At one time it was rival tribes to the north and south, and, on a broader scale, the Ottoman Empire through its local rulers in Iraq, eastern Arabia and Egypt. One such leader, Muhammad 'Ali of Egypt, sent his son, Ibrahim Pasha, to capture the Saudi capital at al-Dir'iya in 1818.

In recent times, a large number of real, potential, and perceived antagonists have been incorporated into the Saudi encirclement syndrome, though never all at the same time. They have included Zionist Israel, Nasserist Egypt, Marxist South Yemen, Somalia and Ethiopia, Ba'thist Iraq and Syria, and Hashimite Jordan and Iraq (the Hashimite ruling families of Jordan and Iraq [until 1958] are, for example, descended from a rival royal house expelled from Mecca by the Saudis in 1920).

With the fall of the Shah in 1979 and the outbreak of the Iran-Iraq war in 1980, Iran rapidly became seen as a leading adversary encircling the kingdom. Moreover, as with many of the other adversaries of the past and present, the Iranian threat had an ideological, as well as political and military, dimension.

Before the Iranian revolution, Saudi Arabia enjoyed a virtual monopoly on the far right of the political spectrum. Traditionally since World War II, anyone in the region who was disaffected and opposed to a regime turned to the left — to Nasserism, Ba'thism and, more dangerously, Marxism. The Saudis saw proponents of leftist doctrines as atheists and as threats to the Muslim way of life which they, as keepers of the Muslim holy places of Mecca and Madina, were committed to defend.

With the advent of the Iranian revolution, Saudi orthodoxy was challenged from the right. Unaccustomed to being outflanked from this direction, Saudi Arabia quickly interpreted Iran's militant brand of revolutionary Islam as a heretical threat to its own Islam-based political system. The ideological threat was given form and focus by Iran's record of support for subversion and terrorism in the Gulf states since 1979.

Kuwait, which has suffered an airliner hijacking, bombs set off in oilfields, restaurants, government offices, and the US and French embassies, and an attempt on the life of the amir, has been the greatest victim of Iranian terrorism in the Gulf. But there were bombings in Riyadh in 1985, and several Saudi diplomats have been held hostage in Beirut. The most recent provocations by Iran against Saudi Arabia occurred during the 1987 *hajj*. At their government's instigation, Iranian pilgrims incited bloody riots in Mecca, killing over 400 pilgrims. The incident was followed by the sacking of the Saudi and Kuwaiti embassies in Tehran to "protest" at Saudi behavior in suppressing the rioters. Of all their responsibilities, both domestic and foreign, the Saudis take most seriously their guardianship of the holy places and their responsibility for holding the annual pilgrimage. The Iranian actions were seen not only as political provocations but as a desecration of Islam's holiest city as well.

Saudi political rivalry with Iran actually preceded the Iranian revolution. The Saudis had been ambivalent about Iran even under the Shah. Although the Shah's regime was anti-Communist and pro-Western, the Saudis always were concerned about Iranian imperial ambitions in the Gulf. Persian-Arab rivalries were never far beneath the surface, as evidenced by the acrimonious argument over the name of the Gulf itself — Persian or Arabian.

Saudi concern over Iranian ambitions were rooted in concrete issues over the years. For example, Iran's claim to Bahrain was a divisive element for many years until the Shah recognized the full independence of that state in 1971, and its forcible occupation of the Tunbs and Abu Musa at that time has continued to be an irritant to the GCC states. Saudi Arabia and the other Gulf states also had problems with Iran over the median line in the Gulf, an important issue because of its impact on oil rights. In the late 1960s, Iran seized an Arabian American Oil Company (ARAMCO) oil rig in the Gulf in a dispute over the median line. Finally, agreement was reached a few years ago on a line traversing the entire length of the Gulf. As a result of this long experience with provocative Iranian actions in the Gulf, the Saudis and their Gulf neighbors see Iranian militancy in the Gulf not simply as the result of its revolutionary ideology but as the product of Persian imperial aspirations as well.

The Iran-Iraq war

The event most directly affecting Saudi relations with its Gulf neighbors has been and continues to be the Iran-Iraq war. Iran and Iraq have never been on good terms, politically, ethnically or ideologically. The Ba'thist regime in Baghdad is socialist, secularist, and Arab nationalist. The rulers of Iraq, moreover, have always been Sunni Muslims, despite Iraq's larger Shi'a population. Iran, on the other hand, is conservative, Persian nationalist, at least in part, and Shi'a.

The fragile truce achieved in 1975 between the two countries quickly deteriorated following the fall of the Shah. In September 1980, after a series of Iranian border incursions, Iraq launched a full-scale attack, calculating that the internal chaos in Iran following the revolution would give it a temporary strategic advantage. Iraq's hope of a quick victory soon evaporated, however, and once Iran had driven Iraq from its territory, the war settled into a stalemate.

Facing the prospect of debilitating, protracted hostilities, Iraq announced that it would abide by a negotiated settlement. The Iraqis may have calculated that such a settlement would also be in the interests of Iran, since the latter was also incapable of an all-out victory, and, with its economy severely dislocated since the revolution, the war effort was bringing severe hardship to the Iranian people.

The Iranians, however, with a larger country and more resources, believed that time was on their side. So great was the hatred of the Islamic regime in Tehran for the Iraqi Ba'thist regime of Saddam Hussein that it was willing to put up with the hardships brought on by the war in order to cause Saddam's downfall. The only terms Tehran would agree to were ones totally humiliating the Iraqi government: admission of war guilt, payment of reparations, and the removal of Saddam Hussein and the rest of the Ba'thist leadership.

Iraq's economic position was even more precarious. Early in the war, Iran destroyed Iraq's offloading facilities in the Gulf, forcing Iraq to rely on pipelines to export its oil. Syrian President Hafiz al-Asad, a bitter rival of Saddam, had at times refused to allow Iraq to use the old Iraq Petroleum Company pipeline through Syria. As the war progressed, Asad increasingly sided with Iran and cut off Iraqi use of the pipeline.

The only remaining pipeline transited Turkey. When the war broke out, it had a throughput of only 750,000 bd. Although the pipeline's capacity has subsequently been doubled, it still cannot provide enough oil revenues to maintain the war effort. Thus, Iraq increasingly has looked to Saudi Arabia and the Gulf states for financial support.

Prior to the war and the fall of the Shah, the Saudis and their neighbors regarded the radical Ba'thist regime in Baghdad as a major potential threat. A number of dissidents fleeing the Arabian Peninsula had been granted refuge in Baghdad, from which to continue their subversive operations. Moreover, in the 1970s Iraq had actively pursued a territorial claim to two Kuwaiti islands, Warba and Bubiyan, near the Iraqi border. Furthermore, its strident foreign policies in the mid-1970s had virtually isolated Iraq from the rest of the Arab world.

By the late 1970s, however, Iraq had begun to break out of its isolation in the Arab world, hosting two Arab League conferences dealing with reactions to Egypt, the Camp David accords and the Egyptian-Israeli peace treaty. Thus, when Iraq looked to the Gulf states for help in 1980, and after, they were much more disposed to be responsive than they might have been a few years before. This attitude, of course, was quite apart from their growing antipathy toward Iran. Since the war began, Saudi Arabia and the other GCC states have contributed over $30 billion to Iraq.

Not only did Iraqi relations with the conservative Gulf states improve, but overall Iraqi foreign policy became more moderate as well. In 1983, for example, the Iraqi government expelled the Abu Nidal Palestinian terrorist organization, which had made Baghdad its headquarters since its leader, Sabri al-Banna (Abu Nidal) broke with the PLO in 1974. In 1985, Iraq resumed full diplomatic relations with the United States, the last major Arab state to do so since the rupture of relations in the aftermath of the June 1967 Arab-Israeli war.

The Iran-Iraq war continued to keep tensions in the Gulf high, so high in fact that they enveloped domestic and regional politics like a blanket. Out of that atmosphere came a renewed impetus for Saudi Arabia and its Arab Gulf neighbors to increase cooperation, not only for mutual defense and security, but on a broad spectrum of political and economic issues as well. On May 25, 1981, the Gulf Cooperation Council was created in Abu Dhabi.

It would, of course, be a gross oversimplification to say that the GCC was solely the result of the Iran-Iraq war. As has been stated earlier, the idea of a regional organization had been around for a long time, and the mutual realization of interdependence required for its establishment did not begin with the war. Nevertheless, the war was definitely the catalyst which turned a need into a reality.

Even after the creation of the GCC and the overriding threat of the Iran-Iraq war, security cooperation took time to develop. Some of the smaller states, particularly Kuwait, feared that their freedom of movement could be impaired by working collectively with Saudi Arabia and insisted that the GCC should occupy itself primarily with economic and social development matters. Others, such as Oman, which had just put down a protracted insurgency in Dhufar, were frustrated by the apparent timidity of the GCC and sought direct support from the British, and increasingly from the United States. The Saudis occupied the middle ground, wanting the GCC to become involved in security matters but not to the extent of forcing the kingdom to assume additional defense commitments to fellow GCC members. Because of Saudi Arabia's predominant defense position in the GCC, its strategic military planning will continue to be based predominantly on unilateral considerations. In so doing, however, its experience with the GCC has given it a greater sensitivity for its neighbors' concerns and a greater appreciation for the need to coordinate security policies with them.

Despite these constraints, progress has been made toward more security cooperation. In October 1983, the GCC states conducted their first joint military exercises, held in the UAE. The growing intensity and expansion of the Iran-Iraq war to the Gulf itself greatly encouraged the process. By 1987, Kuwait, the victim of Iranian-sponsored terrorist attacks and missile attacks as well, asked the Soviet Union and the United States to protect its shipping through the Gulf, opening the way for the United States to reflag Kuwaiti vessels and provide naval escort. The Kuwaiti initiative was apparently supported, albeit quietly, by most of its fellow GCC members.

IN CONCLUSION: TOWARD MORE COOPERATION

Saudi interests in common with the GCC states are obvious and longstanding. They include commonalities as traditional, Islamic, tribally-based societies, with oil-based economies and few other natural resources, small populations in proportion to revenues, small military establishments in proportion to potential external threats, and a shared threat from revolutionary Iran and the Iran-Iraq war.

Saudi behavior towards its neighbors is complex, a paternalism based on respect for the lineages of its neighbors, and a demand for the respect it believes it deserves as both the largest state in the Peninsula and its tribal and spiritual heartland. This behavior is reciprocated by Saudi Arabia's neighbors with an amalgam of respect and resentment present in a special relationship that is closed to outsiders.

Despite this tradition, the Saudis never systematically explored their interests in collective cooperation with the Gulf states until after the British departed. Since then, a combination of external and internal political, economic and military factors have led them toward more cooperation, culminating with the creation of the Gulf Cooperation Council.

This cooperation by Saudi Arabia still does not constitute a formal Gulf policy. Although all the elements are there, Saudi Gulf policy is still at the prepolicy stage. Given the continuing sense of crisis arising out of the Iran-Iraq war, however, a full Saudi Gulf policy is emerging with a multilateral approach, using the GCC as a principal focus.

Looking beyond the present crisis atmosphere of the war, one can speculate about the degree of cohesiveness of Saudi Gulf policy in the future. Unless another security crisis follows on the heels of the present one, it is very likely that the Saudis will very quickly again become preoccupied with broader Arab-world and East-West issues. The Arab-Israeli problem flared again with the Spring 1988 riots in the territories. A further tension in that arena or progress in the peace process will demand more Saudi attention. The ever-present Communist threat will also probably receive more attention, whether manifested by nearby neighbors such as South Yemen and Ethiopia or more distant threats such as Afghanistan.

It is also likely, as the world oil market bottoms out and the glut ends in the next few years, that OPEC will again become more active, and Saudi oil interests once more will take on a much broader perspective than that of the other Gulf producers. Despite the economic, as well as political, costs absorbed by the Saudis in maintaining their role of price setter, both during the energy crisis and the oil glut, they are not likely to give up that role easily.

There could also be other economic differences with the Saudis and their Gulf neighbors. For example, all the Gulf states seek to diversify their economies and, lacking significant resources to do so, some have invested in petrochemicals. Once all these plants come on stream, it is quite likely that the Saudis will some day find themselves in competition with their neighbors in an oversupplied market, yet unable to reduce production for a variety of reasons, including prestige, political pressures from Saudi entrepreneurs and labor, and domestic economic dislocations.

That said, the level of cooperation already achieved between Saudi Arabia and its fellow GCC member states appears to be self-sustaining, and the chances for continued and expanded cooperation are good. The Saudis and their colleagues have become accustomed to cooperating, and habit is still a primary motivating factor in this part of the world. Secondly, the experience has demonstrated to the Saudis just how many mutual interests they do have with their Gulf neighbors, interests that can best be served by mutual cooperation. As a result, there is a genuine willingness on the part of Saudi Arabia to expand the area of cooperation to a broader range of issues.

FOR FURTHER READING

Akins, James E. "Saudi Arabia, Soviet Activities, and Gulf Security." In Z. Michael Szaz, ed., *The Impact of the Iranian Events Upon Persian Gulf and United States Security* (Washington: American Foreign Policy Institute, 1979), pp. 89-110.

Beling, Willard A. *King Faisal and the Modernisation of Saudi Arabia.* London: Croom Helm; Boulder, CO: Westview Press, 1980.

Bligh, Alexander. *From Prince to King: Royal Succession in the House of Saud in the Twentieth Century.* New York: New York University Press, 1984.

Cordesman, Anthony H. *Saudi Arabia, AWACS, and America's Search for Strategic Stability in the Near East*. Washington: Smithsonian Institution, 1981. Woodrow Wilson Center for International Scholars.

——*The Gulf and the Search for Strategic Stability: Saudi Arabia, the Military Balance in the Gulf, and Trends in the Arab-Israeli Military Balance*. Boulder, CO: Westview Press; London: Mansell, 1984.

——*Western Strategic Interests in Saudi Arabia*. London: Croom Helm, 1987.

Dawisha, Adeed. *Saudi Arabia's Search for Security*. London: International Institute for Strategic Studies, 1979-1980. Adelphi Papers, No. 158.

——"Internal Values and External Threats: The Making of Saudi Foreign Policy." *Orbis*, Vol. 23, No. 1 (Spring 1979), pp. 129-143.

de Gaury, Gerald. *Faisal: King of Saudi Arabia*. London: Arthur Barker, 1966.

Helms, Christine Moss. *The Cohesion of Saudi Arabia: Evolution of Political Identity*. London: Croom Helm; Baltimore: Johns Hopkins University Press, 1981.

Long, David E. *Saudi Arabia*. Beverly Hills, CA: Sage Publications, for the Georgetown University Center for Strategic and International Studies, 1976. Washington Papers, No. 39.

——*The United States and Saudi Arabia: Ambivalent Allies*. Boulder, CO: Westview Press, 1985. Published in cooperation with the Middle East Research Institute, University of Pennsylvania.

Niblock, Tim, ed. *State, Society and Economy in Saudi Arabia*. London: Croom Helm, for the University of Exeter Centre for Arab Gulf Studies, 1982.

Piscatori, James P. "The Roles of Islam in Saudi Arabia's Political Development." In John L. Esposito, ed., *Islam and Development: Religion and Sociopolitical Change* (Syracuse: Syracuse University Press, 1980), pp. 123-138.

——"Islamic Values and National Interest: The Foreign Policy of Saudi Arabia." In Adeed Dawisha, ed., *Islam in Foreign Policy* (Cambridge: Cambridge University Press, 1983; published in association with the Royal Institute of International Affairs), pp. 33-53.

——"Ideological Politics in Sa'udi Arabia." In James P. Piscatori, ed., *Islam in the Political Process* (Cambridge: Cambridge University Press, 1983; published in association with the Royal Institute of International Affairs), pp. 56-72.

Safran, Nadav. *Saudi Arabia: The Ceaseless Quest for Security*. Cambridge, MA: Belknap Press of Harvard University Press, 1985.

Shaw, John A., and David E. Long. *Saudi Arabian Modernization: The Impact of Change on Stability*. New York: Praeger, with the Georgetown University Center for Strategic and International Studies, 1982. The Washington Papers, No. 89.

10

The Future of Federalism in the United Arab Emirates

J.E. Peterson*

The United Arab Emirates (UAE) is the Arab world's most success-ful unity scheme to date. December 1986 marked the UAE's fifteenth anniversary, amid justifiable self-congratulations for the longevity and continued promise of an experiment that many ob-servers at its inception gave little chance of succeeding. The fifteenth year of independence also provides a convenient benchmark for evaluating the success of the federal experiment in the UAE and prognosticating upon its likely future course.

All other attempts at Arab unity have been dismal failures. The UAE experiment differs from most of these in that it has been a real attempt at unification, rather than simply an empty political state-ment. Any attempt to explain the success of the UAE compared to the modern Arab world's only other serious attempt at unity, the short-lived United Arab Republic between Egypt and Syria (1958-1961), would have to take into account the social, economic, and political similarities among the members of the UAE and their relative equality in population size, wealth and level of development.

But the confederal structure of the union, though often over-looked, may have been just as important in ensuring a successful first fifteen years. Areas of sovereignty not specifically assigned to the UAE government fall to the individual amirates, which jealously guard their autonomy. Even when certain powers, such as defense, constitutionally come under the jurisdiction of the federal government, local control persists in practice.

* Research in the United Arab Emirates for this article was assisted by a Senior Research Grant in the Fulbright Islamic Civilization Research Program, under the local sponsorship of the UAE Cultural Foundation, Abu Dhabi.

Map 6: The United Arab Emirates

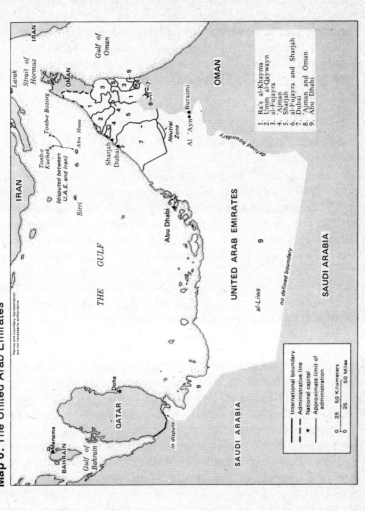

Names and boundary representation
are not necessarily authoritative

IRAN

THE GULF

IRAN

Strait of Hormuz

Larak

Gulf of Oman

Tonb-e Kuchek
Tonb-e Bozorg

(disputed between
U.A.E. and Iran)

Sirri

Abu Musa

Sharjah
Dubai

OMAN

1. Ra's al-Khayma
2. Umm al-Qaywayn
3. al-Fujayra
4. 'Ajman
5. Sharjah
6. al-Fujayra and Sharjah
7. Dubai
8. 'Ajman and Oman
9. Abu Dhabi

Neutral
Zone

Al 'Ayn   Buraimi

OMAN

defined boundary

Abu Dhabi

UNITED ARAB EMIRATES

al-Liwa   9

no defined boundary

SAUDI ARABIA

QATAR

Doha

Manama

BAHRAIN

Gulf of
Bahrain

SAUDI ARABIA

in dispute

9

international boundary
Administrative line
National capital
Approximate limit of
administration

0   25   50 Kilometers
0   25   50 Miles

As time goes by, however, the limitations inherent in the confederal approach become more apparent. The flexibility it initially provided, in encouraging the seven rulers to cooperate without sacrificing their sovereignty, was essential to its early success. Indeed, most likely it was the only workable formula. But what constituted necessary pliancy in the beginning may be evolving into an unwieldy and possibly uncontrollable looseness that thwarts attempts at further political evolution. Furthermore, it seems increasingly archaic as the society and economy of the UAE change and serious questions emerge about the next generation of UAE leaders.

THE POLITICAL BACKGROUND OF THE SEVEN AMIRATES

The longstanding British presence and the discovery of oil played inordinately key roles in the modern development of the United Arab Emirates. The area now comprising the UAE traditionally was regarded as part of Oman and was sometimes called Peninsular Oman. It became more commonly known in the West as the Pirate Coast after Britain became concerned with maritime attacks by the Qawasim of Peninsular Oman, and then received the interchangeable sobriquets of Trucial Oman, Trucial Coast, and Trucial States after Britain pressured the various tribal shaykhs along the coast to enter into a general truce against maritime warfare.[1]

British involvement gradually intensified from simple concern with the protection of shipping through the Gulf to recognition of certain key shaykhs as territorial rulers and eventually their being given British-protected status. Throughout much of the twentieth century, Britain assumed responsibility for the foreign affairs and defense matters of the Trucial Coast, and exercised increasing influence over domestic political and economic affairs.

The evolution from simply powerful tribal shaykh to ruler of a political and territorial entity depended on British recognition, and the final shaping of the Trucial States into its present seven shaykhdoms or amirates did not appear until the 1950s. With impending British withdrawal from the Gulf, the seven Trucial States — and also, for a while, Bahrain and Qatar — began negotiations in 1968 toward an independent union. As a consequence, the United Arab Emirates came into existence on December 2, 1971, with six members; the seventh, Ra's al-Khayma, joined in February 1972.

In addition to permitting the UAE to achieve one of the world's highest per capita incomes, oil has been responsible for determining the relative wealth and influence of the member states of the UAE.[2] Oil came late to the Trucial Coast, compared with elsewhere in the Gulf: exports first began in Abu Dhabi in 1962. While Abu Dhabi remains by far the largest exporter in the UAE, oil is also exported by Dubai (discovered 1966), Sharjah (discovered 1969), and Ra's al-Khayma (discovered 1983). Umm al-Qaywayn receives a small income from an offshore field shared with Sharjah and Iran.

Despite their historical, cultural and tribal connections, the seven member states of the UAE display considerable diversity in the recent political convolutions of their ruling families. Since the seven hereditary rulers comprise the highest authority in the UAE, the quality of individual rulers and heirs apparent, internal family divisions, and issues of succession have crucial implications for the future of the federation.

Abu Dhabi

Abu Dhabi is not only the largest oil producer in the UAE (and therefore enjoys the largest income of any of the amirates), it is also the geographically largest and tribally most complicated member.[3] [See Table 10.1.] The largest and predominant tribe is the Bani Yas, which is composed of over a dozen sections. Over the last several centuries, the Al Bu Falah section gradually achieved political predominance and the present ruling family, the Al Nahyan, derive from this section.

Through alliance with other prominent tribes (such as al-Sudan, al-Manasir, and al-Dhawahir) and primacy over other Bani Yas clans (such as the Al Bu Mahayr, al-Qubaysat and al-Mazari'), the Al Nahyan were gradually able to strengthen their control over the stretch of coastline from Khawr al-'Udayd in the west (at the present border with Qatar) to the southern shore of Dubai Creek in the east, as well as over the important inland regions and oases of al-Zafra, al-Liwa, al-Khatam and al-Buraymi. Water was discovered on Abu Dhabi Island in 1761 and the Al Bu Falah subsequently settled there and made it their capital.[4] By the end of the 19th century, under the dynamic leadership of Shaykh Zayid bin Khalifa (r. 1855-1909), the process of Al Nahyan consolidation of authority over the entire present territory of the amirate was virtually complete.

201

Table 10.1: The member states of the UAE (a)

Amirate	Population (1980)	Population (1985)	Size (sq. m.)	GDP at Factor Cost (1982) (in b dh)	Crude Oil Production (bd) (June 1987)
Abu Dhabi	451,848 (44%)	670,000 (42%)	26,000 (87%)	73.1 (63%)	880,000 (70%)
Dubai	276,301 (27%)	419,000 (26%)	1,500 (5%)	30.2 (26%)	380,000 (30%)
Sharjah	159,317 (15%)	269,000 (17%)	1,000 (3%)	6.7 (6%)	5,000 (0.4%)
Ra's al-Khayma	73,918 (7%)	116,000 (7%)	650 (2%)	2.9 (2.5%)	— (b)
'Ajman	36,100 (3%)	64,000 (4%)	100 (.3%)	.9 (0.8%)	—
al-Fujayra	32,189 (3%)	54,500 (3%)	450 (1.5%)	1.3 (1%)	—
Umm al-Qaywayn	12,426 (1%)	29,000 (2%)	300 (1%)	.5 (0.4%)	—
UAE	1,042,099	1,600,000	30,000	115.6	1,265,000

Notes:

a. Figures in parentheses represent amirate's proportion of UAE total.

b. Sharjah also produces approximately 50,000 b/d of condensates and Ra's al-Khayma approximately 14,000 b/d.

Sources:

a. Population figures for 1980 are from the 1980 census, derived from United Arab Emirates, Ministry of Planning, Central Statistical Department, *Annual Statistical Abstract, 1984* (Abu Dhabi, 1985), p. 23; 1985 figures represent preliminary results from 1985 census, as reported in Sarah Searight, "The UAE: A Special Report," *The Middle East,* No. 138 (April 1986), p. 29.

b. Size and GDP figures are derived from the UAE *Annual Statistical Abstract, 1984,* pp. 8 and 427 respectively.

c. Crude oil production is derived from US Central Intelligence Agency, Directorate of Intelligence, *International Energy Statistical Review* (Washington, August 25, 1987), p. 1.

Four sons of Shaykh Zayid followed their father to the Abu Dhabi rulership in quick and often violent succession until Shaykh Shakhbut bin Sultan came to the throne in 1928. A true conservative and traditionalist, Shakhbut presided over the first inklings of change in Abu Dhabi and the discovery and export of oil. His failure to utilize his new income to develop the state led to a British-supported *coup d' etat* by his younger brother, Zayid bin Sultan, in 1966. Zayid not only initiated the process of rapid change that has completely altered the face of the amirate but he also served as a principal architect of the new UAE, of which he has been president since its inception. [See Table 10.2.]

After twenty years of ruling Abu Dhabi and fifteen difficult years of pushing the cause of federation with his fellow rulers, Shaykh Zayid seemed to become less and less interested in affairs of state. Much administration of Abu Dhabi State was left to

Table 10.2: Leadership of the UAE member states

Amirate	Date of Trucial Recognition	Ruling Family	Ruler	Date of Accession
Abu Dhabi	1820	Al Nahyan	Zayid bin Sultan (a)	1966
Dubai	1820	Al Maktum	Rashid bin Sa'id (b)	1958
Sharjah	1820	al-Qawasim	Sultan bin Muhammad	1972
Ra's al-Khayma	1921 (c)	al-Qawasim	Saqr bin Muhammad	1948
al-Fujayra	1952	al-Sharqiyyin	Hamad bin Muhammad	1974
'Ajman	1820	al-Na'im	Humayd bin Rashid	1981
Umm al-Qaywayn	1820	al-Mu'alla	Rashid bin Ahmad	1981

Notes:

a. Also President of the United Arab Emirates.
b. Also Vice-President and Prime Minister of the United Arab Emirates.
c. A shaykh of Ra's al-Khayma was one of the original trucial signatories in 1820 but the shaykhdom was incorporated into Sharjah for a period in the early 20th century.

Khalifa bin Zayid, his eldest son and the heir apparent. As Deputy Commander-in-Chief of the UAE Armed Forces, Khalifa is nominally in charge of Abu Dhabi's military, but is not regarded as particularly dynamic or charismatic. Shaykh Zayid was forced to conduct more official business himself, however, when Shaykh Khalifa suffered a cerebral hemorrhage in early 1987.

Zayid's second son, Sultan bin Zayid, has a military background and, as an 18-year-old, was appointed commander-in-chief of the UAE Armed Forces by his father in 1978. But he has given up that position, in part because of a personal scandal, and dropped out of the picture in recent years. A third son (Shaykh Zayid has at least 19 sons), Muhammad bin Zayid, is an air force major and de facto commander of the air force; although promising, at about 28 years of age he is too junior to figure heavily in amirate politics. A fourth and even more junior son (he is in his mid-20s), Hamdan bin Zayid, is well-regarded as undersecretary in the Ministry of Foreign Affairs.

Given the weakness of the Bani Sultan (descendants of Shaykh Shakhbut's and Shaykh Zayid's father), there is considerable speculation that the rival Bani Muhammad (sometimes known as the Bani Khalifa after their grandfather Khalifa, uncle to Shakhbut and Zayid) might try to wrest away leadership of the Al Nahyan after Zayid's death. The half-dozen brothers of the Bani Muhammad are well-represented in the amirate and UAE hierarchies: Hamdan as UAE deputy prime minister; Mubarak as titular UAE minister of the interior;[5] Tahnun as the ruler's representative in the Eastern Region (and chairman of al-'Ayn Municipality, vice-president of the Abu Dhabi Executive Council, and titular chairman of Abu Dhabi National Oil Company); Sayf as chairman of the Abu Dhabi Department of Planning; Khalifa as the former UAE minister of hydraulic and electric power; and Surur as presidential chamberlain (and chairman of the UAE Central Bank and chairman of the Abu Dhabi Departments of Water and Electricity, Organization and Management, and Purchasing).

Of these, Surur appears to be the most capable and energetic. Alone among the Al Nahyan, Surur tends to play an even more active role on the federal level than in Abu Dhabi, serving as something of a de facto prime minister during the sickness of the appointed prime minister, Shaykh Rashid of Dubai. He also displays the best relations with Dubai's Al Maktum of any of the Al Nahyan. Surur has been mentioned as a possible successor to the

Abu Dhabi rulership after Khalifa bin Zayid, if the situation should arise in the next few years.

Dubai

In contrast to Abu Dhabi, politics in Dubai has been relatively more straightforward. Although a fishing village has existed on the site of Dubai Town since the 18th century, it only became independent of Abu Dhabi's Al Bu Falah in 1833 when another Bani Yas section, the Al Bu Falasa, seceded from Abu Dhabi and took up residence in Dubai. Dubai's new leaders, the Al Maktum (a family from the Al Bu Falasa), tended to rely on good relations with the British in order to protect themselves from their stronger neighbors in Abu Dhabi and Sharjah. But by the turn of the twentieth century, Dubai began its rise as a commercial center for the entire Trucial Coast.

Much of the amirate's prosperity was due to the acumen of its last two rulers, Shaykh Sa'id bin Maktum (r. 1912-1958), who put down a family-led challenge to his absolute authority in the late 1930s, and Shaykh Rashid bin Sa'id (r. 1958-present), who took over most leadership responsibilities from his father in 1939. While Abu Dhabi's oil-fueled growth and development has resulted in a large, cumbersome bureaucracy dominated by expatriate Arabs, the development of Dubai has evidenced a more commercial approach, with minimal bureaucracy and the ruler's personal involvement and partial ownership in all major schemes.[6]

Shaykh Rashid has served as UAE vice-president since independence and as its prime minister since 1979. For several years, however, he has been unable to carry out either his Dubai or federal duties because of terminal illness, and the running of the amirate has been left to his four sons. The eldest of these is Maktum bin Rashid, presently heir apparent and UAE deputy prime minister. Maktum will undoubtedly succeed his father as ruler of Dubai but the quality of his leadership is questionable. He was generally uninspiring as federal prime minister before his father took over and, as an introvert, he does not like playing a political role. Muhammad bin Maktum, the third son, is far more dynamic and ambitious. A trained pilot, Muhammad has been the UAE's only minister of defense and has taken over responsibility for Dubai's internal security, armed forces, finance, investments and civil aviation — all the things that really count.[7]

A positive scenario has the two brothers reaching a modus vivendi on Shaykh Rashid's death, whereby Maktum reigns while Muhammad rules (not unsimilar to the recent relationship between King Khalid and Crown Prince Fahd in Saudi Arabia). The negative scenario would be another intense struggle for power as happened so frequently in the Trucial States' past. Rashid's other two sons are less likely to challenge Maktum or Muhammad. Hamdan bin Rashid is the UAE's minister of finance and industry, as well as being nominally in charge of Dubai Municipality and the amirate's business affairs; he is most interested, however, in horseracing. Hamdan does not get along well with Muhammad and he has a bitter feud with Ahmad bin Rashid, the youngest brother. Ahmad is also a horseracing enthusiast, which commands more of his attention than his official position as commander of the Central Military Command (Dubai's armed forces).

Sharjah

The ruling families of both Sharjah and Ra's al-Khayma belong to competing branches of the clan of al-Qawasim, the old aristocracy of the Trucial Coast. In the eighteenth and nineteenth centuries, the Qawasim succeeded in imposing their control over most tribes in the northern half of Peninsular Oman, and also controlled a number of ports on the Persian littoral of the Gulf. Unlike the Bani Yas of Abu Dhabi and, to a lesser extent, Dubai, the Qawasim have been a minority in their own realm and have had to rely on strong leadership and diplomacy to maintain their pre-eminent position.

Ra's al-Khayma served as the traditional Qasimi capital and was burned on several occasions by the British, insistent on stamping out what they saw as piracy. Subsequently, rivalries within the clan led to a brief Sharjan independence in the mid-eighteenth century and later Sharjah rose to predominance over Ra's al-Khayma. Ra's al-Khayma gradually gained independence from Sharjah until it was finally recognized as a Trucial shaykhdom by the British in 1921.

Following a period of intra-family squabbling, Saqr bin Sultan acceded to the rulership of Sharjah in 1951. From the British point of view, Saqr was far too sympathetic to Arab nationalist ideology and his efforts to open an Arab League office in Sharjah eventually led to his deposal in 1965 and a life of exile in Cairo. Saqr was replaced as ruler by a cousin, Khalid bin Muhammad, who had been a small merchant in Dubai. Although personally likeable, Khalid was widely seen as a weak ruler and his agreement to Iran's take-over of Sharjah's Abu Musa Island in 1971 did not help his popularity. As a consequence, Saqr bin Sultan returned to Sharjah in January 1972 in an unsuccessful attempt to regain leadership; in the course of the fighting, he killed the ruler Khalid. Saqr was captured and imprisoned by the federal government.

Leadership of Sharjah thereupon went to Sultan bin Muhammad, Khalid's younger brother and a young agricultural graduate of Cairo University. Sultan's experience abroad has given him a relatively more liberal outlook than his fellow rulers and he has been a strong federalist, as well as an advocate for greater political participation in the UAE and a supporter of the arts.[8] He recently received a Ph.D. in history from the University of Exeter for a thesis appropriately refuting the view that his Qasimi forebears were pirates.[9] While Shaykh Sultan is sometimes described as a liberal ideologue or philosopher, his elder brother 'Abd al-'Aziz is seen as the practical figure in Sharjah, serving as deputy ruler and commander of the Amiri Guard. The alleged neglect of duties and profligacy by Shaykh Sultan were cited by Shaykh 'Abd al-'Aziz in his abortive coup attempt of June-July 1987. The eldest surviving brother, Saqr bin Muhammad, is resident in and responsible for Khawr Fakkan (Sharjah's port on the eastern Gulf of Oman coast).

The first coup attempt since the beginning of the oil boom occurred on June 17, 1987, when Shaykh 'Abd al-'Aziz ordered the Amiri Guard to seize control of Government House while his brother was in London. A hard-headed businessman, Shaykh 'Abd al-'Aziz cited Shaykh Sultan's alleged neglect of duties and profligacy, claiming the amirate was $1.3b in debt, as reasons compelling his action. Success was forestalled, however, by Shaykh Sultan's quick return to neighboring Dubai, and the full support given him by the Al Maktum.

Abu Dhabi, which initially seemed to support 'Abd al-'Aziz — and, by some accounts, to have encouraged his action — was forced to convene non-stop meetings of the Council of Rulers at Shaykh Zayid's palace in al-'Ayn. Finally, third-party mediation produced a solution whereby Sultan was confirmed as ruler while 'Abd al-'Aziz was formally recognized as heir apparent (in addition to deputy ruler) and deputy chairman of the Sharjah Executive Council, a new combination of cabinet and consultative council.

The two brothers met face-to-face before the Council of Rulers on June 23, bringing the crisis to an end, at least for the time being.

Sharjans have tended to be the best educated and regard themselves as the most cultured of the UAE's nationals. As the first site of the British political agency and the location of a British RAF base up to 1971, Sharjah had a head start in the race to development. Its meager oil resources and stiff commercial competition from Dubai has meant that the amirate has had to take a back seat in UAE matters to Abu Dhabi and Dubai. Given the glories of the Qasimi past, this has been a galling experience and has led Sharjah to a sometimes ambivalent attitude toward the federation.

The amirate's rush to development also left it heavily in debt, which is only gradually being reduced by the amirate's recent good fortune in producing crude oil condensate. In addition, leadership in Sharjah is complicated by the amirate's geographical separation. Although Sharjah Town is located on the Gulf coast, it has major dependencies at Hamriya (on the coast between 'Ajman and Umm al-Qaywayn) and al-Dhayd (the agricultural settlement inland from Sharjah), as well as three non-contiguous enclaves on the Gulf of Oman coast of the UAE: Khawr Fakkan in the center, Dibba in the north and Kalba in the south.

Ra's al-Khayma

While Sharjah is on the verge of being a "have" amirate, like Abu Dhabi and Dubai, Ra's al-Khayma is clearly the most important of the "have-nots." The decline of what had been the most important town on the Trucial Coast began with the loss of Qasimi supremacy to Sharjah in the mid-nineteenth century. Its independent status was recognized in 1921. But Shaykh Sultan bin Salim, who had acceded on his father's death in 1919, increasingly alienated his subjects and relatives. In March 1948, Sultan's nephew, Saqr bin Muhammad, was able to take over with popular support and he has remained Ra's al-Khayma's ruler ever since.

Like Sharjah, the Qawasim of Ra's al-Khayma have always been a minority in the tribal composition of the shaykhdom. This has presented problems in governing the various dependencies from the Qasimi stronghold in Ra's al-Khayma Town. Sha'am (at the northern end of the coastal plain where the mountains come down to the sea) is inhabited by the Shihuh tribe, traditional Qasimi rivals. The Za'ab tribe predominates in Jazirat al-Hamra' (on the coast south of Ra's al-Khayma Town) and in 1968 the Za'abi shaykh quarrelled with Shaykh Saqr and relocated to Abu Dhabi with a number of his tribesmen.[10]

Shaykh Saqr is regarded as the most truculent of the UAE rulers. Like his namesake Shaykh Saqr bin Sultan of Sharjah, he favored closer relations with the Arab republics during the heyday of pan-Arab nationalism in the 1960s and he nearly sabotaged the 1968-1971 federation negotiations by abruptly walking out of a meeting of the rulers. Shaykh Saqr bitterly resents the turn of fate that has given the upstart Bani Yas "bedouin" the lion's share of wealth and power in the UAE, while the aristocratic Qasimi states remain powerless and poor.

His eager hope of oil discoveries in Ra's al-Khayma, and the greater autonomy and influence it would bring the amirate, led him to postpone joining the UAE until February 1972. The continuing failure to achieve oil prosperity in the amirate has embittered him and he feuds incessantly with Shaykh Zayid and fights any extension of federal authority (which invariably is perceived as Abu Dhabi intriguing) over Ra's al-Khayma.[11] The grandiose plans to develop Ra's al-Khayma as a modern commercial center have evaporated, leaving a bleak skyline of half-completed hotels, office buildings, and residential blocks. The heir apparent is his son, Khalid bin Saqr, the only UAE heir apparent to have been educated in the United States and a rising star in federal affairs through his frequent role as emissary between the amirates.

Al-Fujayra, 'Ajman, and Umm al-Qaywayn

The remaining three amirates have even less opportunities and importance within the UAE. Al-Fujayra, the only amirate located entirely on the eastern Gulf of Oman coast, is slightly better off than 'Ajman and Umm al-Qaywayn, with relatively greater development opportunities due to its deepwater port (which has the advantage of being located outside the Strait of Hormuz) and tourism potential.[12] The Fujayran ruling family comes from the tribe of al-Sharqiyyin, one of the biggest in the UAE and certainly the most important tribe on the Shamayliya (Gulf of Oman) coast.

Sharqi size and unity enabled al-Fujayra to free itself from Qasimi domination (including al-Fujayra Town, part of Dibba [at the northern end of Shamayliya], and various tiny enclaves between al-Fujayra and Dibba) but the amirate was not recognized as being independent until 1952. Shaykh Hamad bin Muhammad served as the UAE's minister of agriculture and marine resources before succeeding his father as ruler of al-Fujayra in late 1974. While by all accounts a capable and energetic ruler, his task is complicated by al-Fujayra's remoteness, lack of money, traditional rivalry with Qasimi Sharjah (whose dependencies surround the amirate), and lack of prestigious family status within the Council of Rulers.

Both tiny 'Ajman and even smaller Umm al-Qaywayn are tribally homogenous. 'Ajman's native inhabitants are largely from the Al Bu Khayraban section of the large tribe of al-Na'im, which is concentrated in Abu Dhabi amirate and the Sultanate of Oman around al-Buraymi and the Jau region and also has members in Ra's al-Khayma. The 'Ajmani ruling family, drawn from the Al Bu Khayraban, also controls the inland enclaves of Masfut and al-Manama. Umm al-Qaywayn is the smallest and poorest of the seven amirates, and the UAE's only amirate, apart from Abu Dhabi, with totally contiguous territory. The Al 'Ali tribe forms almost the entire indigenous population of the amirate and its inland oasis of Falaj Al 'Ali; a number of Al 'Ali tribesmen have also settled in Ra's al-Khayma. The Mu'alla ruling family come from this tribe.

Besides their small size and poverty, another similarity between the two amirates was the longevity of their previous rulers. Shaykh Rashid bin Humayd al-Na'imi of 'Ajman ruled from 1928 to 1981 while Umm al-Qaywayn's Shaykh Ahmad bin Rashid al-Mu'alla ruled from 1929 to 1981. They were succeeded by their sons, Humayd bin Rashid al-Na'imi and Rashid bin Ahmad al-Mu'alla. The significantly different policies and outlooks followed by the two amirates are partly the consequence of the opposing styles of these two long-lived previous rulers. Shaykh Rashid's physical courage, impressive stature and engaging personality, along with his relative success in playing Abu Dhabi off against Dubai, gave 'Ajman respect and a somewhat independent posture within the UAE, while Shaykh Ahmad's introverted nature and lack of interest in state affairs has resulted in a near-total dependence on and subservience to Abu Dhabi.

THE FIRST FIFTEEN YEARS OF THE FEDERAL EXPERIMENT

Not surprisingly, the UAE had a difficult birth. Relations between neighboring shaykhdoms were marked by intense rivalry and often overt hostilities. Relations between ruling families were similarly strained and only British encouragement ensured a minimum of cooperation, particularly through the Trucial Council. Abu Dhabi, Dubai and Sharjah had already experienced the beginnings of economic change and they were in the process of forming prototypal financial and administrative organs before independence, in contrast to the other four shaykhdoms. Negotiations on the larger, logical combination of Bahrain, Qatar and the Trucial States fell through and even the union of the remaining seven smaller states was not completed until three months after independence.[13]

Nevertheless, three years of protracted negotiations bore fruit in the union of six shaykhdoms at independence in December 1971. Agreement was reached on a provisional constitution and a number of necessary executive and administrative organs for the new state.[14] The provisional constitution specified the name of the new state (the United Arab Emirates), the "temporary" location of its capital in Abu Dhabi,[15] the composition of the flag, and, most importantly, the relationship between the federal entity and the individual shaykhdoms (henceforth known as amirates) and the structure of federal institutions. Articles 116 and 122 guaranteed the federal nature of the state, by leaving all powers to the individual amirates except for those explicitly reserved for the federal government. Thus, sovereignty and most existing political, economic and administrative institutions were left in the hands of the members.

In general, the most effective federal institutions have been those that did not exist on the amirate level. The most important of these institutions is the Council of Rulers, representing the supreme authority in the state and consisting of all seven rulers or their deputies. As the highest authority, the council reviews and approves (or disapproves) all important matters within the UAE. Its decisions require a high degree of consensus: approval of at least five of the seven members, including the two most important amirates, Abu Dhabi and Dubai.

The council is empowered to delegate authority to other institutions. It elects the president and vice-president of the state for five-year terms. Given the rarity with which the council has met in recent years, the president acts virtually alone. Once again, reflecting the predominance of the two largest members, the ruler of Abu Dhabi has always been the president and the ruler of Dubai the vice-president. The president has the authority to appoint the prime minister, deputy prime minister(s) and the other members of the cabinet.

The actual composition of the cabinet, however, is the product of an arduous process of negotiation and compromise among the seven members. Thus, in the first cabinet, the portfolios were carefully allocated to representatives of all seven states. Six were reserved for Abu Dhabi (including foreign affairs, interior and information), three each for Dubai (including defense, finance, and economy and industry) and Sharjah, two each for Umm al-Qaywayn and 'Ajman, and one for al-Fujayra; Ra's al-Khayma's subsequent admission required an expansion of the cabinet. In addition, the office of prime minister went to Dubai's heir apparent and members of the seven ruling families filled most of the positions in the cabinet. More emphasis has been placed on merit in more recent cabinets.

At the time of independence, the British had left virtually no institutional structure that the federal state could build upon, and so all federal ministries had to be built entirely from scratch. For example, the Ministry of Foreign Affairs, an obviously new and necessary body, began with only the minister and a staff of three. The federal civil service exploded from less than 4,000 employees in 1971 to more than 24,000 by the end of 1976 and over 38,000 by the end of 1983 (not including armed forces personnel). Nevertheless, the capability and effectiveness of many of these ministries and bodies remained questionable.

Given the lack of proper federal foundations, it is not surprising that a number of economic, development and other institutions established by individual amirates before independence have continued to survive. In many cases, it took years for the federal government to create capabilities to assume functions in a particular field, thus forcing the amirates to go ahead on their own. Recently, however, the northern amirates have been able to go to the Ministry of Planning, for example, and present their requirements for schools or roads and realistically expect the federal government to provide them.[16] Nevertheless, where amirate administrative departments already existed, especially in Abu Dhabi and Dubai, federal ministries either never really took root or simply and ineffectually duplicated amirate departments. This is particularly true in the fields of oil, finance, and defense.

None of the oil (and gas) producers, regardless of whether production began before or after independence, have shown any desire to hand over control of oil resources to the federal government, and matters of exploration, production and pricing are exclusively handled by the respective amirates. Dubai even retained its separate membership in OAPEC until well after independence.

As oil is the predominant source of national income, the amirates have also been reluctant to give the federal government control over finances. Even in the case of Abu Dhabi, the amirate with by far the largest oil production and therefore the largest income, the federal government is reduced to begging the amirate government for its pledged payments to the federal budget. When an amirate does honor its commitment to the budget, its actual contribution is minimal since the amirate's expenditure in such supposedly federal fields as roads and schools is deducted from the ledger account of what it owes the federal government. As a consequence, the federal government is almost completely dependent on the goodwill of the member states to meet its expenses.

Defense is another contentious area.[17] The origins of the armed forces date back to the creation of the British-officered Trucial Oman Levies, later Trucial Oman Scouts (TOS), in the early 1950s. Upon independence, the Scouts were the logical choice for conversion into the armed forces of the new UAE state. They had grown in size from 500 in 1955 to 2,500 in 1971. But the Union Defense Force (UDF), as the TOS was rechristened, was not the only armed force in the new UAE nor was it even the largest.

Over the decade of the 1960s, the continuing competition between the seven shaykhdoms had evolved a new form: the development of competing military units. Thus in 1971, the Abu Dhabi Defense Force (ADDF) far eclipsed the UDF with over 9,500 men, including a small naval force and developing air wing. In addition, there were also the Dubai Defense Force (DDF, with 500 men, a patrol vessel and small air wing), the Ra's al-Khayma Mobile Force, the Sharjah National Guard, and the 'Ajman Defense Force (in the process of formation). Rather than serving as the armed forces for the entire state, the UDF merely existed as a somewhat neutral element among competing forces, which were lineal descendants of the shaykhs' traditional armed retinues.

While logic dictated the merger of all these units, politics prevented it. Abu Dhabi and Dubai had fought a border war as recently as 1948, and all the shaykhdoms — especially Ra's al-Khayma and Sharjah — resented Abu Dhabi's newfound wealth and muscle. As modern versions of shaykhly guards, these individual forces not only performed police duties but protected the rulers and their families from attempted coups, which more often than not derived from within the ruler's family, as well as from threats from their neighbors.

The infusion of new wealth into traditional rivalries resulted in arms races within the UAE. By 1975, the ADDF had grown to 15,000, equipped with 135 armored vehicles, two squadrons of Mirage IIIs and Vs, some Hawker Hunters and helicopters, Rapier and Crotale SAMs, Vigilant ATGWs, and Vosper Thorneycroft and Fairey Marine Spear class patrol craft. The DDF had also expanded to rival the UDF in size, with 3,000 men, Ferret and Saladin armored cars, several kinds of helicopters and patrol craft. Only the UDF had tanks, however.

Despite the creation of a federal Ministry of Defense and the existence of the UDF at independence, merger of the armed forces was continually postponed. It was not until mid-1975 that the first serious discussions on merger took place, and formal unification was delayed until the constitutional crisis of 1976. At the end of that year, the UAE Armed Forces formally came into being: the ADDF became the Western Command, the DDF the Central Command, and the Ra's al-Khayma Mobile Force the Northern Command; the UDF was renamed the Yarmuk Brigade, and the Sharjah National Guard was merged with the federal police force.

Nevertheless, the merger was still only on paper: the shaykhdoms continued separate arms-purchasing policies, and each force was commanded by the appropriate ruler's son. The chief of staff at the time was able to function effectively only because he was a seconded Jordanian. Important steps were made in subsequent years to strengthen the UAE's military unity by unifying expenditures, upgrading the central headquarters, and redirecting lines of command to federal authorities, yet effective control over those armed forces located in each amirate remained exclusively in the hands of that amirate's ruler.

Most of the fundamental accomplishments of the federal process date from the first few years of independence. The present constitution remains the original provisional one of 1971, although subsequently amended. The essential administrative structure is unchanged, even though ministers have switched chairs and the number of portfolios increased. The reservation of powers not explicitly granted to the UAE government is jealously guarded by all seven amirates and most even seek to take back functions originally granted to the union.

The uncertain balance between federalism and amirate sovereignty has provoked serious crises on more than one occasion.

In early August 1976, Shaykh Zayid threatened to step down as UAE president at the expiry of his term in December 1976, unless his authority was reinforced and certain measures were undertaken to enhance the strength of the federal experiment. In November, the Council of Rulers adopted a series of measures along those lines, including steps toward the merger of military and security forces and the formation of a high financial commission to prepare the federal budget and determine each amirate's contribution.

As a result, the terms of the president (Shaykh Zayid) and vice-president (Shaykh Rashid) were extended for another five years, as was the validity of the provisional constitution. The denouement of the crisis was marked by the formation of a new government at the beginning of 1977. The reduced size of the new cabinet, including less representation from Abu Dhabi, sent a clear message that more emphasis in cabinet selection was to be placed on rationality and competence and less on formulas aimed at representing all amirates.

Bickering within the Council of Rulers and tension between the pro-federal and anti-federal blocs sparked a similar crisis in 1979. Shaykh Zayid and the allied rulers of Sharjah, al-Fujayra, 'Ajman and Umm al-Qaywayn pressed for greater progress in federalization, while Shaykh Rashid of Dubai and Shaykh Saqr of Ra's al-Khayma resisted. In frustration, Shaykh Zayid unilaterally took several steps to increase federal powers. In particular, his appointment of his 18-year-old son Sultan as commander-in-chief of the UAE Armed Forces provoked the rage of Shaykh Rashid, and Dubai and Ra's al-Khayma began to pointedly ignore federal government decisions.

To deal with the deepening rift, the Council of Rulers was forced to meet formally for the first time in three years, to the accompaniment of the first demonstrations in UAE history demanding total unity. The impasse was ended only with Saudi and Kuwaiti mediation. As part of the compromise, Shaykh Rashid took over as prime minister, thus giving Dubai a stronger voice in federal administrative affairs (and forcing Rashid into more direct involvement in UAE matters). The government resigned and a new one was formed with considerable difficulty.

In many respects, the first fifteen years of the UAE experiment have been surprisingly successful.[18] The problem of continuity of the union's leadership, to date, has been handled by the simple expedient of extending the terms of the original officeholders. In theory, the federal budget has been given a more balanced look through all the oil-producing amirates' assumption of responsibility for contributions in addition to Abu Dhabi, and particularly the 1980 agreement by Dubai to join Abu Dhabi in contributing 50 percent of its income to the UAE. A first five-year plan was drawn up, a central bank belatedly created, and a university built.[19] Even though many of the outstanding contentious issues were still to be resolved, they at least seemed to be manageable.

On the surface, at least, the process of federalization had slowed to an imperceptible crawl but no one questioned the underlying legitimacy of the federal state. While the tension between the opposing blocs of rulers continued, reluctant agreement was reached on extending the terms of the president, vice-president and provisional constitution for another five years. Even as such ministries as health, education, and planning extended their jurisdiction over all seven amirates, the crucial areas of oil, finance and defense remained kept far away from federal interference.

But the state of temporary equilibrium between federalism and autonomy existing in 1987 cannot last forever. Continuing progress for the process of federalization is by no means assured and the danger of a drift away from unity still exists. Indeed, a wide range of positive and negative factors which in combination will determine the future of federalization are discernible. These factors are examined below.

POSITIVE FACTORS LEADING TO FEDERALIZATION

1. *Homogeneity of Society*. The UAE possesses a considerable reservoir of strength in the homogenous outlook of the great majority of its indigenous population, which is largely Arab, Sunni Muslim, and of tribal origin. On the one hand, UAE citizens tend to share religious, social and economic goals and values, and are nearly universally supportive of the existing political structure based on ruling families. This also means, on the other hand, that internal security threats from UAE nationals are negligible while the large expatriate population, highly vulnerable to arrest and deportation, generally steers clear of local politics.[20]

2. *Gradual Acceptance of the UAE*. The UAE exists, it has survived despite the misgivings of its detractors, and there are plenty of reasons to suppose that it will continue to exist. The doubters have been turned into grudging acceptors, if not enthusiastic supporters. Nearly an entire new generation (almost

half of the UAE's indigenous population) has grown up knowing nothing else but a UAE government, the UAE flag, UAE passports, and UAE sports teams. The press and television and radio stations tend to reinforce a UAE identity. Many nationals, especially from the northern amirates, have taken employment with the federal government; they may complain about Abu Dhabi's highhandedness and federal inefficiency but not necessarily against the federal idea itself.

3. *Climate of External Threats.* All the UAE members are highly conscious of their small size and fragility to external threats, and the last decade has produced a significant upsurge in serious potential threats. As the threat from secular radicals, as posed by the Popular Front for the Liberation of the Oman (PFLO), receded in the mid-1970s, a new threat emerged from the politicized Islamic right. The Iranian revolution generated considerable excitement on the Arab littoral, the new revolutionary regime actively undertook to foment subversion in the Arab monarchies, and the Iran-Iraq war periodically raises the potential for the spread of warfare to the UAE's shores. In the circumstances, the rulers and citizenry of the various amirates are fully appreciative of the relative advantages of collective security within the UAE framework.

4. *Financial Necessity.* Economically, the UAE's members fall into three categories: the wealthy states of Abu Dhabi and Dubai (although Dubai's wealth is far less than that of Abu Dhabi), the largely self-sufficient state of Sharjah, and the remaining four — basically small towns, too small and too poor to go it alone. While possessing numerous grievances against the federal government, Sharjah would not be able to absorb such necessary functions of an independent state as foreign affairs and defense. Even for Abu Dhabi and especially Dubai, the costs of "going-it-alone" would seem to outweigh the advantages of leaving things as they are. Thus, the majority of UAE members have been heavily dependent on federal financing in order to meet current expenditures as well as development costs. But federal financing is often simply a euphemism for Abu Dhabi largesse, which creates its own problems, as discussed below.

5. *Effective Federal Institutions.* The growing competence and effective jurisdiction of such ministries as education, health and planning points to an incrementalist approach which is bound to have a positive effect on the ability of the federal government to carry out all the functions normally expected of a state, as well as on the UAE citizenry's perceptions of the federal government as a

worthwhile entity. The growing legislative impact of the federal government in the implementation of criminal, commercial, and civil codes is a further step toward a unified legal environment.

The unified administration of foreign affairs, integration of economic affairs, standardization of commercial regulations, and steady amalgamation of the judicial system all provide an incremental enhancement of the UAE's legitimacy. The robust vitality of the Federal National Council (FNC), an appointed assembly of 40 members drawn from all seven amirates, also helps to forge a common identity and viewpoint on a wide range of issues.[21] Faced with increasing problems due to over-capacity in the UAE's banking sector, the UAE Currency Board was converted into a Central Bank in 1980. The Central Bank has proved its effectiveness in straightening out the recent collapse of the Galadari brothers' business empires.

NEGATIVE FACTORS WORKING AGAINST FEDERALIZATION

1. *Traditional Amirate Rivalries.* Mention has already been made of such endemic rivalries as the longstanding enmity between Abu Dhabi and Dubai and the abiding resentment of Ra's al-Khayma's al-Qasimi ruling family over their fall from their historic status as the aristocrats of the lower Gulf to the poor relations of today. Far from subsiding, these rivalries continue in the attitudes of the ruling families toward each other. There are few among the Al Nahyan of Abu Dhabi who will even make the effort to speak to members of the Al Maktum of Dubai and vice-versa. Al-Qasimi truculence in Ra's al-Khayma has intensified in the present troubled economic climate, when resented but necessary Abu Dhabi handouts have virtually ceased and various unfinished development projects give the town of Ra's al-Khayma a ghost-town look. Even al-Qasimi Sharjah is expressing growing doubts about its previously pro-federal policy.

2. *Unresolved Boundary Disputes.* Even a casual glance at the map will quickly demonstrate the UAE's territorial complexity and the entanglement caused by a plethora of non-contiguous enclaves. While many conflicting claims were settled in the years prior to independence, there are still at least a dozen outstanding disputes. These have the same potential to erupt in violence in the future as they often did in the past.[22]

These disputes are particularly thorny since territorial sovereignty is tightly bound up with notions of tribal honor. Furthermore, boundary problems between one amirate and an external neighbor threaten to involve the entire UAE in an international crisis, as happened in the late-1970s dispute between Ra's al-Khayma and Oman, which was solved through negotiations between the UAE and Omani foreign ministries. In addition, in the oil age, boundaries can spell the difference between prosperity and poverty. Umm al-Qaywayn, after settling its offshore boundary dispute with Sharjah, found itself receiving only a small portion of the revenue from the disputed area's small oilfield (which it shared with Sharjah and Iran), rather than all the income.

3. *Unrequited Hopes for the Discovery of Oil.* Experience has shown that the key to power and influence in the UAE is oil. Those amirates that have it control the federation; those that lack oil are dependent on the others. As a consequence, the "have-nots" are reluctant to tighten permanently federal bonds which leave them in an inferior position as they continue to anticipate the future discovery of oil. This attitude is particularly acute in Ra's al-Khayma, which delayed joining the federation at its inception in anticipation of oil finds and has dragged its heels ever since on the same grounds.

4. *Amirate Indebtedness.* There has been considerable pressure on the smaller amirates to engage in large-scale development and prestige projects to keep up with their neighbors inside and outside the UAE, and to demonstrate their independence from Abu Dhabi. The consequence has been rising levels of amirate indebtedness, particularly on the part of Sharjah and Ra's al-Khayma, and the necessity on occasion of advances by Abu Dhabi. Sharjah's debts were prominently cited as a reason for the abortive coup attempt in June 1987.

The economic recession of the last several years has made it far more difficult for these amirates to pay back their loans or to get wealthier neighbors to bail them out, and there is a fear in federal circles that the UAE might end up paying off what are seen as irresponsible amirate debts, much as the Central Bank has had to do with individual citizens and businesses.

5. *Domination by Abu Dhabi.* There is still considerable feeling in the northern amirates that Abu Dhabi has been too overbearing, insensitive, and secretive with the federal budget, especially in defense. Growing resentment of Abu Dhabi policies and ways has even led to grudging cooperation between Dubai and Sharjah, as

exemplified by the ending of their territorial dispute, Sharjah's supplies of gas to Dubai, and Dubai's support of Shaykh Sultan during the 1987 coup crisis. Furthermore, the Abu Dhabi-dominated and -identified federal bureaucracy is seen as largely inefficient and even incompetent. This bloated structure is the object of much derision from "Dubai Inc.," which is run much more smoothly with far fewer people.

Abu Dhabi has tended to take over responsibility for most foreign-policy decisions, and the other amirates seem to have acquiesced as long as the decision does not affect business. This is particularly true of Dubai. Dubai may not have liked the decision to establish diplomatic relations with the Soviet Union in late 1985 (permission for a Soviet consulate in Dubai was refused) but this decision will not have that much impact on the amirate, particularly as Bulgarian and East German trade missions are already located in Dubai.

On the other hand, Abu Dhabi agreed in 1971 to make Gulf Air the UAE's national airline (in partnership with Bahrain, Qatar and Oman) without consulting Dubai. Eventually, Dubai's mounting dissatisfaction with Gulf Air's policies at Dubai Airport — the weekly number of Gulf Air flights were cut from 108 in mid-1983 to 41 in mid-1985, despite growing demand — drove it to establish in late 1985 its own carrier, Emirates Airlines, with the advertising slogan, "your very own airline!"

6. *Autonomous Armed Forces*. There probably are few countries where the minister of defense (Shaykh Muhammad bin Rashid of Dubai) rarely visits the General Headquarters, where the chief of staff — previously a seconded Jordanian officer with a naturalized UAE citizen, Maj. Gen. Muhammad Sa'id al-Badi, appointed only recently — actually works for the deputy commander-in-chief (Shaykh Khalifa bin Zayid of Abu Dhabi) and sees the minister about once a year, and where the two top military officials, the minister of defense and the deputy commander-in-chief of the Armed Forces, do not even speak to each other at official functions.

The ballyhooed merger of the UAE, Abu Dhabi, Dubai, Sharjah and Ra's al-Khayma armed forces in 1976 has taken place only on paper. Separate command structures, recruiting policies and arms purchases continue the same as before. Coordination between the various "commands" is nonexistent. Furthermore, momentum seems to be swinging away from integration, rather than toward it. Sharjah, which merged its police force with the federal force years ago and accepted federal troops in its territory, recently formed its own Amiri Guard for internal security and to protect its oil installations.[23]

Even more disturbing, the top titular officials rarely display any interest in their prescribed duties. The commander of the Central Command (Dubai) (Shaykh Ahmad bin Rashid) rarely shows up at his office, while the titular head of the Western Command (Abu Dhabi) (Shaykh Khalifa bin Zayid, also UAE deputy commander-in-chief) is little interested in military affairs. The minister of defense (Shaykh Muhammad bin Rashid) has his hands full with most administrative functions of the state of Dubai, not to mention one of the world's most extensive racing stables. The lack of interest shown at the very top is reflected in a lack of professionalism among both the various units' national officer corps and their largely non-national ranks.[24]

7. *Weakness of Federal Institutions*. The resolute refusal to transfer additional sovereignty to the federal government handicaps, if not paralyzes, innumerable federal bodies. As a consequence, an abundant number of institutions are duplicated at the amirate level; these generally exercise the real authority within each amirate, as opposed to the paper authority of the federal in-stitution. Even Abu Dhabi, the most pro-federal amirate, demonstrates such prominent examples of duplication as an Executive Council (essentially an Abu Dhabi cabinet), "depart-ments" (which act as ministries on the Abu Dhabi amirate level), and an appointed National Consultative Council (similar in function to the FNC). In addition, most ministries still face the problem of being staffed by nationals of the amirate from which the minister comes.

8. *Federal Finances and the UAE Budget*. Since oil income began before the UAE was established, control over income and expenditure remains in the hands of the individual amirates. Theoretically, each member is supposed to contribute 50 percent of its income to the federal budget. On a more practical level, this really applies only to the significant oil exporters: Abu Dhabi, Dubai, and now Sharjah. The budget-making process is complicated additionally by the provision that each amirate may deduct from its federal contribution the cost of those services it already provides but for which the federal government theoretically has responsibility (such as building or maintaining roads).

Despite these budget-sharing agreements, only Abu Dhabi really has provided substantial additional funds (i.e. beyond expenditures pledged to the federal government but actually spent within the amirate). But this financial assistance to other amirates often comes with burdensome strings attached. In addition, federal ministries often find themselves in the predicament of having to go from amirate to amirate with cap in hand in order to collect overdue amirate installments on pledged contributions to the budget.

In recent years, approval of the budget has come later and later, as the Council of Rulers fails to reach any agreement, and thus the budget has become increasingly meaningless. The 1985 budget was not approved until late October of 1985, and approval of the 1986 draft budget similarly was delayed until late October 1986. Meanwhile, ministries are told to plan monthly expenditures on the basis of 1/12 of their spending over the previous year.

9. *Dependence on Expatriates*. The UAE has sought to build a modern state based on Egyptian, Syrian, and Iraqi models (which themselves were based largely on Western models). This approach produces two problems. First, the state finds itself heavily dependent on foreign workers and experts, who naturally perpetuate the foreign model without really determining whether it is best for the people of the region. In many respects, the modern administrative machinery exists to regulate the affairs of the expatriates, while the nationals conduct their affairs in the old way, by going to their shaykhs and relying on personal relationships.

Second, it is obvious that eventually UAE nationals must take over the administration of their state themselves, a real necessity as oil revenues decline and expatriates leave for economic reasons. The rational response is to prepare nationals to take over positions from the highest level to the lowest. But that has not been done in the UAE. All too often, nationals employed by government agencies are found only in the top positions and serve as titular heads without any real knowledge of or interest in their jobs. In education, for example, nationals account for only 2 percent of the UAE's male teachers. In terms of training citizens to replace expatriates, the fifteen years since independence largely have been wasted.

In part, this emerging political problem is a product of the abundance of oil income and its lavish distribution. For many people, it destroyed the incentive to work except in highly prestigious positions. At the same time, there has been significant criticism of the overemphasis on university education. Everyone wants a university degree for prestige reasons when the state's need for indigenous engineers and especially technicians at all levels is completely ignored.

10. *The Oil Price Plunge.* The world oil situation has had a double effect on the UAE: the federation's oil production, which peaked in 1977 at 2 mbd has dropped to about 1 mbd, while the income per barrel has fallen by nearly half, and briefly by three-quarters in early 1986. The federal budget was reduced by 7 percent in 1984, 10 percent in 1985 and 15 percent in 1986. The poor members of the UAE are still overwhelmingly dependent on Abu Dhabi's generosity in funding development projects in their amirates, as well as its assuming responsibility for most of the federal budget. Yet, with rapidly dwindling oil income (Abu Dhabi's production has been halved in the last ten years), pressures are growing in Abu Dhabi to cut back on expenditure everywhere. As a result, the poorer members largely have been left on their own in financial terms, as Abu Dhabi cuts off the flow of money. This can generate additional resentment of Abu Dhabi and has led to certain anomalies.

The problem was illustrated recently when Abu Dhabi cut off its subsidy to Emirates General Petroleum Company (EGPC) for the supply of electricity and gas to the northern amirates and insisted that the amirates should pay for their own supplies. When Ra's al-Khayma refused to pay, EGPC cut the amirate off; after the resulting blackouts, Shaykh Saqr was forced to ask Shaykh Zayid to restore power. Al-Fujayra also found itself unable to pay EGPC when Abu Dhabi cut off the subsidy. Since in this instance the company actually purchases the gas for al-Fujayra from Sharjah, the latter state has been stuck with al-Fujayra's bills, and once again Abu Dhabi emerges as the villain in the eyes of both sides. Dubai's refusal to join the EGPC system because of fears that the amirate would find itself in Abu Dhabi's grip now appears justified.

11. *The Problem of Sovereignty.* The description of the UAE as a confederation, rather than a federation, follows from the jealous reservation of sovereignty within the individual amirates, except where explicitly granted to the federal government. This compromise, so necessary to get the UAE established fifteen years ago, never has been overcome. If Dubai objects to excessive commercial regulations proposed by the Abu-Dhabi-dominated federal bureaucracy, it simply does not enforce them. If Sharjah wishes to create a new armed force, even though the constitution forbids it, it simply goes ahead and does it. If Ra's al-Khayma disagrees with federal criteria on immigration, it follows its own visa policy. The Council of Rulers, the institution charged with bridging the gap between central authority and local autonomy, is

frequently unable to convene formally for a year or more at a time, let alone take any initiative designed to deepen the federal ties.[25]

12. *The Constitutional Issue.* The considerable ambiguity and lack of enforcement power embodied in the thrice-extended provisional constitution, combined with the adverse psychological impact of continuing to rely on a "temporary" constitution for a permanent state, has provoked considerable dissatisfaction. Nevertheless, no steps have been taken to write a new one. As a consequence, the provisional constitution was once again extended for another five years from its expiry in December 1986.

13. *The Leadership Crisis.* As one diplomat has put it, the art of diplomacy in the UAE is finding the government. Shaykh Zayid, the president of the country, has spent considerable time abroad in recent years and appears to have lost most of his past enthusiasm. Shaykh Rashid, the vice-president and prime minister, is in the final stages of terminal illness and is incapable of carrying out his federal duties. Further progress in federalization requires aggressive advocates. But the key, ardent proponents of federalism in the past are rarely heard from these days. Shaykh Zayid basically has been in semi-retirement, as has been former Foreign Minister Ahmad al-Suwaydi, while Mahdi al-Tajir's fortunes have fallen with the incapacitation of Shaykh Rashid, and Tiryam 'Umran Tiryam, Sharjah's pro-federal speaker of the FNC, has been replaced.

The leadership crisis on the federal level is duplicated in the amirates. In the near future, both Abu Dhabi and Dubai will face the prospect of transition to new rulers for the first time since the UAE was formed. The quality of leadership is particularly crucial, given the dual role these successors will face as rulers of rapidly evolving amirates and key players in the future of the union. Yet the heirs apparent in both cases appear less capable and less interested in affairs of state than their fathers and even less able to get along with each other.

The uncertainty in Abu Dhabi could lead to a succession struggle between the sons of Shaykh Zayid and the Bani Muhammad. There is no certainty in Dubai that Shaykh Muhammad will be content to rule only in a *de facto* sense while his less dynamic older brother Shaykh Maktum reigns. In Sharjah, Shaykh 'Abd al-'Aziz's dissatisfaction with the ruler and his younger brother led to an abortive coup attempt in 1987.

While amirate matters are likely to be sorted out and taken care of in any future arrangement, that is not necessarily the case with the federal government. The federal process has already been drifting with Shaykh Zayid's lack of attention. The drift is certain to be more pronounced with an uncertain Shaykh Khalifa as president, and there is the question of what role Shaykh Muhammad bin Rashid will play when he is unlikely to have a prominent federal position. In addition, Sharjah is likely to insist that its new-found oil income entitles its ruler to be named as a third deputy prime minister (in addition to Shaykhs Maktum bin Rashid of Dubai and Hamdan bin Muhammad of Abu Dhabi).

THE BALANCE SHEET

The future of the federal experiment in the UAE can be capsulized in a three-part prognosis. In the short-term, everything remains on hold while the questions of leadership and cooperation within the Council of Rulers remain unsettled. Over the medium-term, the prognosis is neutral, or balanced more-or-less evenly between the positive and negative factors enumerated above. The long-term gives cause for a rather optimistic outlook. But important, definitive decisions must be taken for this positive scenario to come to pass.

Knowledgeable observers contend that several steps are necessary for further demonstrable progress in the integration of the UAE beyond its present confederal status. One could point to the functional model of integration and expect that increasing federalization will come over the course of time as people and amirates learn to work together.

This undoubtedly holds true for many areas of federal concern, but the drawback of this model or approach is that some outstanding problems need to be settled immediately. The impasse over the federal budget is one such problem. The federal government can never become independent of the largesse (and recalcitrance) of individual rulers until it acquires its own source of income. The most logical source is an oil tax, defined as a percentage share of all revenues from crude oil and natural gas production, which would be paid directly by the operating companies to the federal government.[26]

The uncertainty of leadership is just as pressing as the budget crisis. On one level, of course, leadership is an amirate matter, involving succession within the seven ruling families. But the problem on the federal level involves the conflict of interest and only part-time commitment of high-ranking government officials.

The federation requires a full-time president, vice-president, prime minister and cabinet ministers. The present device of appointing the rulers of Abu Dhabi and Dubai to the two top positions in the UAE is guaranteed to make meaningful federalization impossible, as both are duty-bound to put their amirates' interests before federal necessities.

A partial remedy would involve the appointment of a neutral, "professional" (technocratic?) prime minister to run the government on a routine basis. But even this step is prevented by the occupation of the prime minister's office by Dubai's Shaykh Rashid (and his son before him). Full-time appointments are not only necessary for any chance of neutrality but also would eliminate the present problem of ministers and other officials putting in limited time at jobs that require full-time attention. At least one minister holds three full-time positions in his home amirate and so spends only one day a week in his federal job.

Furthermore, a constitutional means must be found to resolve opposing interests, disagreements, disputes and the like between amirates, instead of relying on mediation by a third party. Since most of these disputes are political and not juridical, involving opinions and views of rulers, they lay outside the province of the courts.

Boundary disputes provide an apt illustration of the limitations at present. In the tribal society of the UAE, boundaries are a very sensitive issue, being bound up with the honor of the tribe. Terms reached through outside mediators have little effect and only agreements between the rulers involved are respected. The territorial dispute between Dubai and Sharjah languished before an arbitration panel in The Hague for more than five years before an award was reached in Sharjah's favor. Dubai's refusal to recognize this decision meant that settlement of the dispute could come only when the ruler of Sharjah relinquished his claims.

By its very requirement of neutrality, any dispute-resolving mechanism must rely on its federal authority and impartiality. A congress of several hundred individuals, consisting of the rulers, the cabinet, the FNC, various chambers of commerce, municipal councils, and similar bodies has been one suggestion. This congress could discuss outstanding problems and decide on a uniform course of action, as well as establish guidelines and directions for the future of the UAE.

Such a comprehensive body would provide widespread political participation at the federal level in a traditional social environment that is not suited to deciding matters by referendum. It would also have the additional advantage of providing a framework for debate on alternative courses of action, rather than simply allowing approval or disapproval of previously chosen options.

These steps require action and agreement on constitutional revisions. Continued delay in formulating a permanent, viable and effective constitution leaves papering over the cracks in the federal foundations as the only recourse. Eventually, these cracks will bring down the entire edifice unless they are firmly addressed and repaired. Given the present financial climate and the seriousness of impending leadership problems, the UAE is likely to remain a confederal state for the foreseeable future — until and unless basic circumstances change dramatically. Only a return to world oil shortages and thus another surge of oil income in the 1990s, positive changes in the leadership situation, and a gradual deepening of nationals' attitudes toward the legitimacy of the UAE itself give cause for a cautious optimism on the long-term viability of the federal experiment.

NOTES

1. On the history of the Trucial States and the formation of the UAE, see Donald Hawley, *The Trucial States* (London: George Allen and Unwin, 1970); K.G. Fenelon, *The United Arab Emirates* (London: Longman, 1973); John Duke Anthony, *Arab States of the Lower Gulf* (Washington: Middle East Institute, 1975); idem., "The Impact of Oil on Political and Socioeconomic Change in the United Arab Emirates," in John Duke Anthony, ed., *The Middle East: Oil, Politics, and Development* (Washington: American Enterprise Institute, 1975), pp. 79-98; Rosemarie Said Zahlan, *The Origins of the United Arab Emirates* (London: Macmillan, 1978); Frauke Heard-Bey, "Le developpement d'un Etat-Cité maritime dans le Golfe: l'exemple de Dubayy," in Paul Bonnenfant, ed., *La Péninsule Arabique d'Aujourd'hui* (Vol. 2; Paris: Centre National de la Recherche Scientifique, 1982), pp. 523-559; and idem., *From Trucial States to United Arab Emirates* (London: Longman, 1983).

2. Oil revenues still account for 90-95 percent of total government revenues in the UAE.

3. Population figures for the UAE can be misleading, as some 80 percent of the UAE's inhabitants and approximately 96 percent of the labor force are foreigners.

4. The principal town and capital of each of the seven amirates also bears the name of the amirate, thus leading to potential confusion. In this paper, the appellation "Town" is given whenever just the capital settlement and not the entire amirate is meant.

5. Mubarak suffered considerable brain damage in a London car accident several years ago and so is unable to act effectively. His son Nahyan is president of the UAE University at al-'Ayn.

6. For example, the Dubai Electricity Company was created in 1959 as a private company when demand for electricity began to outstrip the capability of individual generators to supply it. It is still a private company, with Shaykh Rashid as probably the largest shareholder. It should also be noted that while Dubai is heavily dependent on commerce for its prosperity, recent oil production levels in excess of 350,000 bd have also provided sizeable income.

7. Muhammad has also been at the center of the Al Maktum family's extensive horseracing empire in Britain, where all of Shaykh Rashid's sons spend a considerable amount of time and are said to have invested £500m.

8. Shaykh Sultan recently made the suggestion that Sharjah's six representatives to the 40-member Federal National Council (the UAE's national assembly) should be indirectly elected, rather than simply chosen by the Ruler.

9. The thesis has been published as *The Myth of Arab Piracy in the Gulf* (London: Croom Helm, 1986).

10. Another, more tranquil, dependency is the inland agricultural center of al-Diqdaqa.

11. Oil was finally discovered in Ra's al-Khayma in early 1983 and production of condensates had reached 14,000 bd by late 1985.

12. The waters off al-Fujayra became a preferred anchorage in the mid-1980s for ships waiting for an opportune time to run the gauntlet of Iranian attacks in the Gulf. It also gained some notoriety in the summer of 1987 when Iran apparently mined those waters.

13. On the negotiations on and formation of the UAE, see John Duke Anthony, "The Union of Arab Amirates," *Middle East Journal*, Vol. 26, No. 3 (1972), pp. 271-287; and Heard-Bey, *From Trucial States*, pp. 336-369.

14. The political and administrative structure of the UAE is detailed in Ali Mohammed Khalifa, *The United Arab Emirates: Unity in Fragmentation* (Boulder, CO: Westview Press; London: Croom Helm, 1979); Ahmad Khalil 'Atwi, *Dawlat al-Imarat al-'Arabiya al-Muttahida: nasha'tuha wa-tatawwuruha* (Beirut: al-Mu'assisa al-Jami'iya lil-Dirasat wa-al-Nashr wa-al-Tawzi', 1981); and Heard-Bey, *From Trucial States*, pp. 370-377.

15. The creation of a new capital at al-Karama, midway between Abu Dhabi and Dubai Towns, has been abandoned.

16. Under the leadership of former Ambassador to the US Sa'id Ghubash, the Ministry of Planning was able to prepare a draft five-year plan for the years 1981-1985 but the economic recession provided a convenient excuse for shelving the plan, which would have required considerable coordination between the amirates. When Ghubash resigned to become chairman of the Arab Monetary Fund in 1982, the Planning Ministry was placed under the charge of the minister of state for cabinet affairs and did not receive its own separate minister until late 1985.

17. On the background of UAE military forces, see J.E. Peterson, *Defending Arabia* (London: Croom Helm; New York: St. Martin's Press, 1986), pp. 210-212.

18. Recent surveys of the political climate of the UAE include: John Duke Anthony, "United Arab Emirates: Sociopolitical Developments," *AEI Foreign Policy and Defense Review*, Vol. 2, Nos. 3-4 (1980), pp. 56-60; idem, "Transformation Amidst Tradition: The UAE in Transition," in Shahram Chubin, ed., *Security in the Persian Gulf, Vol. 1: Domestic Political Factors* (Westmead, Farnborough, England: Gower, 1981), pp. 19-37; Iskandar Bashir, *Dawlat al-Imarat al-'Arabiya al-Muttahida: Masirat al-Ittihad wa-Mustaqbaluh* (Beirut: Dar al-Kitab al-'Arabi, 1982); Naomi Sakr, "Federalism in the United Arab Emirates: Prospects and Regional Implications," in Tim Niblock, ed., *Social and Economic Development in the Arab Gulf* (London: Croom Helm, 1980), pp. 177-187; Heard-Bey, *From Trucial States*, pp. 378-401; and Malcolm Peck, *The United Arab Emirates: A Venture in Unity* (Boulder, CO: Westview Press; London: Croom Helm, 1986).

19. Recent economic surveys of the UAE include: Carl Bazarian, "United Arab Emirates: Economic Developments," *AEI Foreign Policy and Defense Review*, Vol. 2, Nos. 3-4 (1980), pp. 61-65; Ragaei El Mallakh, *The Economic Development of the United Arab Emirates* (London: Croom Helm, 1981); Adam Nigel, "The Shifting Sands of U.A.E. Banking," *Euromoney*, January 1985, pp. 150-151, 153, 155-156; Middle East Research Institute, University of Pennsylvania, *United Arab Emirates* (London: Croom Helm, 1985); Naomi Sakr, *The United Arab Emirates to the 1990s: One Market or Seven?* (London: Economist Intelligence Unit, March 1986; Special Report, No. 238); and Sarah Searight, "The UAE: A Special Report," *The Middle East*, No. 138 (April 1986), pp. 27-40.

20. Two people were killed when a bomb went off in Dubai's Hyatt Regency Hotel on April 20, 1981. It was thought to be the act of Islamic extremists, possibly with the assistance of Iran. Since, then, however, the extremist threat seems to have ebbed, although the Ikhwan al-Muslimin has some strength in several federal ministries, particularly education. Other incidents, like the 1984 assassination attempts on several UAE diplomats in Europe, were likely the product of the UAE's foreign policy.

21. For more information on the FNC, see J.E. Peterson, *The Arab Gulf States: Steps Toward Political Participation* (New York: Praeger, for the Center for Strategic and International Studies, 1988; Washington Papers, No. 131).

22. The 1972 attempt by al-Fujayra's ruler to present an oasis, the ownership of which was disputed with Sharjah, as a gift to the ruler of Abu Dhabi ended in battle between the two amirates, with significant loss of life; the fray was ended only when UAE troops were permanently stationed at the oasis and the federal government purchased the oasis to ensure access by citizens of both states. Tensions between Sharjah and Dubai escalated a few years ago when Sharjah announced plans to build a commercial center on disputed land, momentarily leading Shaykh Zayid to throw up his hands and refuse to continue as UAE president. Additionally, the inability of these two states to connect their ends of the principal

highway between them provides evidence of long-standing boundary disputes.

23. One bright spot recently has been the seeming willingness of the various amirates to cooperate in the installation of a US-supplied I-Hawk system. In order for American survey teams to visit all the projected sites, separate permission had to be obtained from each amirate. Surprisingly, not only was permission granted but at least three amirates sent personnel to the US for training on the system.

24. The officer corps contain a number of non-UAE Arabs, Pakistanis, and Westerners, especially British (in Dubai), while 80-85 percent of the enlisted ranks are thought to consist of non-UAE nationals, drawn from approximately 28 nationalities, with Omanis in the great majority. The glamor associated with flying and their small sizes give the air forces the highest concentration of nationals. The total size of all the UAE armed forces is estimated at between 40,000 and 50,000 personnel. Omanis also predominate in the police forces.

25. A joint cabinet/FNC committee, meeting in mid-1985, decried the vacuum in leadership at the top caused by the absence of a functioning Council of Rulers. The committee charged that the failure of the Council, the executive body of the state and the locus of decision-making authority, to meet rendered the government unable to make any long-term plans or to tackle effectively the problems caused by the economic recession.

26. The introduction of a federal income tax has been broached privately and in the FNC, but such a measure seems politically impossible.

Index

Abadan, 101
Abd al-'Aziz, Shaykh, 207, 224
'Abdullah Bishara (GCC Secretary General), 44
Abu Abbas, 131
Abu Dhabi, 117, 201-5
  coup d'etat (1966), 203
  dominance in UAE, 219-20
  dominant tribes, 201
  Executive Council, 221
  leadership, 201-5
  National Consultative Council, 221
  water, 201
Abu Dhabi Defense Force (ADDF), 213-14
Abu Ghazzala, Muhammad, 106
Abu Musa (Palestinian leader), 130
Abu Musa island, 94, 186
  Iranian occupation of, 192
Abu Nidal Organization (ANO), 130-1, 193
Afghanistan, 93
  US policy concerns, 4, 9
Africa, 142
Ahvaz, 101
'Ajman, 209-10
al-Abdali, 97
al-Asad, Hafiz, 103
Al Bu Khayrahan family ('Ajman), 210
al-Da'wa party, 128-9, 140, 145, 149n4, 150n5
al Dir'iya, Saudi capital at, 190
al-Faw offensive, 96, 98, 103
Al-Fujayra, 209-10
  deepwater port, 209, 228n12
al-Hakim, Ayatollah Sayyid Mahdi, 140
al-Hakim, Muhsin, 140
Al Khalifa family (Bahrain), 145
al-Kurdi, Ma'mun, 45
Alliance for Progress, 183

Al-Maktum family (Dubai), 205-6, 218
al-Maskari, Sayf (GCC), 45
Al Nahyan family (Abu Dhabi), 201-5, 218
  Bani Muhammad clan, 201-5
  Bani Sultan clan, 201-5
Al Sabah, Amir Shaykh Jabir al-Ahmad, 128-9, 137
Al Sabah family (Kuwait), 145
Al Sabah, Shaykh Sa'd al-Abdullah (Kuwaiti Prime Minister), 128-9
Al Sabah, Shaykh Salem, 97, 104
al-Sadat, Anwar, 130
al-Sadr, Ayatollah Sayyid Muhammed Baqir, 145
al-Salmiya, 129
al-Sharq, 129
al-Sharqiyyin family (al-Fujayra), 209
al-Zulfiqar group, 130
Amiri Guard (Sharjah), 207, 221
Alexander the Great, 142
Algeria, 115, 121-2, 125
Allah Akbar Heights, battle of, 101
Angola, 124
ARAMCO, 116, 192
Arabian Peninsula, 99, 184
Arabism, 131, 184-5
Arab-Israeli dispute, 25-6, 31, 188
  1973 war, 111
Arab League, 193
Arab Revolutionary Brigades Organization, 129
Armenian terrorists, 130
arms sales, 24, 56-7, 70-1
  Great Britain-Oman, 166
  Soviet-Kuwait, 71-7
  US-Saudi Arabia, 189-90
assassins (hashashashin), 131
AWACS, 98, 101

231